THE ONLY WOMAN IN THE ROOM

THE ONLY WOMAN IN THE ROOM

*Episodes in My Life and Career
as a Television Writer*

RITA LAKIN

Applause Theatre & Cinema Books
An Imprint of Hal Leonard Corporation

Published in 2015 by Applause Theatre & Cinema Books
An Imprint of Hal Leonard Corporation
7777 West Bluemound Road
Milwaukee, WI 53213

Trade Book Division Editorial Offices
33 Plymouth St., Montclair, NJ 07042

All images and photographs are from the author's collection.

Printed in the United States of America

Book design by John J. Flannery

Library of Congress Cataloging-in-Publication Data

Lakin, Rita.
The only woman in the room : episodes in my life and career as a television writer / Rita Lakin.
    pages cm
Includes index.
ISBN 978-1-4950-1405-5
1. Lakin, Rita. 2. Television writers--United States--Biography. I. Title.
PN1992.4.L28
[A3 2015]
812'.6--dc23
[B]
                          2015028676

www.applausebooks.com

This book is about women.
But it is dedicated to men.
The men who helped, who were kind. And cared.
Mel Bloom, Steven Bochco, Eddie Feldman, Michael Filerman,
Freddy Freiberger, Frank Furino, Michael Gleason, Merrill Grant,
Buck Houghton, Mort Lachman, Paul Monash, Sydney Pollack,
Larry Sanitsky, Dale Sheets, Ned Tanen, David Victor,
yes, and even Aaron Spelling.

And most of all,
Douglas Unger,
mentor, author, and dear friend.

Contents

Preface

*"We write to taste life twice,
in the moment and in retrospect."*
—Anaïs Nin

*"You own everything that happens to you.
Tell your story. If people wanted you to write warmly
about them, they should have behaved better."*
—Anne Lamott, *Bird by Bird*

I have written fiction throughout my entire writing career. First for television, and most recently novels. So when it came to doing something personal and auto-biographical, I looked at it as I always have. Is this a good story? Who are the characters? How does it flow? What's the theme? What am I trying to say? And who is my audience?

Many people today don't realize that prime-time network television writers in the 1960s and early 1970s were virtually all men. Generally, it wasn't prejudice—it was cultural. Gender roles, gender expectations. My story is based on the twenty-five years I worked during these early days as a pioneer woman writer in Hollywood, when I was almost always the only woman in the room.

Accurate memory is a challenge for all of us. I'm telling you what I remember to be true, often with vividly recalled details. But at times I took the liberty of recording my adventures in a different chronology, telling my story in a way that makes it more cohesive. Every so often I needed to recreate an event in which details were blurry. In these cases I indulged in a bit of restrained creative recall. All events involving famous people, those whose names you will recognize, actually happened just as I describe. In a few cases, I chose not to use real names. I felt it was important to protect the innocent, and equally important to protect myself from the guilty. If you catch me in a mistake of name, time, or place, it's unintentional.

I also must note that the device of the young reporter is a means of compiling questions asked me by many reporters through the years. Again, this was to avoid tedious repetition and to tell the story as smoothly as possible.

I hope whoever reads my insider journey will be intrigued, entertained, and perhaps even amazed by this slice of life from one woman's unliberated Hollywood past.

Acknowledgments

It took a village and here are my villagers:

First and most important of all, my A-Team family: my sons, Howard and Gavin Lakin, for loyalty above and beyond, patiently reading draft after draft, after draft, after draft . . . There aren't enough adjectives to thank them for all they do for me.

My sister, Judy Van Wettering, the heroine in my memoir. (And hello to Michelle, Chris, and Erik Trolson.)

My beautiful granddaughter in every way, Alison Lakin, who wanted me to write my story so that women would know how it once was. And her brother, my loving (and favorite!) grandson, James Lakin.

Dr. Leslie Simon Lakin, daughter-in-law par excellence—for all those psychological insights and a whole lot more.

In California: It all started with author Rhys Bowen for suggesting that my adventures in Hollywood should be written as a memoir. Camille Minichino, Peggy Lucke, and Jonnie Jacobs—my most valuable writer critique group who willingly read many drafts. (And a special wave to Charlie Lucke.) The Sisters in Crime NorCal branch, every one, including Bette and J. J. Lamb, Simon Wood, Priscilla Royal, Kelli Stanley, and Lisa Lutz.

That amazing dynamite duo, Bill and Toby Gottlieb, for über-encouragement.

Deb Todd, for a multitude of gifts in friendship, and Andy Hoffman, and Jason, too.

My agents: Kimberley Cameron for making my memoir happen; Nancy Yost for her generosity.

My Los Angeles friends and supporters: Frank and Sylvia Furino, and Vanya and Boyden Rohner.

The families of Harriet and Fred Rochlin, Larry and Doris Silverton, Jack Kay, Ellie and Bill Grayer, Fred and Shirley Freiberger, Dolores and Jerry Raimist, Allan and Bobbi Holtzman, Mark Fienberg, Michael Link, Evan Baker, Barbara Minkus, and Susan Holcomb.

And my *machatenista*, Lois Leonard.

Those I mentored, who became my good friends: Cynthia Cherbak, who more than just helped me research *The Rookies*. June Christopher, who assisted me so beautifully. (And hello, Michael Haney.) Lee Schiller, for being the caring, wonderful person he is. All of whom do me proud.

For research: Joanne Lammers, Karen Pedersen, and Bertha Garcia from the Writers Guild of America Foundation Library.

My West Coasters: Karen Williams and Al Reiss, Guia Hiegert, Deb Rice, Matt and Wendy Larson, Joel Drucker, Ann Lyerla, Roger Macdonald, Joan Parr, Lou and Britt LaGatta, Richard Katz, James Rosin (author of *Peyton Place,* the television series, for his helpful hints), and Sofia Gonzales (for my photo collection).

My medical team, literally keeping me going: Dr. John Fullerton, Dr. James Adams, Dr. Sujoya Dey, Dr. Richard Bernstein, Dr. Gary Grossfeld, Dr. Dawn Stock, and all of their staff.

All my loving New York relatives: Sandra Carp, Jay and Maryann Litzman, Joan and Larry Cohen, Peggy and Harold Lakin, Erwin and Shirley Banoff, and all of their families.

My New York and East Coast friends: Elaine Grossinger Etess, Stephen Cole and Peter Rinaldi, Richard Maizell and family, Robert Burton, Thelma Jurgrau, Lori McNichol, and Jerry Minkow.

My former editor, Caitlin Alexander, one of my first loyal readers.

My Midwesterners: Professor Lou Erdman, and the loyal women's book club in Green Bay, Wisconsin, "The Women Who Walk on Water" (with their leader and jolly troublemaker, Margaret Sampson).

And to so many other people I met along the way.

Thank you, one and all.

And in memory of my mom, Gladys, my dad, David, and my aunts Ann and Rose, who understood love and kindness and truly inspired me.

TEASER

watched the young reporter fuss with her smartphone. My college newspaper inter viewer was what, maybe twenty-one to my seventy-five? What could possibly be our mutual frame of reference? What could we have in common?

Finally Chelsea was ready. "Thanks again, Ms. Lakin, for letting me do this story on you. It's really kind of you."

"And you're welcome . . . again."

Interesting, I thought. She wasn't reciting this litany of apologies in deference to my age. She had an "attitude," was confident and entitled, but she was careful not to offend, handling me like something antique and maybe breakable. It was clear to me that Chelsea would be more at ease interviewing women of her own generation.

"Ahem," she began, "I know you've written seven successful comedy mystery books in your Gladdy Gold series about little old ladies who become private eyes, but my editor wants to know what made you stop and decide to write a history of an era."(Translation: She had never heard of me and was feeling her way, because the people in my field worked behind the scenes and seldom had fame. I was surprised she hadn't Googled me, or maybe she had and still wondered who I was.)

"I went to a mystery writers' conference a few years ago."

"Yes? "

"These conferences are made up of authors like myself and our fan base—readers who enjoy mysteries and meeting those who wrote them. They attend panels on various genre topics. On this occasion for fun, one of my panels was called The Liars' Club, the idea being that we writers would make statements describing our career experiences and the audience would decide whether we were telling the truth or lying.

"My fellow panelists did the usual mix of true and false. I related my Hollywood anecdotes. After waiting out the laughs and the shouts of "Liar" from the listeners, I shocked them all: Everything I said was true. The room turned silent and then went crazy.

"People were astonished. On Dynasty, was I really assigned to work with a writing partner who had murdered his wife? Did Omar Sharif really organize a birthday dinner for me in Italy on a movie shoot? Why did Mia Farrow cut off all her hair while on Peyton Place? Because of Frank Sinatra, her husband then? Did someone actually steal my prestigious Edgar Allan Poe award away from me? Did that infamous Mafia don actually offer to buy me a mansion in Beverly Hills if I would sleep with him?

"So the idea had been in me about writing up these anecdotes for a long time. The more I thought about my career, one fact kept striking me over and over again: how few women writers worked in TV in the 1960s. And the 1970s as well. And the 1980s, too."

Chelsea abruptly sat up straighter. "Seriously? You mean, like, television was, like, sexist?"

I had her full attention now. Was it possible her generation was that clueless about mine?

"Tell me all about it. Details!"

I realized what my new young friend and I had in common. We were women, that's what.

So I told her.

As we say in showbiz:
Fade in.

Part One
THE SIXTIES

UNIVERSAL STUDIOS

How I Almost Met Cary Grant, Doris Day, and Alfred Hitchcock, All in One Day

Mid-1961
Universal Studios, Los Angeles

How many words can you type per minute?"

I hesitated. No sense lying. "Maybe ten."

The personnel director's pretty blue eyes looked askance at that. "With two fingers," I added, knowing that would be the next question.

We were seated on plush Italian leather couches in a section of the marble lobby in this newly opened all-black aluminum-and-glass office building. It was huge, awe-inspiring and imposing, and I felt insignificant. Later it would become known as the Black Tower.

I was aware of the other applicants watching and waiting in leather chairs across from us, speculating on how I was doing. They didn't need to worry. I didn't have much chance.

"And your shorthand? Pitman or Gregg?"

I shrugged, embarrassed. "I did take a course in Pitman once. I flunked out. The symbols never made sense to me."

Come on, I urged myself. You've answered a dozen ads by now. And struck out each time. Not that I blamed them. No work experience. No skills of any kind. And I'm sure the sad, pathetic face that greeted those potential interviewers made turning me down easy. You need this job. Say something positive. Say how you'd love to work at a big movie studio.

Her name was Merle Johnson and she was about my age, thirty-one. She had medium brown hair, too, and was also about five foot five, weighing in at 120. And there the resemblance stopped short. Her wavy hair was beauty-salon coiffed and shining. Mine was straight, straggly, and dull, though God knows I'd tried to do something with it that morning. I couldn't remember when I'd had my last hair appointment. Her clothing was perfect. Her makeup, subtle. Jewelry, understated. Perfume, light.

I felt she was able to see right through me. Nothing in my wardrobe worked for me. I'd managed to dig out a black linen skirt and old white cotton blouse from a far corner of my closet, where things I no longer wore lived. And that included the maternity clothes I'd shed not that many months ago.

She was also wearing black and white, but on her it was right. Hers was probably 100 percent wool or even silk. But my skimpy skirt was creased and didn't fit well and had a safety pin holding up a falling hem. Did she see the remnants of a stain on my blouse from nursing my baby? I'd scrubbed it, but that discoloration doesn't come out easily, and I didn't have anything better to wear. I didn't own what might be considered a business wardrobe.

The only jewelry I wore was my wedding ring. And how much longer would I be wearing it?

I cringed as she closed the folder that had my name printed on it. "I'm sorry, Mrs. Lakin, but I don't think this will work out."

Normally, I'd have been spending my afternoon at the Farmer's Market at Third and Fairfax, strolling with my friends Doris and Harriet, enjoying Bennett's delicious ice cream and wheeling our baby strollers while we shopped.

I didn't belong here. I was a housewife. A mother. None of my friends had to work. They felt sorry for me, needing to get a job. Believe me, I felt plenty sorry for myself. I wanted to be home, where I felt safe.

Stop it! Those days are gone. Pay attention. You're losing this Merle Johnson's interest. Don't let her see how scared you are.

Soon she would point me to the exit, and I knew I had to stop her. I couldn't bear another rejection. I had no other choice. I didn't want to do it this way, but I had to play the pity card. I was that desperate. My voice trembled.

"Look, Miss Johnson, I need this job. I know I have no secretarial experience. I do have a degree in English lit. It never prepared me for a husband who would die young. I'm left with three children under nine and no way to earn a living. I was meant to live happily ever after."

Merle stared at me; I saw her respond just the tiniest bit.

"He was thirty-four years old. His name was Henry, but we called him Hank. He was a wonderful man. A good husband and father. He was brilliant, too. A physicist. He was working on the first mission to outer space. . . . He died six months ago." I stopped myself—this was hopeless. "I'm sorry. I'm taking up your time. . . . I guess I should leave."

I saw Merle tear up as she turned her face away. She flicked a bit of lint off the shoulder of her black jacket, hoping I wouldn't notice.

There was no danger of me crying. I hadn't cried yet, not at his funeral, not in my empty bed at night; this was neither the time nor place to pour out my grief. Please don't ask me for details, I silently begged.

There was a pause and I held my breath.

"Well," she said, covering her feelings, "I think I have a position for you."

Was it true? Was she saying what I thought I heard? What possible job was there for someone without skills? I smiled hopefully. Give me anything, anywhere, doing whatever. Just let me be in this magical place and earn a paycheck.

"Allow me to show you where you'll be."

It was happening, really happening. I felt my heart flutter. I told myself I had been unrealistic, going from movie studio to movie studio. I needed a job, but did I go to the telephone company or department stores like JCPenney or Sears? Did I try to get a job selling five-and-dime stuff at Woolworth's? Did I go someplace where I had a reasonable chance of getting hired, of being stuck in a situation of infinite boredom and infinitesimal salary?

I'd had enough of a dose of realism. Even in my pain, I was hoping to be able to work where I might find a little joy. I loved movies. For so many kids like me who grew up during the Depression, those wondrous Saturday matinees were our escape. I was glued to the silver screen. Two features, cartoons, a Western, serials—it was the stories that held me entranced. The noise level in the audience was kept down by an imperious matron in a white nurse's uniform, carrying a flashlight, shushing the rambunctious boys. I never wanted the afternoon to end.

I glanced back at the waiting job applicants, their faces clouding up at the realization the job was now taken. I hurried after Merle.

Since we were on the ground floor, I assumed we'd take the elevator up to one of the tower floors. But, no, she walked me outside and wound me through an adjacent area of small, charming one-story cottages with sweet miniature gardens. If you closed your eyes and pretended that huge black building wasn't there, you might imagine you were in an English countryside.

"These bungalows," Merle informed me, "are the offices of important people." She pointed. "Doris Day, the singer-actress, always brings all her dogs to the studio." Her dogs barked as we passed her door.

"That's Rock Hudson's door; you know he's that romantic leading man. He and Doris are starring in a movie right now, *Lover, Come Back*."

"And next, Edith Head, the famous costume designer."

She paused at a sprawling nondescript building with people milling around in a variety of costumes of different eras. "This is our restaurant. We call it the commissary."

We continued on and Merle identified the soundstages, massive beige concrete square numbered structures with huge doors.

She walked me along what she identified as the back lot. Here was a period New York street, there, a dusty Old West saloon and blacksmith shop. A French chateau around a corner. A cobblestone mews in a Charles Dickens London.

"Recognize that?"

I nodded. Even I knew the familiar gloomy Bates Motel and the spooky house on the hill. Hitchcock's movie had come out the previous year and shocked audiences with its famous, terrifying shower scene.

I sensed she was doing this tour thing to cheer me up. Kind lady.

We arrived back at the cottages and she pointed at one. "This will be your new home."

Did my eyes deceive me? Was that Cary Grant coming out of the door next to where I'd be working?

Merle informed me that my high-ranking executive boss-to-be never gave dictation to his secretary. "He does all his work on the phone. You'll be dialing his numbers for him and taking messages when he's out. There's a minimum of filing."

Me, she was talking about me! Relief washed over me. I'd never have to type. Or even file. I could take messages. I could dial.

What I'd prayed for was a simple job, with no demands on me, so that I'd have time to grieve. I'd found my home away from home. May you have a happy life, I wished Merle Johnson. You've just saved mine.

VAN NUYS

Home Not-So-Sweet Home, Not Anymore

5 p.m. the same day
My house in Van Nuys

I didn't want to get out of my car. But of course I had to.

I unwillingly climbed out of the compact gray 1960 Chevy Corvair, which had formerly been my husband's pride and joy, and which under my care had suffered greatly. I was exhausted from the day's emotional ups and downs. Even though it had ended well, it had taken a lot out of me. I didn't even have the strength to lift the garage door open. Trying not to look around, I was all too aware of the crabgrass taking over my lawn. Some of the sprinkler heads had broken off. The shutters on the windows were peeling. The gutters were filled with dead leaves. The front doorbell hung from its wiring. My little yellow tract house was getting back at me for my neglect.

How it was before: When he was here, everything was spick-and-span. The house shone inside and out and promised welcome. At this hour, Hank would have been getting home from work. I'd have raced around readying the place for him, dumping toys into the toy box, picking up dropped clothes and tossing them into the hamper. I'd have made sure my nine-year-old, Howard—called Ricky, owing to his middle name, Eric—and four-year-old, Susie, were bathed and in their pj's, and that my nine-month old baby, Gavin, was nursed and sleeping. I'd have changed my clothes and put on makeup. Dinner would be ready, the aroma filling the house with its promised comfort. He'd open the door and his two older children would run to hug him. The house in order, the atmosphere peaceful. And for the final touch, I'd have a martini in hand to greet him.

I'd learned all these rules from *Good Housekeeping* and *Ladies' Home Journal*. The 1950s had been happy. I had the soul mate husband. I was content as wife, mother, and housewife. Three wanted babies in a row, a husband in an important career—who would ask for anything more?

After dinner and after the kids were put to bed, while I did dishes, Hank would go into our undersize den, which was his office. The walls held our college degrees: my English lit BA, and his two PhDs, one in math and one in physics. There was a two-seater worn brown corduroy-covered couch, a recliner that didn't recline, an unfinished pine bookshelf containing his texts and reference books, an ordinary desk, and an office chair, though he hardly ever sat in it. One whole wall held a chalkboard where nightly he'd stand and work out mathematical problems. Sometimes I'd curl up on the recliner and watch him. He loved playing with those numbers. And I loved watching him, even though what he was doing looked like hieroglyphics.

How it was now: I walked inside, standing there silently in the front hallway listening, taking the temperature of my home. No sign of the older ones, but I was able to hear them from the playroom, squabbling while the TV blasted *The Mickey Mouse Club*.

Those same toys and clothes were strewn in the hallway and, I imagined, all over the house. I was sure my sister, Judy, had found no time to do any cleaning.

I heard my little guy crying from his high chair in the kitchen, where Judy was attempting to prepare the children's dinner. Probably leftover canned Chef Boyardee spaghetti, red Jell-O, Hershey's chocolate milk and Toll House choco-late-chip cookies. And I remembered:

January 12–24, 1961

My husband died on the twelfth, and then it suddenly was the twenty-fourth, my birthday. Where had I been those twelve days?

I was told later that at Hank's funeral I behaved as if I were hosting a party. Like a Perle Mesta, famous for her lavish soirees, known as the "hostess with the mostest," bouncing up and down the aisle after the services, greeting everyone as a guest, effusively thanking them for coming.

Back at home with a smile pasted on my face, passing a tray of cheese and crackers (Swiss and Ritz) around to friends and family, making preposterous chitchat about the weather and thanking those who had traveled so far. I had no idea where my children were or who was caring for them. Whatever strange spirit moved my body and spoke my words during those bleak days bore no resemblance to the me who had totally shut off and disappeared onto the planet of Nothingness.

I did that? I don't remember. I don't remember any of it.

For days—maybe it was a week—my family and Hank's family, who had come from New York, hovered over us, moving in and out of my house at all hours. My redheaded sister, Judy, had arrived with them, carrying two heavy suitcases, which didn't register at the time. My mother, Gladdy, and her sisters were constantly cooking up a storm. Aunt Rose, the oldest, was in charge; she always took over. Mom and Aunt Ann just obeyed her orders: Go shopping, make beds, do dishes, whatever. They didn't argue—it was easier that way.

My always-shy dad, Dave, said nothing. He touched my shoulder a lot, then moved quickly away. The New York uncles attempted not to be underfoot. They tried for normalcy, watching sports on TV, complaining, pretending as if it mattered; they couldn't get the New York Giants football games on my California TV.

Hank's parents, Lena and Jack, those dear, gentle people who'd adopted him as a child, sat numbly in my kitchen, staring into space, holding hands. She said tearfully to anyone who'd listen, "It shouldn't happen. It's not right for your child to die before you."

Alone, standing in Hank's den, were his two best friends, and fellow physicists, Merrill and John, and their wives. Perhaps they felt most comfortable near the chalkboard, with its recognizable symbols from their own work at the lab.

All the above I was told later. I vaguely recall, like some buzzing in my ears, people giving advice. "This, too, will pass," one after another promised. I knew they'd lied.

Still in my self-protective coma, I saw them vaguely come and go. Many hugs I didn't quite feel, soft words I didn't quite hear. More food in the fridge.

Then—poof!—they were all gone.

Suddenly, awesome silence. No more visitors. The phone no longer rang.

My freezer was full. Each meal labeled and dated, probably by perfectionist Aunt Rose.

And there was my sister, Judy, oddly left behind. I found her sleeping in my tiny den in the small tract house.

This was my greeting to my sister: "Why are you here? Why is there a bed in here? Where did it come from? What happened to the brown couch? This is Hank's workroom. Don't you see Hank's chalkboard? See what he's working on now? Don't you dare erase anything!"

Judy cried. And then I sat down on the bed and held her hand.

And after they all left to go back to their own lives, and for this thirty-first birthday on the twenty-fourth, Judy bought a cupcake and centered a candle in it, and she sang "Happy Birthday" to me as my children watched in confusion. Where was their daddy?

Thank you, my dearest, for not dying on my birthday.

I STOOD IN THE KITCHEN DOORWAY watching my sister place my children's food on the table, and I thought about what she'd come from.

Living in New York in our parents' cramped apartment had been stifling for her, as it once had been for me. But that's the way it was. A nice girl lived at home until she got married, so at twenty-four, surprisingly still single, Judy had a series of part-time jobs to pay for clothes, makeup, and incidentals. Dating and husband hunting was the agenda, which stopped abruptly as she was thrust into flying three thousand miles away to Los Angeles to help her newly widowed sister.

But she'd never had to deal with taking care of three young children. She'd never had to cook or clean a house, but she was trying, with not a complaint out of her.

I'd apologized to my sister for uprooting her. But Judy insisted she was thankful that I'd rescued her from the Bronx and all those loser guys. This gorgeous L.A. was paradise. And she knew for certain that her dream husband was waiting for her just around the corner. However, neither of us could ever have imagined she would be here under such heartbreaking circumstances.

I watched as she called my kids into the kitchen for dinner. She had to call them three times before they obeyed.

Mourning has weight and smell. It was oppressive. The walls would soon close in and crush us all. I had to think. We were going to sink under this morass if I didn't do something.

Listening again to the sounds from down the hall one last time, I backed out of the room, silently closed the front door behind me, got back into my Chevy, and drove away.

I did a lot of thinking as I drove to our neighborhood shopping area on Ventura Boulevard. I knew this was going to be hard. Someday we'd have to deal with our sorrow, but not now. First, we had to survive.

As my mother, Gladdy (she preferred it to being called Gladys), used to say, "You've got two choices. You can be sad and waste your life using it as an excuse to do nothing, or you can talk yourself into being happy and maybe it will come true."

I left my car, yet again, in the driveway. I hurried back into the house, my arms loaded with packages. I shouted, "Hey, everybody, Mom's home!"

They all dashed into the hallway.

My Susie, with her Shirley Temple strawberry-blond curls, was already at the I-can-do-everything-by-myself stage. She dressed herself in layers of mix-and-match clothes, overalls on backward, already making her own fashion statement. Ricky, already too thin and too tense, was the only one old enough to understand that the death of his adored father was a reality. He thought I didn't know it, but he'd been faking illness so he wouldn't have to go to school. His face was pinched with unhappiness, and I suffered silently for him.

Judy, burdened and worried, held my adorable baby on her hip, a spatula in her hand. Gavin wrapped his chubby arms around her, a big smile on his face. My poor baby, never to know what a father meant, was a happy little guy. He was in better spirits since I stopped nursing. Stress made the breast milk sour.

Other than Gavin, my shell-shocked family stared at me, eyes flat and unfocused.

"Guess what! Mom got that job at the movie studio and we're celebrating!" I announced cheerfully. Please, God, let this work. Until I can crawl my way out of heartbreak. I let loose the balloons I was holding and reached into the bags and pulled out some Woolworth's leftover New Year's Eve party favors. Blowers, whistles, silly hats, confetti.

Unsure for a moment, they one by one got with it, grabbing stuff, laughing.

"Teach me that song. The mouse song," I said, singing a few notes off-key.

Judy latched onto a pointy glittery gold hat and plopped it on her head, grinning. "Will we get to meet movie stars?"

"You bet. In fact, I saw Cary Grant today."

"Wow!" said Judy, duly impressed.

"Can we go to Disneyland?" Ricky asked as he flung confetti up in the air.

"Soon. I promise."

Clapping our hands, we sang and talked ourselves into being happy.

FIRST DAY ON THE JOB

Where I Learn About Cottage Industries, Lew Wasserman, and Jules Stein

Next Monday morning
First day at my new job

T hus began my double life.

Dale Sheets introduced himself as my boss. The other guy in the office welcoming me was Ned Tanen. Both were in their thirties and single. Dale was blond and, I thought, had a Santa Monica beach-boy look. Ned was dark-haired, New York sophisticated. They looked like movie stars. Both men were upbeat and well dressed, and I wondered if that was a prerequisite for running a movie studio.

The first thing they told me was that they were executives in the television division.

Ned was involved with the music department, and Dale was the supervisor in charge of the Tennessee Ernie Ford variety show. Ernie Ford was a country-western singer. That's about as much as I knew. I had no idea what Ned's and Dale's job descriptions were.

My desk was situated opposite to that of Melody Meyer, Ned's secretary. She was about twenty, blond, cute, and bouncy, and informed me that her dad was a musician, ergo the name. Once our bosses went into their offices, Melody gave me the lowdown on the job.

"The sweetest gig in town," she informed me. "The guys need their caffeine in the a.m. Ned likes his espresso, Dale takes tea, no sugar. We open the mail for them. We file a couple of pieces of paper once in a while. Our big job of the day is to phone whichever restaurants they want to go to for lunch and make reservations. They have their own private phone lines and they make most of their calls by themselves, especially to the ladies they're involved with at present. They're out of the office most of the time. When they have meetings here, we serve coffee to any visitors till they're called in."

Melody stopped short. I waited, expecting her to continue.

She shrugged. "That's it."

I was hardly able to hide my surprise. "What am I supposed to do all day?"

"Whatever you want," she answered as she opened her desk drawer and took out a bottle of coral nail polish—one of many—and opened it.

The cottage was an unexpected treat. It was beautiful. I learned that each office in the Black Tower as well as in the cottages was decorated with genuine English antique furniture and paintings picked out by Mr. Lew Wasserman's wife, Edie. I realized my French Louis XIV desk was a copy—of course, the secretaries didn't get the real antiques.

Lew Wasserman and Jules Stein were the top dogs at the studio. Obviously very shrewd men. Everything they bought was a tax write-off. Every piece of furniture grew more valuable by the year.

The CEOs were noted for always wearing impeccable black suits, stark black ties, gleaming white shirts, and buffed black shoes. It was not meant as their fashion statement. It meant business, and must have made it easy to get dressed in the morning.

My favorite personal story about them is about the time when I hopped outside the studio one day and, in a hurry, decided to grab a quick bite from a street food vendor. In front of me were Wasserman and Stein, walking away, seemingly enjoying their hot dogs al fresco.

I waited a moment and then stepped up to the cart. Unable to resist, after placing my order, I asked, "Those two men who just left, do you know who they were?"

"Yeah," the hot-dog vendor said, "those guys? Undertakers from O'Callaghan's Funeral Parlor two blocks down. Look at 'em. Grim reapers, they be."

Good thing I hadn't yet bit into my kosher dog or I would have choked, laughing. He had just served two of the most powerful and influential men in Hollywood.

So much for fame.

I discovered that Melody did have something specific to do that kept her busy. She pointed out our mutual window and stated that the cottage next door indeed housed Cary Grant. "I'm in love with him, you know."

I did a double take. "Isn't every woman?" I joked. Cary Grant was the debonair British leading man in such famous films as *North by Northwest* and *An Affair to Remember*. Sigh. Melody had good taste.

But no, she specifically meant herself, and further explained, "And I intend to marry him."

I humored her, thinking, Oops, I'm going to be working alongside a crazy person. "Does he know yet?"

"When we start to date, I'll inform him."

A poster child for anyone who intends to make it in Hollywood. Not a nutcase, but a very sweet, romantic young lady who had high hopes and improbable dreams.

So most of the time, in between sporadic dialing and filing, Melody would lean on her elbows, stare out the window at his cottage, and swoon. A spy in the house of love, waiting for her dream man to appear.

I enjoyed watching her jump up the moment she would see him heading out his door. She'd grab any folder and rush outside to "accidentally" bump into him, pretending she was on her way somewhere. He was elegant but cautious. He would smile at her politely and then move on, and Melody would come back into the office, walking on air.

Amazing, I thought. Just like in the movies.

MY INSTINCTS HAD BEEN RIGHT to lead me to work here. Even though I was still mourning, the pain was reminiscent of a stitch in the side—always there, always dull, always reminding me. But the studio was like an antidote. I was in awe, as a kid might be if allowed to wander over acres of circus grounds. There was so much to gape at.

Melody was my guide and teacher. She pointed out all the players and even introduced me to the guards at the gates, who seemed like tough guys but were really likeable—especially kind to young and pretty women like Melody.

Out the cottage door, walk ten steps and we were in the commissary. I learned the rules of this simple, large, no-frills room with its Formica tables and plain plastic chairs. She informed me that this cafeteria was for studio employees, the ones who did the nuts-and-bolts work, which included gaffers, best boys, grips, script supervisors, greensmen, props, costumers, truckers, DA's (director's assistants,) extras who populated the scenes, film editors, and the hundreds of other people who toiled the multitude of soundstages.

They were the "below the title" workers. Like most viewers, I paid little attention to all those names that flashed by after a TV show or movie ended in what was called the "crawl." And here they were, dining in this basic eatery, the commissary's front room.

Melody pointed out the private executive dining room in the rear: This was for the A-list only. In the parlance of the business, they were the names "above the title." The bosses, producers, directors, and well-known actors lunching with their agents, business managers, and lawyers were respectfully served in a beautifully appointed room at tables with fine white linen tablecloths. Wine was available. Business deals were made.

And the cafeteria eaters got to gaze at their idols and dream their dreams as the elite paraded, invisible blinders on, through the front plain-Jane quarters in order to reach their lofty surroundings in the back dining room.

Melody handed me a tray and led me on line to pick out my lunch. Never would I have dreamed that in less than five years I'd be seated at one of those important tables in the A-list room.

MONTHS PASSED; there was a rhythm to my days. And a year flew by quickly. My kids seemed to have adjusted. Children have a way of being self-absorbed. Little Gavin was now a toddler. Sue had discovered kindergarten. Rick was managing fourth grade.

Since Dale was away at the Ford show quite often, I had plenty of free time, just as Melody had predicted. What to do with these open hours?

I learned there was a distribution list—all recent scripts were sent to those involved in their film production. Something was brewing in my unconscious. I thought, maybe I should be reading those scripts. My bosses weren't on the list, but I found a way to get Dale's name on it—I befriended Steve, the mailroom boy.

Mailroom boys were mostly UCLA or USC college graduates, the idea being that Universal paid them very little, but they had the opportunity to learn on the job and work their way up. It was considered an apprenticeship, so for the most part, mailroom boys were smart, poorly paid, ambitious young men. And Steve was one of the smartest.

I decided to read scripts while Dale was out. Out of curiosity, I learned what movies and TV series were being produced on the lot.

I asked Steve what they paid scriptwriters. I gasped at the going rate of hundreds of dollars. That was a fortune to me.

Today, writers are paid a minimum of $35,000 per episode. A single episode can cost more than a million dollars to produce! No wonder this was a killer business to break into.

I read my first script for a Western TV series called *Wagon Train*. An actor, Ward Bond, played the wagon master guiding the earliest settlers heading from Missouri to California. Scripts were totally unlike books. All I saw was dialogue, pages and pages of people speaking to one another. Fascinated, I began reading all the scripts I managed to get hold of.

I stepped eagerly into a whole new world.

READING IN BED

In Which I Tell You About Friends

1961
My bedroom at night
Phone call from my best friend, Doris

I t had been my habit every night to read a chapter of a novel before I'd fall asleep. But now I was gobbling up scripts. Steve was delivering daily batches, mostly Westerns like *The Virginian*. Then there was the cop show *Dragnet* and a family comedy, *Leave It to Beaver*. They hardly resembled the literature I preferred; I had just recently finished two incredible novels by two amazing writers: *To Kill a Mockingbird* by Harper Lee and *Franny and Zooey* by J. D. Salinger.

But I had found a purpose, even though I admit some of the scripts I read were putting me to sleep.

I snuggled into my double bed and tucked my nightgown around my legs, making myself comfortable. Our patchwork Amish-style wedding-ring-design quilt still covered my husband's side, keeping it pristine. I couldn't bring myself to sleep on his half, which I'd now covered with books, newspapers, and each day a new script—as if these things could help me pretend I was happy with my new life.

Once in a while, I imagined I could still smell him next to me. And I would wrap my arms around his pillow, and sometimes it helped me fall asleep. Most times, it didn't. How I missed him. He had been beautiful inside and out. Sundays had been the best. I'd wake up to a rose from the garden next to my pillow followed by being served coffee and toast in bed. I loved how he'd tumble with giggling Ricky on his side of the bed, and me nearly spilling my coffee. I missed his amazing smile. His black, curly hair and how he worried about a bald spot beginning to appear. I missed his body. I missed our nights together.

The phone rang.

"Hello, it's me. You still up?"

It was my best friend, Doris. "Hi, Dor. Yes. I was just about to turn in."

I reached for a cigarette and lit up. Over the phone I could hear the snap of a match, Doris lighting her cigarette as well. I leaned back against my headboard, ashtray in one hand, phone in the other. Knowing Doris, it would be a long phone call. I knew because she'd waited until her two little daughters, Gail and Nancy, and husband, Larry, were already asleep.

I could picture her at the kitchen table, papers strewn every which way, covering most of the surface. She worked well in chaos, her mop of black hair wild as usual. A pencil would be stuck in that nest, and soon she'd forget it was there and grope for it. The fact that she was using matches clued me in that she'd again lost one of her many cigarette lighters.

Doris, also a former English major, and I had a long-term hobby of writing short stories. Stories we wrote in between babies' naps, kids in school and our husbands at work. And, quite often, late at night. We'd take turns having literary sessions at each other's houses, using our kitchen tables as our desks. The coffeepot was always full. Our husbands had home offices—usually the den. Of course, we didn't. We were wives and mothers, and a kitchen table was good enough for our leisure activity.

In between avid discussions of the latest literature we'd read, we'd critique each other's stories over cups of coffee and packs of cigarettes. (Remember those dark ages? Will anyone of a certain age forget *Now, Voyager*, watching Paul Henreid light Bette Davis's cigarette and his at the same time? And she says the last line, knowing their love can never be, "Oh, Jerry, don't let's ask for the moon . . . we've already got the stars." Fade out. Movie over. Tears flowing. Guys, trying to be sophisticated with their gals, were placing two cigarettes in their mouths and lighting both with one match. We all bought into the glamour of smoking.)

Doris and Larry were such opposites. The lawyer in Larry kept him organized and meticulous. He was a good-looking man, despite being almost bald before thirty-five. He was half a century too early from when men with receding hair-lines would shave themselves bald on purpose! What Larry and Doris did have in common was absentmindedness. She would lose lighters. And misplace keys. And Larry . . .

I can remember a morning when we were working at their opulent Sherman Oaks Mexican hacienda–style house. Larry left for the office, but he came back moments later, having forgotten some legal paper. He found it and left. Then, five minutes later, back again. Forgot something else. By the fourth time he returned, his grin was sheepish. I had a laugh with him by return number six. He played it like a Charlie Chaplin sketch, kicking up his heels, waving the latest found and rolled-up document as if it were a cane and tap-dancing out the door.

He'd finally left for good. Doris, who had the most amazing ability to focus, hadn't noticed any of his comedic returns. She'd just kept on writing.

"So, how's it going at your office?" she asked me then. I could feel her voice tense over the phone.

"Pretty good. It's an easy, enjoyable job."

"Great. When will we be able to get together? I've got my first draft of the Passover story done."

Two years ago I'd made a hot twenty-seven dollars selling a story I'd written to a mystery/adventure magazine called *Manhunt*. My first and, as of yet, only sale. From what other writers had warned, I was aware that action-adventure magazines only bought manuscripts from men, so I used my initials to hide my being a female, and I guess it worked. I sold my tale about a suicide attempt, titled "Jump, Chicken," and I got to see my name on the cover—*written by R. W. Lakin.*

Doris was working on a series of heartfelt stories she'd based on the early years in America of her husband Larry's immigrant family. She was a fine writer and had already sold one of her stories to *The Saturday Evening Post*, a prestigious magazine.

We were part of a small, tight group of close friends. We had met in 1958 at a political rally. There were ten of us—five couples—in Los Angeles, fresh out of colleges across the country: the men, budding lawyers and architects; my husband, the physicist; and all us college graduate wives.

L.A. was our promised land.

The men began their careers. Away from our parents, we formed new family units. We'd invented a tradition of Saturday night dinner parties, the wives coming up with new culinary efforts from the latest cookbooks as we took turns meeting from house to house. *The Joy of Cooking* was my bible. We celebrated holidays and birthday parties and spent New Year's Eves together.

At a Saturday night gathering, when the subject of Doris and Rita selling their stories came up, it was obvious that Larry and Hank were proud of their wives' little hobby. They boasted about our small successes. Our endeavors were treated by the other husbands as being cute and unimportant.

"Maybe someday our wives will support *us*," Larry said one night, and that got a big laugh. From the men.

Their wives, our women friends Annette, Harriet, and Ethel, paid close attention.

Of course then the important dinner subjects to discuss took precedence. Updates of what was new in the men's careers. The latest architectural project, the newest law case. Hank's new project was top secret. He would reveal nothing, regardless of teasing. After dinner we'd split up. Sports for the guys around the built-in bar while we wives retired to the kitchen, did dishes, and gossiped about our children, fashions, and book clubs.

All in all, we were happily looking forward to the 1960s.

Three years later, Hank died.

With our devastation, the Saturday night parties died too.

Over the years, all the men became highly successful, while the women stayed home and raised their children.

Ethel's lawyer husband, Ben, eventually became a prominent judge. Harriet's husband, Fred, and Annette's Ephraim, partnered up and became world-class architects. Larry branched out into real estate.

My husband, had he lived, would have been part of the group who sent a man up to the moon.

≈

Now here I was, forced to leave the cocoon. Not willingly. I was scared. Unsure. Unable to imagine surviving on my own with no husband to support me.

Doris pulled me out of my reverie with a question. "So how about we meet Thursday night or next Saturday?"

"I don't know, Dor. Nights and weekends are now full of all the stuff I can't get done during the week. I'm trying to spend more time with the kids. And hopefully maybe getting some rest as well."

"But you have to make time. We need each other's input."

I was getting cold. The temperature in the bedroom was cooling down. I pulled my half of the blanket up around my chin. "I've been reading a lot of scripts they produce at the studio."

"So?"

"They pay writers hundreds of dollars per script. I can't depend on an occasional twenty-seven-dollar stipend from the short-story market to help fill out my small secretarial paycheck. I've been thinking I might want to try to learn to write scripts. Maybe someday, hopefully sell one for television."

There was a silence, and again I could hear her lighting up.

"You want to write for TV?"

"I'd have a better chance there than trying to write for the movies. TV has to fill up a whole lot of hours on the air. Maybe there'll be a place for me."

"You can't mean what you're saying."

"Doris, every day I have to find ways to scrimp. Rick wants to eat in the school cafeteria. I insist on packing sandwiches to save money. Birthdays are hell. Their friends have the usual big parties and my children are embarrassed if I don't buy nice presents for them to bring. Short stories be damned. This could be a godsend."

I had to make the mental transition. I was no longer in the wife-who-had-a-hobby category. I was in the saving-our-lives business. What Judy and I had going was my full-time job, which paid a minimum wage, and her equally minimum-wage part-time keypunch-operator job so she could be there when the two oldest came home from school. All of which barely paid the mortgage. Plus we had to pay a babysitter to take care of the baby until Judy arrived home. I had cashed in Hank's small insurance policy to cover the rest of the expenses—the food, clothing, taxes, and anything else.

What if we didn't make it? Then my little family group, as well as my sister, would end up having to leave always sunny, always expensive L.A. and move back east to icy winters and galoshes, living with Mom and Dad in their tiny four-room box of an apartment in the unfashionable East Bronx. My worst memory was of an unidentifiable smell coming out of the kitchen wall from the basement dumb-waiter. How could I ever forget the dumbwaiter? The apartments had enclosed elevator shafts where tenants placed the day's garbage on its shelf and pressed the button to send it down to the basement, where our resident nasty super would unload it.

That was a fate I wouldn't wish on anyone. I didn't want to go back to the Bronx.

Doris interrupted my thoughts again. Her voice had turned bitter. "How can you waste your talent on writing for schlock TV?" With that, she hung up on me.

I FELT AS IF my best friend had kicked me in the gut.

CLUSTER THEORY

Bad Day, Bad News

July 26, 1962
One year later
(Kids are 2, 6, and 10)

The morning began with me being startled out of a nightmare, dreaming of Hank, pulling myself awake and jumping out of the bed as if chased by demons. The realization hit. It was his birthday. He would have been thirty-six today. My head began to ache.

It was already a scorcher, another record-breaking hot day. The dreaded Santa Ana winds were blowing, an ill wind that would blow no good.

I could hear the children, already in the kitchen, grumbling. I assumed Judy was getting their breakfast and then I remembered she was away for the weekend with a friend. I hurried toward the cacophony of silverware being beaten against plates.

I was met with "The pool. We gotta go swim." The evolving drama queen, Susie, emoted, already in her bathing suit.

"Yeah, Mom," echoed Ricky. "Or we'll die of the heat."

My little guy, seated by his caring brother in his high chair, made faces and mewling noises to indicate his unhappiness.

I didn't want to go anywhere. I just wanted to go back to bed and cry.

But I knew they'd pester me all day, so I gave in.

THE CITY POOL WAS MOBBED. An endless blanket of gleefully screaming kids splashed in the water. Parents shouted warnings. Kids ignored them. Hundreds of couples with the same idea: Get the children out of the house.

I found a minuscule spot to park us, jammed between other family units. Susie and Ricky jumped into the water the moment I removed their outer clothes. I parked Gavin on his blanket next to me, but he was cranky. He was not his usual happy self. I sat, sweating and miserable, and fanned myself with a magazine, trying not to think of Hank. But that was not to be.

"Rita, is that you?"

I heard a familiar voice. I looked up to see a heavyset man standing with two pre-teen boys who were the spitting image of him. They carried towels and picnic baskets.

"Merrill. Of all people."

Hank's physics lab partner smiled down at me. "I see you got talked into this zoo as well."

With one eye firmly on my kids in the shallow end, I paid attention to Merrill, who leaned down on his haunches close to me.

"How are you?" he asked.

I shrugged. "As well as can be expected."

"I must apologize for not keeping in touch—"

"Don't. I understand," I broke in to change the mood. "So, you guys must really be excited—JFK announcing. Congratulations."

"Yes, it was pretty awesome."

Merrill recognized my reference to President Kennedy telling Congress in May of his commitment to sending a man up to the moon . . . and bringing him safely back.

"What are you doing these days?" Merrill inquired.

"I'm a working woman now. Got a secretarial job at Universal Studios."

"Good for you. I always meant to tell you back then—you were very brave."

I stiffened. "I couldn't save him."

"But at least you tried." An awkward silence. His obedient sons stood quietly by, watching the swimmers.

Merrill shook his head. "He was crazy to go down there. It was too risky."

"What risk?"

"The radiation."

"What are you talking about?" Suddenly I no longer felt the sun; I was chilled.

"The facility in San Diego. Not only Hank but two others also died of leukemia. All of them were warned it could be dangerous. Later the government tried to cover their asses with some half-baked rationale about a cluster theory—that diseases happen in groups. As if there was no connection with the substances they were handling."

I felt my throat closing, my mind in turmoil. "But Hank worked with chalk . . . numbers on a blackboard. . . ."

"Not down there."

"Oh God, tell me it's not true."

Merrill tried to hide his distress. "I'm sorry. I've said too much."

I grabbed at his arm. "Finish it, Merrill, you can't stop now."

"When Hank told me he volunteered, I begged him not to go. But always the hero, he felt it was his duty."

Merrill stood up, troubled at having upset me. "I'm so sorry. I thought you knew. I was positive the company told you." He managed a bark of a laugh. "Yeah, sure they did."

My kids were climbing out of the pool calling for drinks. Merrill's sons were pulling at their dad.

"Please call me," he insisted. "I can suggest some lawyers. . . . You can fight them." Giving in to his restless sons, he was moving off. "Please stay in touch."

I don't remember taking my unwilling children home or anything else from the rest of the day. Numbness had set in. All I kept hearing were Merrill's words through a piercing ringing in my ears. *The radiation . . .*

Ricky and Susie went to bed complaining of their unfair mother, the boring day, and the heat.

I paced my bedroom. There was no way I could sleep. I felt like a bomb waiting to detonate.

"Mommy . . ." A pitiful wail. I went to Gavin's nursery—really only a small alcove adjoining my bedroom. My little boy was standing up at the rail of his crib, grasping at his throat. Seeing me, he opened his arms wide. He wanted comforting. "I hurts."

I found the cough syrup prescribed to him by our pediatrician, hoping that would help. But he didn't want to be put back in his bed. So I carried him down to the laundry room, stopping only to turn on the lights in the adjoining kitchen. I decided I might as well do a load of diapers. The laundry basket was piling its way up toward the ceiling

With my toddler squirming under my arm, I managed to load the washer. Then I decided to boil his baby bottles. In the kitchen, I turned the gas on under the huge bottle sterilizer and filled it with the six empties. Soon, soon, I begged. Let him be old enough for training pants and drinking out of a cup. Clutching his throat, he started to cry. "I more hurts."

Beads of sweat were sticking to me. Suddenly there was the smell of acrid burning. Thin spirals of smoke began curling up from the inner workings of my vintage Sears washing machine. I held Gavin tighter in my slipping hands, which made him cry all the harder. I pulled switches and turned dials frantically, but the water rose steadily over the top, running wildly down the sides of the machine. I watched almost stupidly as the suds traveled from the laundry room onto the kitchen floor.

Then a worrisome sound—hissing and bubbling. I turned to see the pot of boiling water cascade over, edging down with a life of its own to meet the soapy river below.

Through all this Gavin howled.

"Hank," I cried out toward a mute heaven. "Hank, damn you, you crazy fool, you didn't have to die! How could you have done this to us? Never mind me, your children. For them never to have a father again! Why did you go and leave us!"

It's all right, my darling. I heard a voice gently inside my head.

"It's not all right," I screamed. "I can't go through it again. I won't go to a lawyer or confront your company. I can't relive those unbearable days again!"

The imaginary voice persisted. *You don't have to. Everything's going to be all right.*

I could feel the muscles loosen slightly in my shoulders and the tension lessen.

"How!" I demanded, softer now.

First, put my son in his high chair, the calm voice told me, with warm remembered humor, *before he slides down into the sudsy water.*

I had been holding my breath. I lifted Gavin, lowered him into his feeding table, and offered him a zwieback biscuit. As children do, he reacted to my renewed confidence and food he liked, and stopped crying.

Now, said the voice, *careful not to step into the water. Pull the plug out of the washer and turn off the gas under the bottles.*

As in a dream, I did his bidding. How easy it was now. One rational act followed another. Like a mathematician solving his theorem, I mopped and scrubbed and quickly restored order.

Something has to change, I said to the voice in my head. I must move forward. I have to focus on that job and earn more money. Tell me what to do, my love . . .

You'll do what you have to do.

I closed my past and put it away. Smothered the memories. I was truly alone, for the first time in my life. The children would have to come second. I could already imagine the guilt.

Decision made.

LIFE AT THE OFFICE

And How I Taught Myself to Write

1963
(Kids are 3, 7, and 11)

I continued to hungrily grab and study every script Steve delivered to me. Now I had a chance to read material from the film department. So much better quality than the TV shows. But I was beginning to understand the difference was in the amount of money and time spent on these different media. I got to read Alfred Hitchcock's thriller *The Birds*. Scared me even reading it. And *That Touch of Mink*, one of the many Doris Day romantic comedies. And then, oh my, the script version of my favorite book, *To Kill a Mockingbird*. Of course, I'd seen the movie, and it was wonderful.

I was intrigued by the number of versions of the shooting script that arrived in the mail. Each new draft would appear, all with different-color pages. Sometimes there would be major changes. I'd study each one to see what they'd altered to make it better. Sometimes they made it worse. I heard an amusing pithy showbiz expression—just don't improve it to a failure. I wondered how many people got to decide what would be considered a final script.

SINCE I DIDN'T FEEL I was right for any of the Universal TV shows, I picked a show by watching all three networks, ABC, CBS, and NBC. I chose *Ben Casey, MD*, a well-written medical show. Partly because it was on at 10 p.m., well past bedtime, so I wouldn't have to fight the kids over our one small ten-inch TV. It was bedtime that was the fight. "Aw, Mom, do we hafta?" They'd trip off, moaning about parental cruelty, complaining pathetically, and making vapid excuses to stay up—"I'm still thirsty. I'm still hungry"—all the while yawning and dragging their slippered feet.

I practically inhaled every week's episode. I liked the *Casey* show's dramatic storytelling. The lead character, played by ruggedly handsome Vince Edwards, was the gritty, macho doctor fighting the medical establishment with bearded, benign Sam Jaffe as his supervisor-mentor and calming influence. I made copious notes. (Remember, no VCRs back then on which to save the programs.)

Besides dissecting the shooting scripts that came in Dale's mail, I also absorbed the few books available then on how to write scripts. A teacher, Coles Trapnell, wrote a text called *Teleplay* suggesting what seemed like good advice: Always have a sample TV-show script available. Write the best you can, even though the odds were that script would never be produced. Write what you know. When opportunity knocks, be ready to walk through the door. And so on and so forth. I made Trapnell my bible. So *Ben Casey* was my sample show.

A PILE OF SCRIPTS were stacked up in Dale's in-box. Usually I got them out before he arrived at the office, but this time, I'd been too slow.

Dale walked in and was surprised to see the stack. "Did the mail boy make a wrong delivery?"

Uh-oh. Caught. I walked over to the pile and covered them with my hands as if that would make them invisible. I sheepishly confessed, "I ordered them."

Up crept his blond beach-boy eyebrows. "Oh?"

"I would like to learn how to write scripts, so, I thought, by reading them . . ." I broke off and stiffened, expecting to hear a gentle lecture on secretarial boundaries.

"Really?" He smiled. "Well, you're in the right place. Plenty of those around here." I had underestimated him. Dale was too nice a person to belittle my hopes.

"I promise I won't let it interfere with anything you need me to do."

Just then Ned walked in. He saw my serious expression. "What's up? Don't tell me you want to quit already now that we've gotten used to you?" he quipped. "How can we bribe you to stay?"

"No, nothing like that." I was embarrassed and I knew I was blushing.

Dale smiled. "Our girl is a secret writer."

"Not yet," I said timorously. "I'm just learning."

Dale commented, "I think it's a fine idea. Keep studying. Someday I'll be able to say I knew you when."

"Me too," Ned added. "And if you need help with anything, just let us know."

Off they went into their offices to start their next round of phone calls.

Melody had listened in to the whole exchange. When I sat down at my desk, grinning happily, I heard her make a sound like "Hmmmph."

"What?" I asked, turning to her, knowing she'd have an opinion.

"You'd be better off looking for a rich or handsome guy for a husband." She actually winked at me. She parroted, "'You're in the right place. Plenty of those around here.'"

I was blessed. What a perfect job. What decent people. I was safe here.

Not only did Steve, the cute mail boy, get me on the script mailing list, but he and I had many conversations about what went on in television. We gossiped, too, and had lots of laughs. He told me my first showbiz joke.

He'd heard it on the radio the previous night, told by comedian Henny Youngman. Could I deal with one a little off-color?

"Yes," I said, but I wasn't sure. I hoped it wouldn't make me blush, something I did easily.

He could hardly keep from breaking up while reciting it. "Did you hear about this TV producer who had his vasectomy done at Sears? Now when he makes love to his wife, his garage door opens."

We both laughed. Having Steve around was fun.

Oh my, all the new language I made myself learn. Shots and Dissolves and Cut-To's and Fade-Ins and Exteriors and Interiors. And the correct way to type a script. What an odd format. I'd find out later just why.

To my delight, I discovered that I really liked writing in script form. Dialogue came easy to me. As did the structure. I had found my métier. My niche. Two fancy French words to say I knew I wanted to write scripts from then on.

One aspect of our jobs was becoming an annoyance. We secretaries, as well as all the mailroom boys, were at the beck and call of the VIPs on the lot.

The suits, as we call them nowadays, had friends. The friends all wanted tours of the studio, and to meet movie stars and see how movies were made. And to be able to boast to *their* friends about whom they'd met. These people were constantly calling.

The studio big shots naturally had no time to be bothered parading people around, but they didn't want to offend them by turning down those requests. So any mailroom guy or secretary was on moment-to-moment call to stop what they were doing and "do the tour."

The tours took hours of our time as we walked our feet off, stopping at many stages to watch scenes being shot, dropping in on major star dressing rooms, looking at the sets, explaining, explaining, explaining. The tour always ended with a tram ride, after which a special lunch was waiting in the special rear section of the commissary.

No free lunch for us guides. The secretaries were forever falling behind, and the intrusions were resented. And the mail boys were unfairly chided for late deliveries.

About Steve—and that's not his name. I wish I remembered it. I'd like to know what happened to him. Here's why. So Steve commented to me one day that something had to be done about these annoying tours, upsetting our schedules and taking us all away from our work. He had been giving it some thought. "Why don't they build some phony 'studio'?" he asked.

"What are you suggesting?" I saw him brighten. He had an idea.

"Here's a way to get rid of all those people we're stuck schlepping around. Remember the back, back lot where there are acres of nothing but dirt?"

"Yes, but what do you mean by a phony studio?"

Steve did a silly little dance around my desk. He spoke excitedly. "We throw in a few dressing rooms and fake stages and build pretend sets and fill them all with props, and they'll think they're visiting the real thing."

I was beginning to get where he was headed. "You mean, maybe have a gift shop where they sell souvenir baseball caps with big star names sewed on?"

Steve jumped in. "And T-shirts, key chains, movie posters, you name it, and the clerks could answer all their questions. Let the big-shot visitors go up there themselves through a separate entrance. We give them a free pass to get in. Hey, and maybe even charge admission . . ."

"Lots of tourists would come to this, too—I'd bet on it."

We were both practically leaping up and down; we were so exhilarated by our business-plan fantasy.

"Steve, you are positively brilliant! You should hurry right up to the top of the tower and go see Mr. Wasserman or Dr. Stein!"

He scowled. "Yeah, sure, like they'll listen to me."

"I bet they will. They'll kiss you for being so smart. You've got to do it." I wasn't going to admit that only I, secretly and personally, enjoyed every minute of touring the studio.

He left in a hurry, pumped up with enthusiasm and bravado.

I never saw Steve again.

I only know that soon after, the multi-gazillion-dollar back lot named Universal Studio Tour was being built. The Bates Motel from *Psycho* was only a small part of it. Eventually they added King Kong, ready to pounce. About thirteen years later, going stronger than ever, they built terrifying rides. From the movie *Jaws*, a boat that broke up in the "ocean" with an attacking shark. Then there was the parting of the Red Sea. Earthquakes. Collapsing bridges, runaway trains, a House of Horrors. For evening pleasures, they added a 5,200-seat amphitheater. Dining. Dancing. Then Universal CityWalk, filled with a mile of stores—need I say more? The lines for each of the exhibits and rides snaked around for miles, and maybe tourists complained, but they accepted the waiting. It was Wasserman and Stein's answer to Disneyland.

That small idea became, and still is, a billion-dollar-a-year business.

I have to admit I took my children once. They had a great time.

I hope Steve didn't get fired. I hope they rewarded him with so much money that he never had to work again. Or at least gave him a better job, maybe on the Tour.

If anyone has information on whatever became of him, I'd like to know.

November 22, 1963
The day our dreams died—a sunny day like any other

IT WAS CHAOS in the studio. People ran haphazardly from building to building, shouting, voices hysterical: "Turn on your TV, the president's been shot." I could see them out my window, people holding onto one another and crying. Horror reflected in their faces. Disbelief.

Melody, having just come inside, joined me and we ran to the TV set in Ned's office. God, they were playing it over and over. President John Kennedy and his wife, Jackie. She, in pink with her signature pink pillbox hat, seated in a convertible waving to the folks in Dallas. The shots ringing out, Kennedy being shot, the secret service man leaping over, willing to take the bullet for him. Too late. Blood all over the shocked first lady's clothing.

I thought I heard someone come into our outer office. I ran out into the hallway thinking it was Ned or Dale, but it wasn't them.

I can't remember their names (hers, maybe Paula?), the studio executive and his secretary/mistress whose office was directly down the hall from ours, maybe because I don't want to. They say you never forget where you were or what you were doing when the president was shot, and this is what I have in my memory bank. The two of them down the hall have forever seared this image into my brain.

They were dancing, and at the same time hugging each other—in their case, for joy. Then kissing, deep, sensual kissing. I'll never be able to erase their shocking words or actions from my mind. He cried out in fervor, with such vitriol, "It's about time someone had the courage of their convictions to kill him."

And she echoed him, hissing, "Yes!" Grinding her body into his. "Oh, yes."

I was standing there, in tears, crushed by sadness, and they were deliriously happy that someone had murdered the leader of our country. How could they be so cruel? It was one thing to disagree with his politics, but to be happy about a young, energetic president's death? I was appalled.

NINETEEN SIXTY-THREE ENDED with a country in deep mourning. Like the millions of other Americans, Judy and I watched the somber funeral from home, crying softly. I clutched my three-year-old, Gavin, on my lap. Watching Jacqueline Kennedy, in black, walking behind her husband's cortege, accompanied by *her* three-year-old, John-John, clutching her hand and saluting the flag. Almost unbearable to see. I looked at the beautiful widow, thinking about what she'd just lost. What I'd lost three years earlier, when I'd walked my widow's walk. Her universe was now shattered, as mine had been; my much smaller universe.

I wondered if Jackie would ever love again and even marry again. I wondered if I would.

GETTING AN AGENT

And I Finish My Sample Script

Welcome to January 1964
Dale's office
(Kids are 4, 8, and 12)

I concluded the last few pages of my third rewrite of my sample script, typing briskly with two fingers. This had been my daily schedule for months. Evenings, I worked at my battered oak kitchen table after my little family had gone to bed, and when I'd finish, mentally and physically exhausted, I'd clear the table for next morning's breakfast rush. I kept my writings on a shelf in the hall closet. My manual Royal portable typewriter lived on its floor among an assortment of family bad-weather boots. That was as much of an office as I had room for.

MY BOSS, DALE, would tiptoe into the office quietly, so as not to disturb me. If anyone else came in, he'd *shh* them. He even brought *me* our morning coffee. Melody was impressed.

Ned Tanen, rushing by, always on the move, would give me a thumbs-up, also encouraging me. At one point Ned suggested I see the new British play, now touring Los Angeles. It was called *Stop the World I Want to Get Off*, written by Leslie Bricusse and Anthony Newley. Ned suggested it would help me as a writer, and that I would closely identify with the story.

It more than helped; it inspired me. Whenever the beleaguered character in the play called Littlechap felt that life was too much to deal with, that it demanded too much of him and he was unable to cope, he'd walk to center stage and cry out, "Stop the world, I want to get off." Those were chilling, telling moments. I, too, felt at times that I wanted to stop the world and just wallow in the sorrow that stayed rigidly locked in my ice-cold heart. But Littlechap also reminded me of the fleeting nature of life, of the importance of love, and that life had to go on, not to be wasted.

At the end of the show, I sat for moments rigid, tearful, unable to leave my seat, deeply touched and affected by what I had seen and heard.

Ned understood me better than I had thought. Such a kind, sensitive man.

AGENTS CONSTANTLY DROPPED BY the office, pitching their writers and actors for Ned's many projects and Dale's guest stars for Tennessee Ernie Ford's variety show. Dale would proudly point each of them in my direction and give a ten-second spiel on my behalf. "Here's a new client for one of you lucky guys. She's a terrific writer." Bless him. What a great fabricator; he never read anything I wrote.

Most of his visitors ignored the not-so-subtle hint, until Mel Bloom waltzed in one afternoon. Mel was a one-man firecracker, small, cheerful, bouncy, and highly energetic, prone to calling his clients *bubalah*.

Curly black-haired head tilted at an angle, he glanced at me without much enthusiasm. The wannabes in this business were legion.

"A writer? Maybe you'd rather be a movie star." He pretended to examine me for my potential in that area. "You're a good-looker."

Mel was flirting. That was a 1960s kind of male thing. Not that he was really coming on to me, but men thought that's what women wanted to hear.

He pinched my cheek. "Good cheekbones."

Next thing he'd want to open my mouth, like I was a horse, so he could examine my teeth.

Mel, leaning over my desk, made a box out of his fingers as if he were shooting me through a camera lens, and grinned. "Did anyone ever tell you you look a little bit like Anne Bancroft?"

Anne Bancroft? My favorite actress? She had just won the Academy Award for playing Helen Keller's teacher in *The Miracle Worker*. Me? Look like her? I told Mel Bloom, "I wish."

Mel pled his case and addressed Dale. "Doesn't she?"

Dale pretended to study my face closely.

"Yes, you do, somewhat. Around the eyes and mouth."

I shrugged. "I don't see it. Anyway, Mr. Bloom, I cannot act. No way. Nohow."

Dale chirped in, again with his pitch, "She's a really good writer."

Mel began to root around his scuffed briefcase. "Dale, I got something hot to show you."

Dale stepped up to the plate. "Don't need anything today. Got a problem with taking on this talented new writer as a client?"

Mel shrugged. "Don't have any female writers. Don't even know of any. Wouldn't know what to do with them." He addressed me. "Do you have some guy to write with? You know, like Fay Kanin works with her husband, Michael. They wrote the movie *Teacher's Pet* with Clark Gable and Doris Day. Or what about Gwen Bagni with hubby Paul Dubov? They're developing a cop show called *Honey West* for Four Star Productions, Dick Powell's company."

"No, there's no guy." This wasn't going to happen. He wasn't interested.

"Won't you at least read something of hers?" My champion wasn't going to let

Mel off the hook. "Be the first in this business to have a lady who can do it all by herself."

Dale was good. I was able to tell Mel was quick. If he wanted to be able to do business with Dale, he figured he should please him. I saw that Mel knew when and how to turn on a dime. "She got something good for me to read?"

And here it was, fidgety Mr. Mel Bloom, my Mr. Opportunity, timidly knocking on my door. Sort of.

With trembling hands I gathered up my sixty pages and passed them over to him. "I just finished it. Of course it needs some work. . . ."

Mel rode over ifs, ands, and buts. "Okay, *bubalah,* I'll give it a read. Catch you later." He tossed my script into the already stuffed briefcase. And with that he dashed out, supposedly on to important meetings.

Clutching my carbon copy, I stared after him like a petrified mother who'd given over her one and only precious baby to some total stranger, maybe never to see her love child again.

DR. KILDARE

My First Appointment, and My Sister Helps Me Pick Out an Outfit

Still 1964
Two weeks later
Dale's office

Mel was a man of his word. He read fast. And what did literary agent Mel Bloom tell me after he'd read my sample script? "Great news, sweetheart, you've got potential and I can always use another talent."

Even though I was *only* a woman? So far the only women I'd met in this business were secretaries and actresses, and a few script supervisors on the stages. The writers who stopped by our office had always been men.

"Okay, let's get down to business. I got you a meeting with executive producer David Victor next Monday. He produces *Dr. Kildare.*"

My heart went pitter-pat. "You did?" But I was puzzled. "Did you show them my *Ben Casey*?"

"Nice work. The *Ben Casey* was well written but didn't work for the *Kildare* people. Never mind that. Meanwhile, think about Richard Chamberlain playing the young, gentle yet sexy doctor. Raymond Massey is his tough, rough mentor. Hot stuff."

"Did you ever show it to the *Ben Casey* people?"

Mel did a little paper rearrangement in his briefcase. A habit he had, I soon realized, when he was about to become evasive. "Well, I didn't go there. I knew David Victor was looking for newcomers." He gave me an "aw shucks" kind of grin. "Besides, I knew we could get in at MGM. They love me over there."

It was my first realization that agents and producers had their own favorites.

And another realization hit me. These characters in *Dr. Kildare* were exactly the opposite personalities of the two from the *Ben Casey* show. I'd have to rethink everything.

I cornered Ned and Dale when they returned to the office at the end of the workday. "I have something to discuss." I was nervous and didn't know how they'd take my news. I didn't want to lose my job.

Before I could start my blurt, "Hey, Mel got you an assignment." This from Ned.

"You'll like David Victor. He's a good guy," added Dale.

Were there no secrets in this town? "I need to take a morning off."

"Take all the time you need," Ned said while scanning his waiting phone list.

"Not to worry," said Dale, heading for his door. "Melody will cover for you."

Melody at her desk called out, in her usual cute, ironic way. "I don't know *when* I'll find the time, I'm sooo busy, but anything for you, *darling*." She laughed.

I loved these people. How did I get so lucky?

Next morning
My bedroom

"Do you realize you've pulled out the same dress twice?" my sister, Judy, announced while sitting cross-legged on my side of the bed. My husband's side of the quilt was covered with my entire wardrobe.

It was early morning and amazingly the children were still asleep. Judy was in pajamas and I was in my slip, standing in front of my open closet door.

I was trying to choose what to wear for my big first meeting on Monday morning. Judy stared at the clothing strewn all around her.

"I did?" I looked at the black-and-white polka-dotted outfit again. "Yes. I did. And I still hate it." I threw it down on the growing pile.

"You're making yourself crazy. And me too. Pick one already."

Judy was snacking on honey-roasted cashews with her orange juice, and I was drinking my morning coffee.

"I can't help it. I need to make a good impression, but I don't know what to choose." I held up a hanger holding a two-piece brown-and-white outfit. Then I tossed it down with the others. "Why did I ever buy this dreary thing? What was I thinking!"

"Good question. Do you realize all those outfits in your closet are black, brown, gray, or beige? What have you got against color?" asked my sister, a bottle redhead whose favorite color was lime green.

What indeed? I never realized that before.

"The man isn't going to pay attention to what you're wearing. He's going to listen to you sell a story."

I plopped down next to her and sighed dramatically. "That's another thing. I've only seen one *Kildare* and it was so different from the *Ben Casey*, in mood, in tone, in character development, in the kinds of storytelling; I don't know the show."

"What's to know? A patient comes in, and brilliant, gorgeous, sensitive Richard Chamberlain saves their life."

"Easy for you to say."

"Well, I watch that program. Sometimes it makes me cry. It gets sentimental." Judy, the expert, she who called daytime soap operas great TV. I was doomed.

"Hmm. Sentimental. I guess they wouldn't be interested in a story about someone stealing drugs."

"What do you know about the world of drugs?"

She had a point. "Nothing." I picked at the store label on a dress I'd never worn, bought only because Macy's had it on sale. Gray, naturally.

"The show's been on for four years. How can I come up with a plot that they haven't done?" I could hear the pathetic whine in my voice.

"Don't worry. You'll think of something. Remember, you're the smart one, I'm the pretty one. I don't need to be intelligent; I only need to be smart enough to catch a husband."

We both laughed. That was how our mother used to describe us. Of course, not in front of each other.

My sister stood up and pretended to inspect me up and down. "I wonder why Mom said that about you? You're pretty enough. You just need to do something with that plain, stringy brown hair and maybe slap on a little makeup."

"Thanks. And you're not too dumb. You're plenty smart for someone who didn't want to go to college."

Judy playfully threw a pillow at me. I threw it back at her. "Speaking about our never-give-up mother, I got another one of 'those letters.'"

"Don't tell me." I laughed. "Let me guess. 'Darling, daughters. You know I don't like to nag, but isn't it time you seriously thought about coming back east to live?'"

"Close," Judy said. "This time, in place of 'I don't like to nag,' it's 'I don't want you to feel guilty.'"

"Right. And what followed? 'For the sake of those sweet, adorable children, they should be living with their grandparents.'"

"Hey, Mom's learning. This time she only said 'living close to,' not 'with' them. Your last lecture must have gotten through to her."

I raised my hand. Judy immediately raised hers. She knew what was coming. "Repeat along with me," and she did. "No matter what happens. Not even if were starving. Not even if we have to move to Anaheim, Azuza, or Cucamonga. God forbid. Not even if we are down to our last fifty cents will we go back home."

We always giggle at those famous lines from *The Jack Benny Show*. But notice I still called it home.

"Why don't you go shopping this weekend and find something new?"

"I don't know. . . ."

Judy grabbed one of the outfits on the pile. "Then wear this on Monday. I can't stand any more of this fashion show. I'll give you some bright beads to gussy it up. I'm hungry and want breakfast now! While it's still quiet, before the rumble of noisy feet beats us down to the kitchen."

"Done," said I, taking the beige skirt with matching beige sweater and cardigan and placing them off to one side.

As we hung up the rest of the clothes, I said, "I'm so selfish. Thinking of myself. What about you? Surely you have plans. You don't want to play nanny-housekeeper for me forever."

"No problem. I have my escape plan ready. As soon as you can do without me."

"Then that'll be never." We closed the bedroom door and headed for the kitchen.

"Fat chance," said Judy, always having the last word.

THE BACHELOR AND THE BOBBY SOXER—BARRY

I Enter the World of Dating, Heaven Help Me

That Saturday morning
The local deli

Talk about tiptoeing into the dating pool. I met Barry in Jerry's Famous Deli in Encino. I was in that suburb of the San Fernando Valley shopping for something to wear at my Monday meeting, and I was discouraged. So far I hadn't liked anything I saw, and I was destined to end up with that beige outfit.

I stopped in for a corned beef sandwich for lunch before I shopped some more.

He was sitting in a booth opposite mine, drinking an egg cream. Though why they call it that, I'll never know; it doesn't have eggs or cream, just chocolate syrup, milk, and seltzer. He was reading from an exceptionally large book.

I did what I usually do when eating alone. I always carried a novel in my car, so I had a book to read, too. I was happily minding my own business when the guy in the booth called across to me, "What are you reading?'

Startled, I turned and answered, just because I was asked. "It's called *From Doon with Death*."

"Haven't heard of it. Who's the author?" He leaned toward me.

I rotated my head so I wasn't straining my neck. "Ruth Rendell. She's a new English mystery writer."

"You like mysteries?"

"Yes, I do. Especially books that take place in England." To be polite, I asked about his heavy tome. "What about your book? Looks like heavy reading."

He laughed—it was a hearty, booming laugh. I realized I'd made a joke. "They say this book may be the longest novel ever written."

"Really?" I countered, not knowing what else to say. I was beginning to get the idea I was being picked up, and it had a vernacular all its own.

"It's *War and Peace*, by Leo Tolstoy? Have you read Tolstoy?"

Honesty was my middle name. "I tried it but got discouraged trying to remember all those long, complicated Russian names."

"You mean you couldn't keep straight the Bezukhovs from the Bolkonskys from the Drubetskys?"

By now Barry, had crossed the aisle and sat down opposite me in my booth, hauling the massive book with him.

"Something like that." I said, startled by his audacity and not knowing how to handle it.

As he was calculating whether or not I was alluring, I looked him over.

I saw an average-enough-looking guy. Slightly pudgy. His age, I was guessing he was forty-fivish, maybe closer to fifty? Thick brown hair and a lot of it. Men were starting to let their hair grow long. Clothes rumpled, so I thought, definitely single and doesn't own an iron. Face, how to describe it, with craggy ridges and lines, reminded me of a grizzly bear. Must be intelligent reading Tolstoy. Come to think of it, he looks sort of Russian.

We went through a routine that I suspected would become more and more familiar if I got into the dating game, and I supposed I should have by now. Where do you live? Where do you come from? What schools, and of course married or single, etc.

Within the hour, once it was settled that we were both available, we decided on going on a date the next night, Sunday night.

I smiled. He seemed interesting, but I wondered—was the book a prop? Did he schlep Tolstoy around, using him as an opening gambit? Did it live at home used as a doorstop?

I told myself not to be cynical. He read books; he couldn't be all that bad.

And then to my shock, I suddenly thought about Hank. I saw my loving husband's face in my mind's eye. What was I doing? I wanted to back out, but I didn't know how.

Sunday night date

I WORE ONE of my boring outfits. What choice did I have?

Barry had picked the restaurant, Mexican, and facing me was a humongous platter of enchiladas, meat tacos, mole, beans, and rice. I had been hoping for a simple salad, but he had done the ordering.

Barry liked to talk, and he liked an audience. He had a full barrel of subjects with accompanied opinions on male-female relationships and a droll litany of dating experiences.

"I'm really into younger babes," he told me. "You want to know why?" He didn't wait for my answer. "It's God's little joke on us. He gets guys to sexually peak at fifteen and women at forty. So young guys learn what they need to know from the older, wiser women, and then they go back to the young ones for their youth and beauty, get it?"

I was taken aback. I was not used to men openly discussing sex in public. Besides, his logic escaped me.

Barry leaned over, his long hair almost dipping into the salsa, winking at me.

I didn't have the opportunity to say much except for the occasional uh-huh, yeah, hmmm, you're right. When he asked my opinion, he didn't listen to my answer and rolled right over me with another sex-filled anecdote.

"You'll love this one. I'm in this bar, see, and a young doll sitting across from me is giving the signal."

"The signal?" I asked, trying to get a word in.

"You know—come on over and let's get acquainted. So I grab my Bud and my smokes and climb on the stool next to her. And right away, I say, 'You look familiar.' I know that sounds like a dumb pickup line, but I mean it, she does look familiar."

"Hmmm," I said, so he'd know I was still awake.

"It turns out I did know her. I used to babysit her when she was six years old. Isn't that a blast!" His raucous laugh filled the room.

Why did I not think it was funny?

"Hey, what can I say, bobby socks turn me on."

The evening seemed endless, but finally the check arrived. He held it aloft. "You read that Betty Friedan book, that *Feminine Mystique*?"

"Yes," I said quickly, before he could interrupt me, "every word."

"Well, now you've got the Equal Rights Amendment and the Equal Pay Act is about to follow. You know why I love women's lib? Guess why?"

I sighed—I was being allowed to get in more than three words. "Because you think it's time for women to be equal to men?"

"Precisely!"

With a grandiose flourish, he handed me the check. "Because I don't discriminate against women. Now you emancipated ladies can pay half the check."

Needless to say, that was going to be farewell, Barry. A dyed-in-the-wool bachelor, though I bet he'd marry someday—if he found a woman who'd pay the full check.

Not a good start. I hadn't wanted to date him anyway. This dating game felt like facing some unnamed danger in uncharted waters. But I should start dating, shouldn't I? My children needed a daddy.

But no one was ever going to take Hank's place. I knew that for a fact.

Besides, tomorrow my career could really be starting. Men were the last thing on my mind.

FIRST *KILDARE* MEETING

Where I Meet David Victor and Sydney Pollack — Color Me Terrified

Monday morning
MGM Studios
David Victor's office

Well, there I was, for the first time in a different studio. MGM had an entirely dissimilar look to Universal. It made me realize just how unique Universal was, with its flowerpot-surrounded cottages and impressive Black Tower and antiques galore. I imagined MGM was like most of the working studios around town. Bland, beige-painted structures, with mostly two-story buildings and matching stages. Workmanlike commissaries. No frills.

Remembering the advice given in Trapnell's handbook, I befriended David Victor's secretary while waiting for my meeting to begin. When I told her I was a secretary too, I made an instant pal. A smart move. After all, she was the one who decided whose calls to put through first. She offered me coffee but I knew to decline, fearing spills.

"Nice lime-green beads," she said. And I silently thanked my sister for her contributions to my boring outfit.

Agent Mel arrived; babysitting his new, unsure client? He'd brought along a basket of fruit and chocolates. Bribery? Did he think I'd need it? Would bribery work?

We were called in. Mel, seeing the panic-stricken look in my eyes, whispered in my ear, "Break a leg," the showbiz expression for "good luck." I guess that was meant to cheer me on. I took a deep breath.

After years of being on TV, David Victor had an office wall filled with show and family photos and shelves holding a number of awards. Piles of scripts covered his desk, also a lot of *Dr. Kildare* medical trivia gifts such as toy doctor sets and old-fashioned pill bottles, I assume coming from fans of the show. The room seemed warm and cozy.

I'd heard David Victor was known for giving writers and directors their first jobs, so I had my fingers crossed. He was warm and welcoming to me. Short, chubby, and gentle. Balding, with wisps of gray circling his head. Like the grandpa you wish you had. Or maybe a jovial Santa Claus.

He introduced us to the other person in the room: Sydney Pollack, who was hired to be the director. Sensing my nervousness, to make me feel better, Sydney mentioned that this was his first job as well. Nice-looking young guy. Thin, and rangy. Curly, light-brown hair. Friendly. Eager. Puppy-dog eyes seemed soulful and caring. Like the kind of guy you'd want to have living next door to you. Someone you could depend on.

After all the intros and pleasantries about the weather, glad it was not a smoggy day, and inquiring about the traffic getting over from the Valley to MGM, finally the four of us sat down. Mel, out of range, pretending to be invisible. David and Sydney looked to me and waited expectantly.

This was it. I'd practiced for hours during most of the weekend in front of a mirror. I must have tried ten different opening sentences. Finally, I started with my disclaimer. "There were so many shows produced ahead of me. Stop me if my idea is one you've already done."

Mel told me later that was a mistake. Never start with a negative. But right now I was pleased that they nodded and settled back in their club chairs. Mel was giving me encouraging nods while unaware that his leg was shaking. Which meant he was tense. Because I was his first woman client? I bet he didn't behave this way with his male clients. Was he worried that I might cry? Or might do something "feminine?" Watching him watching me naturally made me anxious, too.

I read from my one-liner story-idea sheet. "I thought a young, deaf boy might come into the hospital . . ."

To my chagrin, David Victor put up his hand to stop me. "Sorry, dear. We've already done that topic."

I looked at the next one on my list. My voice quaked. "Maybe about somebody suffering with epilepsy . . . ?"

A shake of the head. That too? I felt myself coming across as not being pre-pared. Out of the corner of my twitching eye, I could see Mel scooting to the edge of his chair. Ready to flee? Pretending he'd never seen me before? Ready to lecture me on needing a male writing partner? Ready to hand David the grapes that he'd plucked from the gift basket as a bribe?

Years later, I'd remember this scene when I was the one sitting in the cat-bird seat, a producer of my own show, judging sweating writers tossing out their pitches. But for now, I was one of those sweating writers. "A virus shuts the hospital down . . . ?" Did my voice sound like I was pleading? Because I was.

Another shake of the head. David and Sydney looked grim. Well, that was that. My career was over before it started. Why hadn't Coles Trapnell, that herald of high hopes, warned me that pitching ideas was a minefield? The feeling was similar to getting seasick, where you prayed for relief, preferably death.

David then smiled at me. "Sydney and I rather had something different in mind for you. I hope you don't mind."

He wasn't going to throw me out? Thank God . . . "Sure," I whispered, thinking I'd do anything.

"We haven't worked with a woman writer yet, and we thought a woman's story from her point of view would be welcome. Not a show about diseases, but one based on character. Something touching, poignant."

"Sounds good to me." How about that for quick, recovering repartee on my part?

Sydney added, "Perhaps one of the nurses in the hospital is married to one of the doctors. Both are friends of Jim Kildare."

"Yes . . . I like that." Keep going. Save me. Please.

David continued. "And they have a son, about nine years old." He turned to Syd. "I'm thinking little Ronny Howard."

Sydney agreed. "Perfect. That red hair. Those freckles. Viewers love him."

They looked so happy. Why were they smiling while I was suffering? Why were they casting a show I'd never live to write?

There was a pause. David added, "The nurse? Ruth Roman? She'd be perfect."

Sydney nodded. "She did a fine job in Hitchcock's *Strangers on a Train*."

"The little boy's father dies . . ." said David, his eyes reflecting sadness.

I felt my cheeks flush. Oh my God. Did they know about me? Had Mel told them I was a widow? I looked over at him, but his face was impassive. He suddenly seemed engrossed in reading the text on one of David's Emmy Awards on the wall, still nibbling at the bunch of grapes.

I stared at David and Sydney, telling myself to breathe even as I held my breath.

David Victor leaned toward me. "We had in mind a story about grief and how his wife, who happens to be a nurse, handles it."

"Or can't handle it," Sydney adds.

I knew what to do then. I hadn't just fallen off the turnip truck, to use a bad metaphor about stupidity. I recited as if by rote. "And she can't show how she feels, and she insists upon going to work and Dr. Kildare is worried about her. She can't cry, no matter how much she wants to. He's afraid she'll have a nervous breakdown."

"Yes, that's it!" Sydney said eagerly, as if it had been my brilliant idea.

David stood up. "Perfect! That's the story you should write." Sydney rose also, and instantly, Mel leapt to his feet as well, a man revived.

David put his arm around my shoulder and walked me to the door. "Call us when you have a rough outline."

Mel jumped on the bandwagon. "It will be a four-hankie show, I predict it."

"A pleasure meeting you," said Sydney, vigorously shaking my hand. "I look forward to our working together."

Outside the building, blinking in the sunlight, I stood statue-like, stunned. Whatever craziness had gone on, I'd come out with my first assignment. I wanted to pinch myself. I was going to write a script. A real paid-for script!

But my joy was mixed with distress. I confronted Mel. "You told them about me."

Mel squinted and pursed his lips: his performance of a man thinking. "No, I don't think so. . . . Maybe I mentioned something, but never mind. *Bubalah*, you're in!"

I shivered with excitement. "Now I have to deliver."

"Not to worry," said Mel. "It writes itself."

I was to hear that phrase over and over through the years and, believe me, it's such a lie.

≈

Early evening
At home

"FIVE HUNDRED DOLLARS? WOW!"

Judy and I were in the backyard and she was reacting to my good news.

My threesome were in the living room eating dinner on their new *Bugs Bunny Show* TV trays, watching cartoons as they ate. I could hear them chattering from the open windows.

Judy was leaning back on my weatherworn chaise lounge, painting her toe-nails using the floodlights in order to see. She was so excited, she dropped her nail polish. "Oh my God! That's more money than I make in a month. Now I can stop working and just stay home, lie on the couch, and watch daytime soap operas eating See's chocolates." She grinned at this cliché ideal of the so-called life of a homemaker. "Did I ever tell you how much I hate being a keypunch operator?"

It was not much of a backyard. A small piece of concrete that barely held one small beach chair and the chaise. A handkerchief-size play area for the little ones with a swing and a sandbox. A tiny strip of land for growing things. I was watering what was left of my few plants, trying to look casual about this incredible windfall. But I was equally excited. It was the first real money I'd ever earned. The twenty-seven dollars I'd gotten for my mystery magazine story didn't count.

It had been my husband who could garden; I was the one with the black thumb. Soon the last wilted roses would be gone. Then it would mean either putting in plastic flowers or covering the rest of the backyard in cement. Here was my take on that old line: You can get the girl out of the Bronx, but you can't turn her into a gardener. Cement it would be.

"About time you brought some real dough into the house." Judy grinned, calming down somewhat. "So, when do you get the rest?"

"It works like this: I do an outline. They pay me $500 for that part of it. If they like what I wrote, I get to write the script and that will bring me up to $1,500. If they don't, that's the end of it. Let's say I go on to write the script: When I turn that in, I get the biggest part of the money. And once the final draft is finished, I get the final payment, earning $3,000 altogether. Minus the 10 percent I pay Mel."

We were silent for a few moments, lost in our private thoughts. Visions of checks and residuals danced in my head. What was Judy thinking?

She was about to tell me. "Uhh, sis . . . maybe this isn't the right time to bring this up." She sat straight up on the chaise and began tearing tissues into shreds, bending over and placing one piece between each damp toenail.

"Something you want to get off your chest?"

She reconsidered. "Never mind. Maybe some other time. Not important."

"Out with it."

She hesitated, then jumped in. "I was on the treadmill at the Y today and I met a gal and she told me about this fantastic singles apartment complex. She lives five minutes from here . . . with a pool . . . and a Jacuzzi. . . ."

"Let me guess. And a lot of single sexy guys?"

"That too." Then, poignantly: "It's been three years. . . ."

"I know. It's time. In fact, I've been talking to an agency that has a woman available for a full-time housekeeper job who would do all the housework and cooking and child care." I grinned. "Think about packing."

My sister beamed back. "It's okay? Really? I promise to visit a lot." With the bulky tissues keeping her toes separate, she hopped over and hugged me. "You'll be all right managing by yourself?"

I hugged her back. "Actually, I was planning to leave the kids and move in with you."

Judy's eyes bulged. "What?"

"At least take the kids." I smiled at my little joke.

She gave me a little push. "Cut that out!"

"Just kidding." I pushed her too, reverting back to our childhood behavior.

"Watch out for my wet polish," Judy said, jumping away from me.

A cry from the window. "Mom, Gav spilled his apple juice. Ya better get in here."

I put down the watering can, shrugged, and headed for the patio door. Duty was calling. But things were looking up.

"Sis . . ." Judy called out to me.

I turned.

Her eyes glistened with tears. "You did it. You really did it."

I smiled. "Yes, I guess I did."

"A CANDLE IN THE WINDOW"

In Which I Learn What Makes Me a Writer, and My Sister Checks In

1964
At home and the office
(Kids are 4, 8, and 12)

The weeks flew by. I realized I was writing all the time. In my head. In my dreams. At the office. Everywhere. Anywhere. I had a notebook and I was filling it constantly, with chunks of dialogue, written down before it was forgotten. Character habits. Scene ideas. Hospital scenes with Kildare. Scenes with mother and child. Those were the tough ones for me personally, dredging my own memories back up to haunt me yet again.

Believe me, I was aware of the irony of writing the scenes I hadn't "played" with my own children. In my emotional state of mind, I was not dealing with my own grief. Yet I was building scenes that showed the nurse/mother character falling apart. She suffers a thousand little deaths of her own, coping with finality. Even recognizing the hopelessness, she couldn't stop trying to save her husband from dying, and nor could I. Seeing my children struggling to compensate for their loss. Showing my actor/child in the script doing the same. Writing out of my own experience. My nurse, unable to function at her nursing job. Me, managing as best I could at my job, trying to change my life by becoming a writer. And all the pent-up feelings—unable to get past the grief, unable to help my children with theirs, either.

Invading my mind, even as I was trying not to listen, were the soppy lyrics of Patsy Cline's "Crazy," "I'm crazy, crazy for feelin' so lonely. . . ."

Oh, will you stop feeling sorry for yourself! I yelled in my head. Write it, damn it. Forget you lived it! Turn it into fiction. Let the heroine suffer for you.

IN MY BEDROOM, trying to nap, I heard the sound of bickering children, which could seep through any walls, no matter what the layer of sleep. I staggered over to the window half awake, and glanced down at the patio.

Gavin was in his playpen, playing with blocks. Susie was in the sandbox, kicking sand with her feet, and Rick was wagging his finger at them. "You gotta be quiet and let Mom sleep."

Susie whined, "But I want her to play with us. She never plays with us any-more."

"Because she's busy making money so you can eat all the Cheerios you want. She has to write a lot of words."

"I see her when she's just sitting and doing nothing, but she still won't play."

"She isn't doing nothing. She's thinking. She's writing in her head."

"That's silly."

"You got to listen to me when I give you orders."

Susie pouted. "Why should I?"

"Because I'm the father now. Daddy told me that before he went up to heaven."

Susie looked at him ruefully. She thought about it for a moment. "Okay, I'll be quiet."

Oh God, there it was, the moment I'd been waiting for, an opening to talk to them about their father. To hold them close and say all the things I should have said but hadn't. To let them ask all their questions. Perhaps for us to cry together.

Get up and go down to them, I commanded myself. But my body wouldn't cooperate. I felt as if I were in one of those nightmare scenes where I wanted to move, but my legs remained buried in quicksand. Move, I demanded of myself again, but my body wasn't having any. I agonized—why can't I go to them and talk about their father? But I couldn't. I just couldn't. My poor firstborn, needing to take that burden on himself. I went back to my bed, in tears, feeling like a failure of a mother.

No grief therapy was available in those days to help us through the pain.

HOW NEATLY I WRAPPED UP my entire script. Nurse/Mother almost suffers a nervous breakdown—build to a dramatic final scene in a motel room where Kildare rescues her. Mother and child will be all right from now on. Happy ending, solved in one TV hour. But my own life's trauma would not be solved so easily.

Then it was time to put it all together. The writing flowed, almost erupting from my fevered brain.

A month later
David's office
MGM

DAVID AND SYDNEY went over the last draft of "A Candle in the Window" with me, page by page, line by line, giving me useful constructive criticism, their "notes."

The hours flew by. I was entranced. Every suggestion had something new for me to learn. They were wonderful.

As I listened, I had this quick, guilty unexpected fantasy thought of David as my daddy and Sydney as my lover. In your dreams, dummy.

What *they* wanted was for me to dig even deeper into my characters' emotions to make a good script even better. What *I* wanted was to bury those emotions forever.

Two weeks later
David's office again

I TURNED IN the final draft. I had listened, made the changes, and given them a script that pleased us all. David patted me on the back and then left for another meeting. "Good work," he said at the door.

Sydney stood at the exit as well. "May I say one more thing?"

Go ahead, tell me how beautiful I am. Stop with the fantasies, already, foolish woman! "Oh, no, not another change?" I blurted.

"Definitely not. Just wanted to congratulate you on the sensitive way you wrote the female lead. A dream part for an actress. Ruth Roman will be thrilled."

But I was the one on cloud nine.

A SERIES OF PHONE CALLS with Judy:

"How's the show coming along?"

"From what I hear, I think it's going to be good? How's the job?"

"Boring as ever."

"Why don't you look for something else?"

"And do what?"

"Find something you like better, something that's fun."

"Fun for me would be planning a wedding. That's still my primary goal and I'm working on it."

"Well, when you find Prince Charming, let me know."

"You'll be the first one I call. How's the housekeeper thing? I can't believe you're juggling your job and housekeepers at the same time. Is Chuy working out?"

"Update. Chuy. I rated her okay, but she left after a week because I didn't have enough closet space for all her clothes."

"No, get outta here!" Judy laughed.

"And Maria seemed always to be losing things, and she quit because *los niños* were too noisy and kept singing 'Maria' from *West Side Story* to annoy her."

"Cute kids."

"I was convinced I hit pay dirt with Edna. Even though she's pushing sixty and even though I thought she was a little strange-looking with that wild bleached blond hair always in curlers. And those awful muumuus she wore along with teddy-bear bedroom slippers."

"Okay, so not a fashion plate. Was she good with the brood?"

"Yes, an excellent housekeeper and a super cook. But I had to fire her, too."

"Why?"

"One small problem. I came home one night and found her lying on the couch in the living room, watching TV and arguing with Walter Cronkite."

"What's so bad about that? So she has her own political convictions."

"But did she have to masturbate while expressing those opinions?"

Judy dropped the phone but I could still hear her hiccupping with laughter.

HOUSEKEEPER

Making a Choice, with the Help of the Kids

At home

I sat down at my patio table in the backyard. Another typically warm day in L.A., with its equally consistent thin smog layer floating overhead, always in attendance. A smattering of bees hovered on their way to my pathetically few remaining potted sage plants. My cup of coffee sat at the ready. I could hear my next-door neighbor's lawnmower start up. The neighborhood had an unwritten rule: no noise from mowers until after 8 a.m. And it was as if he had waited, holding his breath, for the second it hit the hour, and mow he did. I could smell his wife's frying bacon. I could smell it from their kitchen window. These houses were in such close proximity, when someone next door sneezed, I could call out, 'Bless you.'

A few sips of coffee and I was ready to tackle my search for a new house-keeper. The employment agency sent me an envelope with photos of the latest batch of available women. I opened the folder. How interesting. These six young women were from Belfast, Northern Ireland, here to seek live-in housekeeper work. Looking for adventure in another country? I assumed the women knew one another.

So peaceful (aside from the mower) this quiet dew-swept Saturday morning. I must have said it out loud—and spoken too soon.

"Watcha doin', Mom?" Rick leaned over my shoulder.

"Yeah, what?" said his chorus of one, standing on her tiptoes in order to see.

My son and his sister were in shorts, T-shirts and flip-flops.

"What if I said I was working?" I attempted to dissuade them from getting involved. "And wanted privacy?"

He countered. "You mean writing work?"

Susie shook her head emphatically. "I don't see no typing-writer."

"And you don't have on your thinking face, so who's in the pictures?" he asked.

I sighed. I had always encouraged curiosity. Oh well. "We're getting a new housekeeper. These are photos of the applicants."

"Hooray, it's about time," Rick said. "That Edna was some weirdo."

I was afraid to ask why. I hope he never saw her watching Walter Cronkite.

"But she made good French *toats*." Susie said with eight-year-old enthusiasm for the important things in her life.

"You see these ladies? They come from far away. Do you know where Ireland is? Susie shook her head. Rick explained to her, "It's in Europe."

"Want to get the globe?" I suggested.

Rick ran back into the house to get the globe he kept in his bedroom.

I twirled it around and pinpointed Northern Ireland. "It's part of the UK and a beautiful place."

They put their fingers on the spot.

"Is that near where Grandma and Grandpa live?" Susie asked.

"No," Rick said. "Not even close." He spun the globe and pinpointed New York. "They live in New York and that's in America. Ireland is across the Atlantic Ocean." He moved his fingers to show her.

But his sister, less interested in geography than in the photos in front of her, pointed. "I like that one." Susie referred to a photo identifying "Margaret."

"I don't," Rick countered. "She's frowning. I bet she's grumpy."

"What about Kathleen? She looks nice," I suggested, pointing to a pretty red-head.

"How tall is she?" My growing-spurt twelve-year-old was going through the stage of being aware of the heights of all the boys and girls in his class. He needed to know.

"Says here, she's five three.'"

"Too tall," he decided. "I like this one." He pointed to "Joan." "But only if she's shorter than me."

"Will five-foot-even work for you?" I asked in my drollest tone. Apparently, he intended to be taller, and therefore in charge.

"Okay with me."

Susie concurred. "She has the same color hair as me and not too much. She looks happy. She even has freckles like Grog." By now the youngest, Gavin, had been given many nicknames by his sibs. Grog. Grub, Gav, Gavie—he answered to any of them.

"Then it's unanimous," I announced. "Joan Reid—five feet tall; short, light-brown hair; smiling; with a good disposition and lots of freckles—gets the job."

"Now can we have breakfast?" Rick pleaded. "I'm starving."

"Yay. French *toats*?"

"The better to grow tall on," I agreed, closing the folder and getting up. "Let's go eat."

THE SHOOT

Where I Sneak onto the Set and Raymond Massey Does Something Mean

Weeks later
MGM Stage 9
(Kids are still 4, 8, and 12)

I couldn't stand the waiting. My first TV show. I wanted to hear how my words on "Candle" were being read by actors. I could have asked David or Sydney for permission to visit the set, but I was too intimidated. I felt like an outsider—especially since Melody once told me she never heard of writers being invited on sets. When I asked why, she said it was because writers got too emotional. They'd assume their work was being mistreated and they'd bother the director and in general hold up production. At least that's what she'd been told—by directors.

So I was nervous as I drove over to MGM on my lunch hour. Luckily, I still had my drive-on pass on my windshield, so the guards waved me in.

I'd found out which stage they were shooting on from David's friendly secretary (I'd known that would pay off). My plan was to sneak inside, check out what was going on, and then slip back out without being seen. And if I was caught, what was the worst they could do—throw me out?

I reached Stage 9, with its closed, daunting steel doors. Since I'd been on a few sets at Universal, I knew that when red lights were flashing accompanied by the sound of an earsplitting buzzer, I was not to open that door. It meant they were shooting a scene and I would have to wait, no matter how long, until they were done. I took my cue from a woman carrying clothing over her arm who was standing in front of me. When the red lights blinked off, she opened the door and I squeezed in almost in her shadow.

And there it was. I was thrilled. I peered through the darkness and stared at the unlit sets on this cavernous stage, looking like ghosts waiting in corners for their entrance. Following the circle of work lights, I recognized the hospital nurse's station, the same set they used on every show. I looked around and couldn't find my amiable new friend, director Sydney. People were moving around, pushing equipment, painting sets, hammering, arranging lights, and drinking tea or coffee.

I spotted the boy who'd be playing Ruth Roman's son. So this was little red-headed, freckled Ronny Howard. He *was* adorable. I guessed him to be about eight or nine. He was seated on a small canvas folding chair that had his name stenciled on the back, at a child's desk. A woman sat next to him. I assumed she was a schoolteacher there to tutor him. There was another woman, probably his mom or maybe his agent. I didn't know how these things were done, but I was interested in everything.

This child actor was going to act out his grief over the death of his father. How could he do that? I assumed the boy still had a father. How does one so young handle such difficult untested emotions? But I was told this little boy came from an acting family and had been performing since he was a toddler!

I had no inkling that that little guy would grow up to be one of the major players in the world of TV and movies. He would become "huge," in the Hollywood lexicon. From becoming known as the child, Opie, in the successful *Andy Griffith Show*, he went on to perform in the musical *Music Man*. Grew up to become famous as a film director and producer, winning the Oscar for directing *A Beautiful Mind*. His credits are legion.

I looked elsewhere and checked out the other actors.

I located Richard Chamberlain, standing next to Raymond Massey. Makeup and hair people were fussing about them, doing last-minute touch-ups as the two actors appeared to be rehearsing their lines. They were deep in concentration.

I crept in closer. Which scene were they reading? If I could hear them, I'd know in a moment where in the script it would be. I'd written so many drafts, I knew the dialogue by heart.

To my horror, Massey suddenly threw the script on the floor and stomped on it. It sounded like a gunshot when his shoes hit the hospital tile. I jumped, my heart in my mouth. The entire crew turned toward him.

"Who wrote this piece of crap?" he said at the top of his commanding voice. He kicked my pages. "What mawkish, maudlin pap!"

What? Kicking my script? Hating it? I backed up, hoping he hadn't seen me. Not that he'd know who I was. What would he say to me if he did? What would *I* say? I knew it! I'd been kidding myself. I'd been found out. I was no writer. I was a fake, a housewife who should have stayed home. Should I apologize to Massey for being such an untalented writer? But Sydney and David said the script was wonderful. Fool, I thought, they said it to make you feel better. They felt sorry for you.

I couldn't run fast enough. I had to get off the set. I didn't want anyone to see me dissolve into a weeping mess.

Perhaps it was better that writers weren't allowed on sets after all.

Once I stood outside, I stared at the closed-to-me-forever door, breathing hard, as if I'd escaped those ghosts I'd seen lurking behind those empty sets.

And then I got mad.

That evening
Judy checks in

"So how was your day?" my sister asked over the phone.

I was lying like a beached mackerel on my bed, a wet cloth on my forehead. I had one hell of a headache. "Don't ask."

"I *am* asking. Mine was so boring, I know yours would be more interesting."

"It was a day full of ups and downs. Which part do you want to hear first, the good or the bad?"

"Let's go for the good."

"Well, the best part was going to the bank and depositing my entire salary for Kildare. Wow."

"Wow is right. We're talking real money, finally. Can you loan me fifty bucks? Kidding. And then what?"

"And . . . hey, listen, the new housekeeper is going to work out fine."

I pulled my beat-up body off my bed and, dragging the phone cord to its fullest, tiptoed over and stood, hidden, near the living room door. "In fact," I whispered, "I'm looking at her even as we speak."

"I'm so glad. Now I can stop feeling guilty that I left you. Tell me."

"Her name is Joan Reid and she's a gem. She came over with a group of other young women from Belfast and registered with my employment agency."

"Belfast? Like in Northern Ireland?"

"Yes. And she was an instant hit with my offspring. Especially since they felt they'd chosen her. She's funny and good-natured and cooks us interesting meals. Last night she made us a traditional Irish dish called pasties, made with sausage, onions, and mashed potatoes, topped with bread crumbs. My gang loved it."

"Sounds yummy."

"She's perfectly happy to be with our family. We get along wonderfully. She's smart and loves reading books. Picture this: She's sitting in my Mission slat rocker. Gav is cuddled on her lap. Rick is leaning over her shoulder. Susie is at her feet."

"A regular Kodak moment."

"She's reading them a bedtime story. *Ulysses.*"

"What?"

"It's a book. Written by an Irish writer, James Joyce. You never heard of him."

"Got that right. If it's not a Harlequin Romance, forget about it."

"Funny though, it's a huge, impossibly difficult book to read and understand. I tried and never got through it. The kids don't understand a word either, but they love the sound of her lilting Irish voice. It puts them to sleep."

"What's wrong with her?"

"Nothing that I can see, yet."

Judy was suspicious. "Gotta be something going on with these girls coming over here to be maids. Let me know when you figure it out."

"I will." I moved away from the door, leaving that tranquil scene behind, and dragged my phone back to my comforting bed.

"So what happened at the studio? You were going to do your spy thing today."

"That's the bad. Call it a mixed bag. It was exciting seeing the sets and the actors. And that darling little boy who's going to play a child like Ricky. But would you believe Raymond Massey throwing my script to the ground and then stomping on it? And calling it names."

"He didn't!"

"Did so."

"But everybody loved the script. One grouch doesn't count."

Talking to my sister brought back the situation at the studio this morning. I saw myself running from the set, horrified and ashamed at what had been said and done by Massey. "I wanted to cry. But you know what? Afterward I got angry. How could he treat someone's hard work like that?"

"I'm trying to picture it and it sounds almost funny. Thinking of that big serious guy throwing a childish temper tantrum."

"When you put it that way, it did look silly." My tender script mawkish indeed. Hah!

"So put it behind you. Hey, I gotta run. My date just arrived."

With that she hung up. Date? What date? Leave it to my sister to toss a hot item like that at me and leave me wondering.

I leaned back and closed my eyes. Then the thought hit me: I'd been through the worst tragedy in my life. My world had totally fallen apart and I'd had to rebuild to where I could function again. Losing your soul mate gives you a *real* perspective on life, as opposed to the *reel* one. An adult had just blown up over something that was so trivial, when put into perspective. Surely anything that showbiz would throw at me should be easy to deal with compared with my reality.

Little did I know that the next day would severely test this theory.

CHRYSLER THEATRE
How I Met Dick Berg, Important Producer — My Big Break

The next day
Dale's office

My *Dr. Kildare* show was almost finished shooting. Apparently Raymond Massey's complaints were ignored, and they shot my script as written. I could hardly wait for November 5, when the show would air. And David called, mentioning thinking about my writing another one for him. But, cautious me, I decided writing one or two TV episodes does not a career make. I didn't give up my day job; I stayed on with Dale and Ned.

My easily excitable agent, Mel Bloom, was on his way to Dale's office, where I was two-finger-typing up story ideas for David to consider. Would I ever learn how to type? (Answer: Let's say, I just trained my two fingers to move faster.)

Mel had news too electrifying to deliver on the phone; he had to tell me in person. He hurried breathlessly into the office, pulling off his Dodgers cap (his favorite team had moved from Brooklyn to L.A., much to the chagrin of their loyal Brooklyn fans) and wiping the sweat from his face. He plopped down on the edge of my desk, exhausted.

Melody, sensing she was in the way of something private, left the office, presumably hoping to run into Mr. Grant again.

From his briefcase Mel dramatically pulled out a copy of *Variety*, one of the two showbiz daily newspapers known as the trades, the other being *The Hollywood Reporter*.

"I ran all the way from the parking lot. You'll never guess what astonishing event's happening on this very lot. You're going to have to start reading the trades."

"I can't afford to buy them. But Dale has a subscription."

"So read his and get educated. Though most of it is gossip and lies. PR hype."

"Then why bother?"

"Because everyone believes the lies. And then they come true. Sometimes."

"That doesn't make any sense."

In a professorial tone he explained: "Here's an example. A production company announces through their public relations people that they are interested in a best-selling book and are planning to film the movie. It's not true, but when the news hits the trades, it gets a lot of attention, which then brings the company investment money, so *then* the company buys the book and makes the movie. Got it?"

"Not really."

He shook his head. "Never mind. Too complicated to explain."

I brought him a glass of water. "Drink. You look like you're having a heart attack."

He gulped it down. "This was in today's *Variety*." He read from a folded-over article. "Writer-producer Dick Berg has just been inked to produce an original TV series of movies on the Universal lot. Using famous stars and famous directors. With original scripts and adaptations written by big name writers. It's being called *Bob Hope Presents the Chrysler Theatre*."

Mel explained: The well-known comedian Bob Hope was the VIP name attached to getting it made, and Chrysler Autos was the sponsor.

Mel continued to read. "Anne Bancroft has already signed on."

That got a rise out of me. "Anne Bancroft! My favorite actress."

"Wait. There's more. They're actively looking for writers."

"So what does that have to do with me? Last time I looked, I was still a secretary, with one unseen TV credit."

"Listen! This is a *huge* opportunity. Dick Berg is *very* important. He started as a writer on high-quality shows like *Playhouse 90* and *Studio One*, an era that's already being referred to as the golden age of TV. And *he* would like to meet *you*. I tossed your name into the ring and I bet David Victor recommended you as well. Dick has a book he wants adapted."

Be still my heart. A television movie instead of an episode for a series! An adaptation! A classy project. Maybe with Bancroft starring? An impossible dream.

I brought Mel more water to cool his thirst. Happily, it didn't chill his enthusiasm.

"But one thing. He wants to interview you first."

"Meet me?"

"He was specific. He said interview."

I knew it. There had to be a catch.

The next day
Dick Berg's office

I MET DICK BERG in his office high up in the Black Tower, which was ten times the size of our quarters, and elegantly designer-decorated with more of Mrs. Wasserman's unending supply of English antiques. Oriental rugs on the floor, English hunting paintings on the walls, and plaques, awards, and photos in the ego section behind his desk. The most prominent photo was of Dick with arms wrapped around Wasserman and Stein. It was lavishly signed by "Lew" and "Jules."

Think caviar, champagne, and Maseratis. This top of the tower was the top of the line. I tried to seem unimpressed.

Dick, over six feet tall, lanky, and intense, had a grayish mop of hair hanging over his forehead. He greeted me by leaning over me, reminding me of a weeping willow tree. Without any formal introductions, he plopped me unceremoniously down on the couch—an island in the middle of the office—and promptly started spouting gibberish while trotting at a fast pace, round and round me as I twisted my head and turned my body to follow him. He quickened his pace, which almost made me dizzy, and his tirade accelerated. Every other word was a curse word. Hard-core curse words, I might add. Words that I'd hardly ever heard anywhere and words I would never, ever say.

F this and S that and C and A that. A lot more of the alphabet, used in ways I could never have imagined. In spite of being shocked by the foul language, I thought him so entertaining, and possibly crazy that I found myself grinning. Finally, out of breath, Dick stopped abruptly and glared at me. Waiting.

Waiting for what? So I applauded. "Very amusing. Do you perform like this for all your authors?"

Dick slid down into a sleek black leather Eames chair across from me, the chair also British but the only non-antique in the room. (I recognized it from a picture in a *Better Homes and Gardens* magazine. I also remembered it cost about $4,000!) Stretching out his long legs, he relaxed. Then he reached over to a side table, picked up a book, and threw it to me.

I caught it. Well, sort of. It landed in my lap. I read the title: *The Shattered Glass*, by Jean Ariss. I glanced up at him, holding my breath.

"That's the novel I want you to adapt. It's a tragic love story. Women all over America will sob at the ending. Right up your alley."

He wanted *me* to turn that book into a script. Wow! I kept rubbing the book to make sure it was real.

He unfolded himself from the chair and I followed him to the door. "Read," he said, "then call my secretary for an appointment."

I started out, happily numb with shock, clutching my new valuable possession. Then I stopped and turned back to Dick. "Mr. Berg, I really would like to know what that hop, skip, and jump around the couch routine was all about."

"Oh, that? It was a test."

"A test?"

"Because I've never worked with a woman scriptwriter."

"Really? Never?"

"Really. In fact I don't know of any women writing in TV. Nor have I wanted to. Sometimes, when deeply involved producing a show, I forget myself and toss out a crude word or two." Here he grinned in what I believe he thought was a self-effacing pose. "I didn't want some prissy nose-in-the air woman sitting in judgment of me for my dirty language. No way for me to concentrate on a movie. You didn't twitch once. You passed my test with flying colors."

First Mel. Now this guy. Women as a keep-away-from species. "Well, thanks," I said nervously. I wasn't sure whether that was a compliment or not. But I wanted out of there before he changed his mind.

With that, he called out to his secretary. "Okay. Turn my phone back on. Meeting's over." Before he shut the door in my face, he winked. "Read fast, doll."

MY MIND TOOK ME BACK to a time when I was fifteen. My mother decided I was the right age to go to her beauty parlor and have my hair "styled." But I wasn't interested. It was Saturday and my father and his pals always went to Belmont Park racetrack in Long Island. And they had invited me to come along. That sounded a lot more interesting than sitting under a hot dryer for an hour and smelling strong bleach that would burn my eyes.

"Daddy invited me to go with him today."

My mother shook her head. "You always pick him over me. What's so good about hanging out with your father? What do you do when he shoots pool?"

"I chalk his cue stick and help arrange the billiard balls."

"And when he plays cards every night in the clubhouse?"

"I empty the ashtrays and bring the guys sodas."

"And what's so wonderful about the racetrack? Better you should pour the money down a sewer."

"Daddy's gonna teach me how to handicap. That uses math, so isn't that a good thing?"

"Hmph," commented my mom, showing remarkable restraint about her opinion of Daddy, her plumber husband, as a mathematician.

"And I'm gonna pick winners, you'll see." Daddy strongly believed in beginner's luck.

She scowled. "And you'll share your winnings with me, like he does. Hah!"

This was a sore spot with Mom. Money was always tight in our modest household.

Ritually, whenever my father came home from the track, she demanded to know how much he'd won. He'd either say he came out even or that he lost a few bucks. Rarely did he ever say he won. Those few times he'd shrug and hand her a couple of crumpled cigar-smelling dollars. She was sure he was holding out on her.

One fateful April morning my mom decided to do what she called "spring cleaning." I helped her move their bedroom mattress so she could drag it over to the open window and lift the mattress up onto the fire escape to "air it out."

As we performed this Herculean feat of mattress lifting and pushing, suddenly you could have heard my mother screech all across the Bronx as we both looked down at what had been hidden under that mattress. There must have been almost a hundred dollars lying on the coiled springs in small, crinkly bills buried there by my father, who didn't trust banks or his wife.

There was a world-record screaming battle that night—one-sided: She yelled, he cowered. "A hundred dollars! I have to drag my tired body from store to store, searching for bargains, and you have this fortune lying under your bony bottom!"

Dad, once outed, was forced to share his ill-gotten racetrack gains with Mom from then on. She taught herself how to read his pencil scratchings on the programs he was now forced to bring home and to figure out how he'd done on any given day at the races. I heard her mumble once, "Too bad the nag only placed. If he'd won, I'd have a mouton coat next winter."

By necessity, not only did Mom study about the track, but I learned a lot hanging out with Dad and his Damon Runyon–esque friends. They pretended to treat me like one of their gang, asking my opinion on potential winners and in the same breath calling my selections glue-factory nags, but then sneaking around the corner to bet my choices just in case "the kid" was right. It was wonderful fun. I learned how to feel comfortable with men and it served me well.

"THE SHATTERED GLASS"

Inge, Serling, Silliphant, and Schulberg: Famous Writers; I'm in Great Company

Another day
Dale's office

The upcoming *Chrysler Theatre* program was hot news. There were articles about it daily in both trades. Mel was phoning hourly with updates. Dale was thrilled for me too. I called him over to join me listening on the speakerphone.

"Mel here, reading from *The Hollywood Reporter*. 'Dick Berg just made his first deal. He signed on Pulitzer Prize–winning playwright and Academy Award winner William Inge to adapt his own story, 'Out On the Outskirts of Town.' This marks the TV debut of the famous writer known for such works as *Picnic* and *Bus Stop*, to name a few.'"

Dale whistled, impressed.

"But wait till you hear the next paragraph." Mel raised his voice with enthusiasm. "'Within the same hour as the Inge negotiation, Berg signed another writer. She is Rita Lakin, a Universal Studios secretary.'"

"Hot dog!" enthused Dale.

"Oh my . . ." I managed. "My name in the newspaper?" I couldn't believe what Mel was reading.

"Sit down," Mel said. "The best is yet to come."

"I am sitting," I said as I dropped down into my desk chair. Dale punched me on my shoulder.

"It goes on: three more paragraphs all about you and Hunter College, where you went to school, and being widowed with three children—and how her agent, that's me, sent him material and that's why he picked you. How about them apples!"

Another "Wow!" from Dale.

We let Mel read on. "'She is not the only unknown (for the time being) . . .'"

"I can't believe they said that!" I interrupted.

Dale commented, "You'll be as well-known as the others soon."

Mel raced on. "'She has now joined such leading scriveners as Inge, Rod Serling, Stirling Silliphant, Budd Schulberg, Lorenzo Semple, and David Rayfiel.' Do you know who those guys are?" He didn't wait for my answer.

"Rod Serling is a famous science-fiction writer. He wrote and narrated *The Twilight Zone*. Stirling Silliphant's done two great series, *Route 66* and *The Naked City*. Budd Schulberg wrote successful novels, and terrific movie scripts like *What*

Makes Sammy Run, and won the Academy Award for *On the Waterfront*." Mel was almost out of breath, but he kept going. "'Lorenzo Semple: He's creating a series about Batman, and David's written important plays in England. Do you realize the company you're in?"

"Stop," I shrieked. "I can't take anymore. What if . . . what if . . ."

"What if what?" Mel asked.

I took a deep breath. "What if my writing isn't good enough?"

"Nonsense!" Mel shrieked over the phone. "Trust me," said the man who disregarded women as writers, "You'll be wonderful!"

Dale was practically leaping up and down in excitement. "Do you realize what this means? There weren't any other women mentioned, only you. . . ."

"Shh, no, stop." I vehemently shook my head. I was afraid if these miracles were mentioned out loud, they would all fade away. It was too good to be true.

Late that night
At home

I ANALYZED what I was reading. The book was riveting. But what was this? Another story about loss and tragedy? Jean Ariss's novel, I assumed loosely based on her own experiences, was about Helen Harper, on the brink of suicide, who meets a loving man, who turns out to be an alcoholic. About a woman with too much passion unable to save her lover from self-destruction. I studied the novel carefully. And read it again and again. I couldn't believe I was dealing with a dead child and an alcoholic lover with a death wish who had severe problems with his father. Talk about complex and depressing.

Did Dick Berg know that I was a widow? Of course he did. From David Victor, who heard it from Mel Bloom. Who heard it from Dale Sheets. My knights in shining armor. Again I would be the author of fate's random acts of pain.

Was this my future? Would I now get typecast to write every woman's tear-drenched story? Next job, *Widow of Frankenstein*?

I had to laugh. But I was laughing with tears in my eyes. My own story was sad enough. Stop it. No matter what, I had to take this job seriously. This assignment was big-time. It was too important. It meant too much.

THE WRITER IN ME TOOK OVER, choosing and editing and combining. Finding the emotional build of the plot. It had everything a dramatist could hope for. I repeated my mantra—I was *adapting a book*!

I rolled the first sheet of paper and carbon copy into my trusty old Royal and stared at the blank page. Then panic set in. Could I do it? Dr. Kildare had been easy. David and Sydney had babysat my entire draft. This time, I'd be flying without a parachute. My fingers trembled.

Whenever I needed help, I'd think of my mother, Gladdy, and the kind of advice she'd given me over the years.

I WAS IN HIGH SCHOOL, sitting at the breakfast table one morning, trying to decide if I should enter an essay contest. "Do it," Mom advised, "and be glad you're a girl."

I'd laughed, surprised at the comment. "What's so good about that, Mom? How many times have you complained, 'It's a man's world?' According to you, most women can't even travel or eat in a restaurant alone, let alone go into a bar."

My timid mother was cooking breakfast. She interrupted the pancake turning, insulted. "Who said I ever wanted to be a bar hopper?"

I knew my mother had fantasies of her own. She'd always dreamed of being a famous world-traveling ballroom dancer, but for her, in her generation, raised the way she was, there was no possible chance. She was trapped into marriage and motherhood by age sixteen. I knew of her secret life, of which my father was unaware. Once in a while she subwayed at night down to the celebrated Roseland Ballroom in Manhattan and danced with strangers until her legs gave out or closing time arrived, whichever came first. She kept it from my father, even though it was all in innocence, mindful of the fact that she knew most women went there to meet men. All that interested her was the dancing, that feeling alive—it was what kept her going year after year.

Our mother gave my sister and I foxtrot, waltz, and rumba lessons in our tiny living room, from records playing on the hi-fi, instilling in us its pleasures. She was a wonderful dancer and a good teacher and those were giggling, happy afternoons. Judy and I passed on the same joyous dance lessons to our own children.

I went over to the stove and gave my mom a quick hug. "Shh, listen. You said men were free to do anything they wanted. Women were supposed to stay home—what a horrible expression—barefoot and pregnant? If they weren't virgins on their wedding nights they were . . . What was it you called them?"

"Not what *I* called them, what *society* called them. Fallen women."

"Whatever. And a wife was supposed to be grateful she had a man to support her. So what's so good about being a girl?"

Mom leaned the spatula against the frying pan and poured herself another glass of hot water and lemon, her morning health routine. She blew on her glass to cool it. "If women fail, who cares? If she burns the dinner, or if she works and gets fired, not such a big deal. And as for you, enter the contest. If you don't win, why worry? If you do win, you just got lucky. It doesn't matter."

So that was my lesson: Women are raised to have low expectations, and men have all the freedom, the perks, and the fun.

Mom countered, "You think it's easy for them? But, remember, it's men who have the heart attacks. All that pressure from the day they're born. All that responsibility. They have to work their whole lives. They're expected to marry and raise children. But most important, they're not allowed to fail."

Then she shrugged and gave me a wicked smile. "That's their problem."

Little did either of us ever guess that when women finally got "liberated," they would also inherit the responsibility, the pressure, and the heart attacks.

ONCE AGAIN out of personal, nearly unbearable pain, I forged this character Helen's experiences from my own life.

I wrote most of the script at the office; so involved was I that I saw and heard little of what went on. Dale and Ned tiptoed around me, Dale dialing all his own calls. Melody left me alone, happily just gazing out our window and doodling on her steno pad, I imagined stuff like *Mrs. Cary Grant*. Or *Melody Grant*.

When I returned home in the evening, I hurried through dinner and getting the children off to bed. I was anxious until I could get back to my script.

A pattern evolved. I would get into my pajamas and robe, sit down at the kitchen table with my trusty Royal, and, my heart pounding, feverishly write late into the night. It was as if I were in a trance. And another month had gone by.

At two a.m. on a Sunday, I finished the script.

I HAD WARNED MEL, no more signed-actor updates until I finished editing my script.

I mustn't be distracted. Although I still wondered which actress I was writing for.

Then Mel knew he had to break the silence with news that Anne Bancroft was taken. She was doing the William Inge script. Oh well, that had been too much to hope for. She would have been perfect for my script, too.

PICTURE THIS: I'm numb and exhausted, waiting to hear from Dick Berg. Apparently everyone else is as well. The lady who served me my tuna melt in the commissary asked, "Well, who's gonna be your star?"

The mail boy delivering the noon batch wanted to know, "Who's directing?"

The guard at the gate welcomed me in the morning with "Way to go, girlie."

Total strangers on the lot knew me, but I had no idea who they were. Faces peeked in our cottage window sending me good-luck signals—thumbs up, fingers formed in *V*s for victory. I was getting more phone calls than Dale. Whenever the phone rang, Melody would hold up crossed fingers; hopefully, the next call would be the right one.

Why all the excitement about me? Because nearly everyone on the lot had the same impossible dream and it was happening to me. I was literally going to be an overnight success.

Scripts were turned in for all of Berg's shows. All the actors and directors got their assignments. Some of the actors announced early were Angie Dickinson, Peter Falk, Suzanne Pleshette, and William Shatner. The Canadian actor, Shatner, was signed to be the tortured love interest, David, in my movie. I was delighted. He'd just come off of shows like *The Twilight Zone*, *The Defenders*, and even *Dr. Kildare*. A few years later *Star Trek* would make William Shatner a household name as Captain Kirk.

Shooting dates were set. Dick Berg loved my script. He called it beautiful and touching. It was an exhilarating time of anticipation.

ON THE AIR

Biting My Nails and Watching My *Dr. Kildare* Show with Judy

TV LOG LINE: November 5, 1964
Dr. Kildare, NBC
"A Candle in the Window"
Kildare worries about nurse Lily Prentice.
Her doctor husband has died,
and she might have a nervous breakdown.
Director: Sydney Pollack. Script: Rita Lakin.
Cast: Richard Chamberlain, Raymond Massey, Ruth Roman, Ronny Howard.

I hurried about the living room, getting ready. Popcorn. Check. Pizza still hot. Check. Cokes. Check. A bottle of wine in case I needed something stronger. Aspirin in case of a headache foretelling disaster. I plumped up the couch pillows, drew the curtains. Lowered the light.

I turned on the TV set to Channel Four. NBC. Fiddled with the rabbit ears, which needed adjusting. Ten minutes to go.

Judy rushed in from outside, red curls flying, having just come from work and her apartment, two miles away. "Am I in time?"

"Just about."

She kicked off her Keds and flexed her feet. "Where are the munchkins?"

"Asleep or busy in their rooms, probably doing things Mom wouldn't approve of."

"You didn't tell them it was your show?"

"Guilty."

I sighed. They were old enough and smart enough to realize how close to the truth this was. I didn't want to deal with their questions. It was easier to pretend it was all just a story I wrote.

"No comment." My sister's tone, sarcastic.

I changed the subject. "How's work?"

Judy tossed her coat on my wing chair and then plopped down on the couch next to me and plunged her hand into the popcorn.

"Not bad, considering that I'm bored silly. Naturally, I'd rather be married and be taken care of." She grinned. That was a line she'd been using a lot lately.

"How's that coming along?"

"Met a cute guy at the mailbox. His name is Paul. Saw him again around the pool on TGIF party night. We gave each other the up-and-down look, but too soon to report." She scooped up a slice of pizza. "Where's Joan?"

"It's her night off." My new Irish housekeeper was out with some of her other women friends from Belfast.

I picked out a piece of the pizza that had mushrooms. "Want to hear some choice gossip?"

"Anytime. Shoot."

"Speaking of Joan, two of her Belfast gals have already broken up the marriages of the couples they're working for and are now marrying the newly divorced guys."

Judy's eyes popped open. "No! Get outta here!"

"Truth."

"What happened?"

"An easy guess. I can see the Movie of the Week now. Bored husband—I'm betting one was the surgeon; they're the worst kind—sees young blood, good-looking, easygoing gal living in the maid's room. Cute accent. Maybe spots Belfast Babe at some time with few or no clothes, maybe in a shower. All part of her plan to entice? Tired wife too involved with the kids, now overweight, no longer hot stuff, and not paying attention. Is that why those gals came to America? It's all about green cards—to get husbands. Anybody's husband!"

"So Joan picked wrong, moving into this house, getting stuck with you. No man around here to steal."

"Our Joan is not like that. She's perfectly happy here."

We both dug into seconds of the pizza, our eyes glued to the screen.

"I still think you should have invited your friends," my sister commented, catching escaping cheese running down her chin in time.

"They understood that I wanted to watch in private."

"Coward."

"I'm not taking any chances just in case that mean Raymond Massey was right."

"Why do you keep letting that bother you? The producer and director loved it."

"Because writers are insecure. What if those guys were wrong? What if the audience hates it?"

"It's still a big night, the first show you ever wrote. It deserved a party."

"I'm happy with just you being here."

Suddenly Judy punched me. "Turn up the sound, quick. It's on!"

We stared at the screen, excited. Here goes. First the theme song, Music by Jerry Goldsmith. Then the *Dr. Kildare* card, followed by *Starring Richard Chamberlain* . . .

"Yummy," Judy ad-libbed.

"Shh," I whispered. Followed by—*Also starring Raymond Massey* . . . And my ad lib, "Boo."

. . . *Guest stars Ruth Roman and Ronny Howard*; then *Norman Felton, execu-*

tive producer, David Victor, producer; then *Written by . . .* and there was my big moment, my name up on the screen . . . *Written by Rita Lakin . . .*

Judy poked me again and jumped up. "Hooray!"

Making me miss the final credit for *Director, Sydney Pollack*. And the show was on. . . .

I couldn't resist. "FADE IN CHAPEL. CLOSE on stained-glass window." As the minister spoke, I said the lines with him: ". . . that this man, a doctor of medicine, dedicated to healing, should himself be cut down so early in life . . ."

Yet another hit. "Are you going to do this through the whole show?"

"Yes, and stop punching me. I'm going to be black and blue tomorrow."

We watched and I continued reciting, and Judy and I kept clutching each other.

By the end of the hour I was hoarse, and my arms ached, but my heart was full.

And Nurse Lily finally says, "That's what it's all about, isn't it?" The end. FADE OUT.

I wanted to jump up and down for joy. It was good. It was actually good. I was a writer. A writer of scripts.

My sister hugged me. And in moments we both were crying.

Then silence. We pulled away. I sat there remembering when Hank died, and my sister, glancing at my face, realized this.

We sighed and started clearing up the pizza mess on the coffee table. Good thing I didn't invite anyone. My sophisticated, highly educated friends probably would have thought my achievement was ordinary.

The phone rang, startling me. I hesitated.

"Answer it. Don't be such a wuss."

I picked up the phone nervously. "Harriet, hi. You liked it? Really? Thanks so much for calling. No, you don't have to get right off. You're the first and probably last call I'll get. You really think so? Okay, we'll talk this weekend." I hung up.

The phone rang immediately after. It was Doris. I repeated her words to Judy. "She actually liked it, even if it was only TV. Larry watched, too. Come on, a guy wouldn't be interested . . . ?" I put my hand over the receiver and repeated what Doris had just said. "Larry cried." Hank was his friend, too.

I was starting to choke up again.

And the calls kept coming. Annette, then Ethel. Neighbors. My old high school friends Jerry and Del. My family on the East Coast who had seen it three hours earlier but waited until I'd seen it.

Then the calls from Dale and then Ned. I was on the phone till nearly midnight. Everyone loved it.

Mel called, but it was a quick conversation, so unlike him. Said he couldn't talk long where he was. But that was all right, so I got "Congrats."

With last-minute hugs, Judy finally went home to her apartment. I was too excited to sleep. I kept laughing out loud with joy. Remembering again my own words from the show:

KILDARE
You must take some time off. Time to grieve for David.

LILY
It's remarkable what the mind will believe when it desperately wants to. Once I stepped across that magic threshold at night, there was no talk of dying. We drew the blinds. Winter in Cannes. Summer in Majorca. No tears. No complaints. No pity. We were living a lifetime in advance.

Suddenly the house seemed almost too quiet. I listened for familiar noises. The dishwasher had just stopped its final rinse. The room grew chilly and the heater clicked on. An ambulance whined outside far away.

I walked over to the kitchen table and looked at my pages and my carbon copies neatly stacked next to my typewriter. I tossed out the leftover paper scraps of all the scribbled notes I'd been scribbling for weeks.

I stretched my aching arms and legs and walked out of the kitchen.

I moved through the living room, hesitated, and then, quickly, because I was afraid I'd change my mind, opened the door to my husband's den and turned on the light.

I waited there on the threshold for a few moments. It had been so long since I looked around this room. I could still smell the chalk and the bit of tobacco that remained in his pipe. I whispered his name under my breath. As if I felt him there.

Do it, Ri, just do it, said the imagined voice in my head.

I walked back to the kitchen, picked up my Royal typewriter, carried it into the den, and put it on my husband's desk. Then I made another trip for my script and placed that on the desk. Next, I brought in the Jean Ariss novel and positioned it on the bookshelf alongside a textbook titled *Boolean Algebra*.

It's all right. I don't mind sharing. The voice was speaking again.

I felt as if he were in the room with me, watching me.

I stared at my husband's chalkboard, still filled with the math problem he'd been working on until the day he went into the hospital for the last time.

I picked up the eraser and slowly, symbol by symbol, sent them out into infinity.

When I finished, I became as a statue, silent and unmoving.

Then I whispered, "I can do it, darling. I can take care of the children now."

And the imagined voice answered back. *Of course you can. I knew you could.*

And I remembered . . . My husband lay dying in the hospital. It was near dawn and I'd been asleep in the chair next to his bed.

"Ri," he gasped, waking me. He beckoned me to come closer. With eyes still half shut, I bent over and touched his dear face.

He managed to murmur his nickname for me. "Ri," over the clatter of the death rattle, and then his last words . . .

Literature and belief systems have canonized the litany of oft-heard dying words: *Goodbye, my love. I love you. Tell the children I love them. Find someone else to marry. I don't want you to grieve long. I'm so sorry to leave you.*

Any one of those.

What my husband whispered to me, straining, with the last seconds of his strength, to get out every word: "Not . . . worry, my Ri. You . . . go . . . write . . . be rich and famous."

That's something I've never told anyone. Ever.

I felt as if a great weight just dropped from my shoulders, for the first time since his death. And then, finally, I was able to cry.

"THE SHATTERED GLASS"

Shattered Me

December 5, 1964
At home

Something had happened two months before the *Dr. Kildare* show was on the air. I didn't find out about it until way too late. There was a conspiracy of silence. Mel Bloom knew, but he didn't want to spoil watching my *Dr. Kildare* show for me, so he purposely kept far away from me. Now I was about to learn why he had been so abrupt. Why Mr. Telephonitus wasn't calling me daily.

I was hearing the rumors. The talented and successful writer Stirling Silliphant having just finished his *Chrysler Theatre* assignment, received an emergency phone call on a Friday morning. He was asked to do a very special favor for his friend, Dick Berg. And it must be done by that weekend, since shooting started on the coming Monday. There were rumblings about how much it cost the studio to pay him on so little notice.

He had been hired to rewrite my script of "The Shattered Glass."

Stirling was commissioned to read the entire Jean Ariss novel and rewrite my sixty-page script in two days. An impossible and preposterous chore.

"Mel! What the hell happened?" I shouted at his flustered answering service operators who gave me the same nonanswers. Mr. Bloom could not be reached.

Finally, Mel could no longer avoid me. He agreed to meet me for lunch at Jerry's Deli. We sat down at a booth in the farthest corner for privacy. Apparently Mel needed a pastrami on rye and two pickles for courage. I ordered a Coke and couldn't swallow a mouthful. Instead, I played with a napkin, methodically tearing it up into little pieces.

"Why? Tell me why! Everything was set to go!"

"I tried to do something about it, but it was too late."

"What was too late? And don't hesitate. Just tell me." I leaned forward over the table, almost nose to nose with his sandwich.

"They hired an actress to play Helen."

"Yes, yes, I saw it in the trades. Shirley Jones. So, Anne Bancroft was taken, I got that."

"So Shirley was a little bit upset."

"About what? Surely not my script. Berg loved it."

A piece of pastrami was stuck in a tooth. Mel took the time to get a toothpick and work on it while my simmer turned into a burn.

"Say it already." I wanted to knock the toothpick out of his cheek and stab him with it.

"I'm not sure she even read it."

I leaned back against the curve of the booth. "Huh?"

"Funny you should mention Anne Bancroft. . . . Shirley found out she was doing the William Inge script and . . ."

Mel stopped to take a long drink of his Dr. Brown's cream soda. He actually slurped through his straw. I reached over and pulled the can out of his hand. "What!"

"Okay. Okay." He blurted. "'There was no way Shirley Jones would appear in a script written by some little office secretary!' That was what was quoted to me when I called and screamed. God knows I tried to handle it. I mean, can you imagine what a mess that was to have to change the whole shooting schedule to match the new draft?"

I didn't want to hear about any damned schedules. "She must not have read mine. She would have seen how good it was."

"Apparently, Bancroft, an Academy Award winner, was rewarded with a script by Academy Award writer Inge. Shirley Jones had her own Oscar for *Elmer Gantry*. And who did she get?"

A nobody, that's who. I sat there, numb. Where the hell was Dick Berg in all this? He hired me knowing who and what I was. Why wasn't my Don Quixote galloping to my rescue?

"Silliphant was the only big name available, and he had enough credits to suit Miss Jones." Mel pushed his half-eaten meal away. Finally, he wasn't interested in lunch anymore. "I'm so sorry."

I really couldn't blame her. I could see it from her point of view. To say I was devastated hardly described my feelings. How would I explain this to all the wonderful people cheering me on? How could a woman treat another woman so badly?

Mel wanted to give me a blow-to-blow description of how hard he would have fought for me, if only they'd let him, but I shook my weary head. I couldn't bear any more of this mind-numbing discussion.

The air date would be coming up soon. I dreaded the thought of watching it.

"SHATTERED GLASS" FINALE
Pans and Praise

TV LOG LINE: December 11, 1964
Bob Hope Presents the Chrysler Theatre, NBC
"Shattered Glass"
A story of loss and tragedy. Helen Harper falls in love with a self-destructive man.
Story: Rita Lakin, based on the novel by Jean Ariss. Teleplay: Stirling Silliphant.
Cast: William Shatner, Dan O'Herlihy, Shirley Jones.

As luck would have it—or, should I say, screening schedules being what they were—my two shows were on the air one month apart. *Dr. Kildare* on November 5 and now "Shattered Glass."

This time I made sure I watched alone. My own pathetic day of infamy.

Telephone calls didn't come that night, nor in the following morning. The silence was deafening. Nobody wanted to beat the already dead horse.

Here's the irony: My *Kildare* show got high ratings and rave reviews, and my nonwritten *Chrysler* show got poor ratings and even worse reviews. Both trades, *The Hollywood Reporter* and *Variety*, ". . . blamed the scriptwriters, Rita Lakin and Stirling Silliphant, for giving the talented Shirley Jones such a bad script," regardless of the fact not one word of mine was left and Stirling had rewritten it under outrageous conditions.

No one would talk about it. No apologies were made. Not a peep out of Mr. Dick Berg. No one anywhere brought up the subject. Ever again. Especially me.

I wondered, had it been an unknown *male* screenwriter who wrote the original Jean Ariss first draft, would they have dared do that to him?

CHRYSLER THEATRE RAN for four years, 1963–1967. One hundred and three episodes of that highly respected dramatic anthology. It was nominated for a coveted Emmy Award twelve times. It won four. Rod Serling won for Outstanding Writing in a Drama. Shelley Winters won for Best Actress. And my darling Anne Bancroft didn't win? How is that possible?

I was never asked to write another one.

I heard that Shirley Jones was really a nice person. I'd like to think that, had someone sat her down and explained what my situation was and what a kind and gracious thing she'd be doing, giving someone worthwhile, with talent, a chance, and since it was a lovely script . . . Or if only I had met her and talked to her. Woulda, coulda, shoulda—that didn't happen.

In retrospect, I wish I knew what words were said behind those closed doors. Did Dick Berg just take the easy way out and shrug it off? There were so many more scripts—no need for him to be concerned about just one.

I'd had the fantasy that someday, I'd meet Jean Ariss after the air date to commiserate with her, and she with me, over our mutual sadness, and that she'd thank me for having so lovingly told her story. But that was never going to happen. The novelist was undoubtedly horrified at the mess made of her book.

I never ran into Dick Berg again. Of course, my disaster didn't hurt his career.

It certainly never hurt Stirling's career.

Or Shirley Jones's, either. Her career also flourished.

And frankly, I didn't do too badly myself either; it just took many more years of hard work for me to once again become an overnight success.

WELL, HAVING A MOVIE shot out from under me had been a lot worse than having an actor kick the pages of my script. Why didn't I fold under such a negative experience as the *Chrysler* show? Answer: I'd lost the love of my life. What could they possibly do to me in that was worse than what I'd already been through? What could hurt more than never again being able to see the person you loved most in the world?

So, a lesson learned. Doors could suddenly slam shut.

And if you weren't strong, showbiz could break your heart.

And loneliness was overrated.

FREELANCE

Learning What That Meant

1965
(Kids are 5, 9, and 13)

Anew year. Wrote another *Dr. Kildare*. Stayed away from Raymond Massey. This one starred Walter Slezak as a loving husband who needed to prepare his wife for his imminent demise, a touching and tender story about an older couple in love. Another good experience with dear David, though I didn't have the same hands-on experience with the director; I never met him.

I started getting a variety of doable jobs, and began earning enough to finally feel secure about leaving my secretarial job. As long as I could take care of my kids and make my house payments, I felt safe. I even treated myself to a brand new IBM Selectric typewriter, the kind with an erasing tape.

It was hard to say goodbye to all the people at Universal who had helped me. We said we'd keep in touch, but I learned quickly in this business that when you worked on a show, the people became "family." You spent endless hours with them, ate with them, struggled to produce a good piece of film, grew close through tears and laughter, problems big and small. But after the show was over, they all moved on to the next "family," the next assignment. Not in all cases, of course. A few friendships lasted, and do to this day.

I was at a chic cocktail party many years later and there was Universal's Mr. Lew Wasserman, in his signature black suit, dazzling white shirt and all. I couldn't resist. I strolled over and thanked him for the year I spent learning my trade at his studio, and actually being paid by him for my education. Of course, he had no idea what I was talking about. But he graciously remarked that he was glad he could be of help.

I thought of telling him story of the hot dog vendor and the undertakers, but I resisted the urge.

In the freelance world, one assignment ended with hopefully another waiting. That uncertainty could, and did, make writers insecure. Most freelancers worried about when the next job would show up. But somehow, I didn't. I bounced along, letting things happen, never actively pursuing assignments. Why I felt everything was going to be all right, I do not know. Did I actually believe I had an angel on my shoulder?

And when would the angel talk to me of love? If ever?

I WROTE AN EPISODE of *The Invaders*. My first and only sci-fi show. I knew little about science fiction. I was assigned to write, so I did. I enjoyed the program's overly dramatic opening voice-over introduction. "Aliens from a dying planet. Destination: Earth. Purpose: Make it their world." And of course, Roy Thinnes, playing the only man who believes in the danger and must prove it to the world.

While I waited in an outer office for my turn to pitch ideas to the producer, I could hear raucous laughter from the room. In a few minutes, a man came out, smiling broadly. He carried a clipboard, so I assumed he could be a writer.

The producer, Alan Armer, seemed cool to me. Quiet guy: I couldn't read him.

My first meeting with him, I'd started my pitch. "We see our hero traveling to yet another town to find people to help him fight the aliens. . . ."

Armer's phone rang. He answered. "I can be at the gym in an hour. Reserve racquetball court number three . . ." Then he turned away and, with his back to me, continued his phone conversation in a muffled voice.

Bored, I looked around the room. The usual. Family photos. Sports awards. Show stills. Finally, the call ended and he glanced over at me as if surprised that I was still there.

"What were you saying?"

"Vincent arrives at another town. Somewhere in the Midwest . . ."

The phone rang again. He answered. I tuned him out.

Then, back toward me again. I wondered if he even remembered my name. "What were you saying? We did the Midwest."

The phone rang again. I'd lost him for good now.

Hey, Alan. Try to treat me seriously. I thought about the laughter with the cheerful guy who'd been in before me. I guessed I wasn't a member of the club. I got up and walked out. I'm sure he didn't notice. I decided next meeting—if there was a next meeting—I'd bring a crossword puzzle.

AFTER I WROTE an episode for *Run for Your Life*, I was asked about being the only female writer on two male-written shows. "Time after time, you were the only woman in the room. How did it make you feel?"

I thought about it for a moment. "Alone, I guess."

Why were these men acting oddly? Because I was a woman? Where were the other women writers? Were there any? I doubted they'd be writing these macho guy shows.

Dick Berg had tested me to make sure I wouldn't be offended at his potty language, because he hadn't any experience working with women. Was this a coincidence? No. These guys were hiding their discomfort working with me, their first woman writer. And maybe the only one ever, if they had it their way. Neither show asked me back.

What I was most aware of was that I still hadn't met other women writers.

THE FLYING DUTCHMAN— PIETER

Picking Up a Guy While Flying

Still 1965

I met Pieter on a plane coming back from an emergency family trip to New York. We sat next to each other.

At first I paid no attention to him; he was in the window seat, engrossed in a sheaf of papers, pen in hand, perhaps editing pages.

I'd rushed home because my mom had become ill. But, thank goodness, it was a false alarm, nothing serious. One evening the whole family had dinner together, sitting around the old scarred kitchen table. Aunt Rose had cooked her famous pot roast. My aunts and uncles teased me for having left "home."

Uncle Hy bombastically asked, "So, what's the big deal about living in California? You get all those earthquakes."

I countered with, "And what about your icy, miserable winters? And horrible hot summers? Complete with mosquitoes?"

My dad shyly contributed, "In California you have mudslides and floods. You sent us pictures of houses falling off cliffs."

Aunt Rose jumped in with, "I saw it on the news. A Volkswagen floating down a street."

I addressed my parents, serious now. "The Bronx is changing. It could become dangerous to keep living here."

My mom excitedly replied with "Dangerous? You want to talk dangerous? What about the time I came to visit for the children's birthday party, when the children were out in the backyard eating ice cream and a police helicopter flew over and a cop with a megaphone yelled down for us to get the children inside the house because a panther was loose?" She took a deep breath after that huge, dramatic outpouring.

Aunt Ann said, "Yeah, try and top that!"

I shrugged. "It turned out not to be a panther but an overlarge pet dog."

Everyone screamed with laughter at that.

And so did I, laughing out loud on the plane, remembering.

My seatmate stared up at this woman next to him seeming to be laughing at nothing. I smiled sweetly to prove I wasn't some nutcase. He returned a quick, tight smile and went back to his work.

I opened the novel I'd bought in the terminal just before leaving. Agatha Christie was one of my favorite mystery writers. However, by page eight, I realized I'd already read that one. I hated when that happened. Now I had five hours to fill without a book. And I'd already finished my reveries as well as my *New York Times* crossword puzzle. What to do?

Out of boredom I tried to inconspicuously study my neighbor.

He was deep in concentration. Nosy me side-glanced over, trying to read what was captivating him. All I could surmise was that it wasn't in English. I guessed German but wasn't sure—too many double vowels in the words.

He was whip-thin, pale skinned, severely clean-shaven, with short, brush-cut whitish-blond hair, a narrow aristocratic nose, and thin, pursed lips. His rimless glasses crept down over his nose as he worked. He wore a starched and stiff white cotton shirt. His suit pants had a razor-sharp crease and his black shoes had been polished until they glistened.

In half an hour in the air, I already felt sweaty and creased; he looked immaculate, pristine, and cool.

I wondered if he spoke English.

He became aware of my attention. "Is there something?" he asked, speaking with a slight accent, his speech clipped.

I was embarrassed at being caught. "No, just looking past you out the window."

"Would you like to exchange seats?"

"No, really, no thanks."

"I am Pieter," he offered.

"Peter?" I repeated, pronouncing it with one less syllable.

He explained that his name was the Dutch equivalent of the American Peter. Dutch, I thought, not German.

So that got us started. I told him my name and a little about my trip home. He was interested that I was a writer. He was not professionally a writer, actually a tax consultant, but he was composing an article. He indicated the sheets of paper in front of him.

He was doing this article for a Dutch magazine as a tribute to a man who had just died but who had once saved his life over twenty years ago. The trip stopped seeming long once Pieter explained his subject matter. I was fascinated.

I sat listening, mesmerized. His story was similar to that of Anne Frank, the Dutch girl whose diary was found in an attic in Amsterdam after her death in a concentration camp in World War II.

Pieter, too, hid out in an attic like Anne Frank. He was there alone for five years, unlike Ann, who was locked up with her whole family. He was never discovered and so he survived, thanks to his brave friend living downstairs.

All he had to keep him company in this empty attic were stacks of old newspapers. In the first year, he read every single word in every edition. The second, he began to memorize the articles. By the fifth year, he had built a paper city out of the pages and fantasized people living there.

I was amazed at how remote Pieter sounded relating those horrendous days, as if he were speaking about someone else.

And then the way I responded after Hank died flashed through my mind: Yes, I understood remote.

Before I knew it, we had landed in L.A. I gathered up my belongings, rose from my seat, and said, "Goodbye, nice chatting with you." But before I could move down the aisle . . .

. . . Pieter asked for my phone number.

PIETER—PART TWO

A Very Black-and-White Dinner Date

Weeks later

Pieter's pristine apartment in wealthy Bel Air reminded me of a modern museum. Nearly everything was white, or off-white with black accents. The furniture was Scandinavian. Sharp lines. Few curves or corners. Stark. Simple. Functional. Minimalist.

The artwork hung on white walls was modern, no surprise. Paintings were all black on black or white on white. Was that a real Robert Rauschenberg, the artist who became famous for his "white paintings?"

I instantly thought of newspapers, the newspapers in his Amsterdam attic. Five years of black and white.

Cool. And formal. That's how he was dressed, that's how he greeted me. All in black. He blended into his home.

Before stepping one inch into that immaculate environment, I took off my shoes. I sat on the edge of the sleek and shiny black-and-white striped modular sofa, because it seemed wrong to lean back. I thought I should be wearing white gloves, so as not to mar anything, and then—silly thought—realized I would match the room.

Everything seemed brand-new, although Pieter insisted it wasn't. Nothing looked as if it had ever been used or sat on.

He had a manservant who cleaned and cooked for him and served us excellent gourmet four-course dinners, silently and efficiently, with calm classical music playing in the background. So proper and intimidating, I never spoke a word while he served. I sat apprehensively hoping I wouldn't disgrace myself and drop a crumb on the floor.

At the last sip of my perfect Kona coffee, the cup and saucer were whisked away. The kitchen door then closed and all that was left was the gentle whir of the dishwasher. Finally, I heard the back pantry door closing. And then we were alone.

I spent many evenings at Pieter's place, but he never suggested visiting my house, not that I could imagine him in that hectic environment. Pieter sidestepping a maze of toys, being blasted by a deafening TV, overwhelmed by the thundering of little feet?

He knew I had children, but he never asked to meet them.

Why was he interested in seeing me? Why did I go to him?

I wasn't sure. Perhaps I craved order. Perhaps he desired company in his shrine?

This lasted three weeks.

He phoned me one evening, as I was in the middle of chaos. A pipe had broken under the kitchen sink; the dog, Linus, (named by his original owner) and cat, Robespierre, (precocious Rick came up with that one) were slipping and sliding around in the flood, barking and mewling while the children turned disaster into a wading pool adventure. I hardly paid attention to what Pieter was saying, since I was busily mopping up with Joan, who was bending and stretching to English Petula Clark, on the radio singing, Joan informed me, "Downtown."

But then he repeated the invitation, announcing it would be a special evening, an important event. I asked why—was it his birthday? Immediately I wondered, should I bring a card? A cake? A gift? What would the man who had all he needed want for anything else?

He told me he intended to propose to me.

I dropped the mop.

WRITERS GUILD MEETING

Guys and Two Dolls

One week later

Not wanting to think about Pieter and tomorrow night, I decided to distract myself. Besides, it was about time I met other writers, so I attended my first Writers Guild of America meeting. I was excited. Now that I had screen credits, I officially belonged to an elite membership with special privileges. These included the ability to attend important union meetings and private movie screenings. Tonight's get-together was being held in a local hotel ballroom and I eagerly looked forward to it.

My first reaction was that I had entered a medium-size, nondescript, bland room at best. Ordinary metal bridge club–type chairs were lined up in rows in front of the dais, set up for the meeting at 7 p.m. That was it. No noticeable décor in this disappointing Hollywood ballroom.

There must have been thirty or so writers, all men, stampeding to a bar that served beer and wine. The air was heavy with cigarette smoke. The men were dressed in Levi's, sweatshirts, and sneakers, casual. Even sloppy. A few were in suits, those who probably had studio jobs and came straight from an office.

I immediately thought of what my sister would say. *Hey, sis, a room full of men. Go get 'em.* But this was not date night. These were my contemporaries. We were all professionals here to discuss matters of heavy importance to writers.

I wondered what to do. How was I to behave? Was I to ease my way into a chatting group and talk my way in? Try to look interested?

Overdressed in my pastel-pink slender A-line dress with its skirt hem down to the middle of my knee, I felt like the kid who'd arrived at a summer sports camp having only packed a pink ballet tutu.

These were literate men, and surely I could find humorous conversation and clever repartee in every nook and corner, because writers were smart.

Visions of the famous New York Algonquin Hotel roundtable group swirled through my memory. Robert Benchley, the humorist; George S. Kaufman, the playwright, director. And the women, yes women, were important in this amusing club. Drop-in quick minds like actress Tallulah Bankhead and novelist Edna Ferber. But the sharpest wit of them all was Dorothy Parker, poet, short-story writer, lover of puns, who said of their Vicious Circle, "It was the twenties and we had to be smarties."

I entertained myself, quoting in my head, as I strolled around, looking for some group to join. I had memorized so much of Parker's drollery, delicious lines like "Beauty is skin-deep; ugly goes clean to the bone" and "This novel is not to be tossed aside. It should be thrown away with great force."

I giggled as I nearly bumped into a threesome of men who were in midst of an animated conversation. They were bandying names about, so I moved in closer to bandy along with them.

"They actually pay Maury Wills fifty thousand bucks!" said one of them, his frizzy red hair bobbing over his forehead.

"That's nothing. Sandy Koufax is up to a hundred grand." said another, pulling at a skimpy Vandyke.

"Jeez," croaked the third, a skinny Woody Allen look-alike. "*Quel* do re mi."

I piped up, joining in, eager to belong. "What shows did those men write to earn so much money?"

The three of them stared at me for a moment, then burst into laughter. "Sandy writes, you betcha! He writes his own ticket," snorted the gleeful, frizzy redhead.

More hilarity.

The Woody wannabe felt sorry for me and wanted to save me from more embarrassment. "Yeah," he said pointedly, "that's more money than any L.A. Dodgers player has ever made."

I backed away, horrified. They were talking baseball! Clever writer repartee, indeed. I whirled about frantically looking around the room for a female to save me. Any female.

There were a few women. Each part of a couple, probably married.

Finally my eyes caught probably the one lone woman in attendance, seated by herself on one of those metal chairs. I practically galloped in her direction.

Her name tag read LEE. Since mine said RITA, we both smiled and repeated our names aloud, thus introducing ourselves. She informed me she was sipping a white-wine spritzer, her third so far. And what was I drinking? I informed her that the line at the bar was so daunting, I hadn't bothered.

What got the conversation easily started was that we were wearing similarly styled dresses. "Where did you buy yours?" Lee wondered.

"I got mine at Macy's."

"Nordstrom's," she countered. "You're from New York, of course." New Yorkers always recognized each other by accent, an identifying code.

I nodded. "A nice Jewish girl from the Bronx."

"Ditto. I'm a sometimes-not-so-nice Italian girl from Queens. "College? Brooklyn for me."

"Hunter."

We formed an instant solidarity.

She was about five years older. People might have seen her as handsome rather than beautiful. Choppy black hair. Matching heavyset eyebrows. A face with irregularities that missed being beautiful. Wide, toothy smile.

"Hot-looking guys around here, smart dressers." She smirked sarcastically, waggling a finger every which way.

"Regular dreamboats."

We both hooted with laughter.

The meeting was called to order. The men sat down and Lee and I turned to listen.

It was established that there were no threats of a union strike, which had been a concern. Many overly long reports on annual earnings were read. A few complaints were voiced about the issue of late payments from production companies, and that took care of the night's agenda. The meeting broke up early.

Outside, before heading for our individual cars, we glanced at each another. I wasn't ready to go home. She seemed to feel the same.

"It's the shank of the evening," Lee decided.

"Absolutely, the shank." Dorothy Parker would have groaned.

We agreed to continue on to dinner.

La Masia was a popular Spanish restaurant across the street, so we headed there and Lee graduated to margaritas, with some tapas on the side. I ordered the same.

We were delighted with our coincidences. We'd both dreamed of being writers since we were teenagers, though we'd never believed it would be more than a hobby. We were each the editor of our high school newspaper and contributed to our college magazine. We wrote short stories. We both had favorite books that inspired us.

"I discovered Ruth Fielding," I told Lee. "It was a series of books this early-twentieth-century author wrote about a young woman in 1916 who had many adventures writing 'scenarios' in the world of 'moving pictures.' I'm sure it resonated with me about becoming a writer myself."

Lee told me how she'd been consumed by Nancy Drew and wanted to be a detective. The closest she came? Writing a cop show.

She waved at the waiter and ordered yet another drink. This was her fifth, but who was counting?

It didn't take long until we got onto the subject of women writers in TV.

She, too, was aware that at the guild meeting tonight, all of the women we'd seen had been part of a husband-wife team.

"Where are the women who write on their own?" I wondered. "I never seem to run into them. Surely we're not the only ones."

"Honey, it's a men's club. Women aren't invited."

"But why not?"

"They don't want the competition. Women don't belong in the workplace. It confuses the issue. They want their women at home, waiting on them and treating them like gods."

Lee noticed I had finished with my margarita.

She was about to signal the waiter, but I shook my head. "No more for me. Any more and I'll have to take a taxi home."

"My car has radar and could find its way home in a tornado."

Lee was pretty tipsy by now. I realized I'd eaten all the tapas and she'd not touched any.

She asked me what I'd done so far in TV and I filled her in.

"Pretty impressive."

"And what about you?"

"Me, I'm a one-trick pony." When the waiter looked our way, she lifted her empty glass and signaled for the next. The waiter came back and she immediately guzzled half the new drink.

I was surprised at her attitude and worried about all her drinking.

"Let me tell you my experience as an executive story consultant."

Before I could exclaim how impressed I was, she stopped me. "Don't get excited. It was only a title. A meaningless one. I thought I was lucky. I found an agent easily, based on my short story I wrote about a rogue cop. Then got to pitch it as a series idea to a producer. I was even hired to write the first draft. So far so good. Right?"

I gave her the expected nod.

"I had a sharp agent," she continued. "He put it in my contract that if they bought my series idea, I went with the job. But they'd already put on a male, non-writing producer. I sat around in my office twiddling my thumbs."

She licked the salt around the edge of her glass.

"When I showed up for the story conference in a room full of men, they just blabbed endlessly about baseball. You know how guys are about baseball."

Yes, I knew about guys and baseball, I though grimly, my face turning red.

"They would get quiet until I got the message and made an excuse to leave. The minute I left the room, I could hear them talking and the real meeting began. They wrestled with my story until they brought it to its knees. By the time my script was rewritten, there wasn't a word of my original left. I was so disgusted, I was almost tempted to marry the guy who asked me and quit the whole damn rat race."

By now Lee was slurring her words. I wondered if she had a drinking problem.

We were both tired—me from listening, she from all that tequila. I raised my hand for the check.

We walked outside and gave the valet parking guys our tickets. When her ride pulled up, I noticed it was a sleek new Jaguar. "Nice car, huh?" she said, climbing in. "As Mel Brooks said in *The Producers*, 'When ya got it, baby, flaunt it.'"

"Are you sure you should drive?"

"No *problema*, I was voted the safest driver in my AA group."

From her window she called out, "Nice meeting you. Let's do lunch sometime." We both laughed at that silly, but trendy, ungrammatical cliché and made promises to do so.

I INTENDED to look her up again later. But I realized I only knew her as Lee and didn't know her last name or the name of her show. I wondered if the booze had gotten to her or if her show ever made it or if maybe she'd quit showbiz and just married that guy and let herself be taken care of.

But thinking of guys and marriage forced my mind back to Pieter, a subject I was trying to avoid. Tomorrow was my "engagement" dinner with Pieter. And I hadn't thought of any way to get gracefully out of it.

PIETER — PART THREE
What a Way to End a Relationship

All week long I agonized about the upcoming dinner. What was he thinking? Whatever gave him the idea I was interested in him romantically? Besides, it was ridiculous. There was no romance. There were no indications other than quiet dinners. How did he imagine our so-called married life would be? I'd live in Bel Air with him while my brood and animals and housekeeper remained on the other side of the hill?

What was I supposed to say to him? What would he say to me? Why couldn't I just phone him and say, no, thanks? Had he bought a ring?

So, there I was dressed in a three-quarter-sleeve V-neck cocktail dress and matching heels, a black-and-white chiffon number. Was I trying to blend in with his wallpaper, for heaven's sakes?

My Chevy and I made the journey along Mulholland Drive, that miles-long curvy road, the demarcation between the city of L.A. and the San Fernando Valley.

I was still thinking how stupidly I'd planned this ridiculous endeavor. I should have phoned him and nipped this in the bud, but I didn't know what to say. I didn't want to hurt his feelings.

What was I afraid of? That I'd say yes?

That unexpected, unbidden thought threw me, and at that moment, I realized I'd just turned off Mulholland onto Beverly Glen Canyon instead of Benedict Canyon, missing the turnoff and going the wrong way. Not thinking clearly, I swerved sharply back onto Mulholland, oversteered to charge down onto Benedict, and landed not on the road but on the shoulder edge. Going too fast, I was inches away from plummeting off the cliff. I slammed the wheel hard as I could to the right, and instead of moving correctly back onto the road, my car climbed a steep incline on the other side of the hill at sixty miles per hour.

And then I heard the *pop pop pop pop*.

It took me a few moments to realize that all four of my tires had blown out, as at the same time, my car came to a heartrending, smashing stop.

I sat there trying to calm my breathing. I felt my body; nothing was broken, except my ribs hurt from hitting the steering wheel. Luckily I'd been wearing my seat belt. The belt had been newly installed; remembering to buckle it had not become an automatic habit yet.

I groaned and pulled myself out of the car and stood still, looking around. There I was, in the middle of nowhere, surrounded by mostly coarse shrubbery and a few trees, which, thankfully, I'd missed. I realized how high up I was, and I shivered thinking of where I'd be and what would be left of me had my car gone over the cliff.

The shivering was not only from fear, but the night had grown cool and I had no jacket. I looked down at my ridiculously fancy black-and-white cocktail dress, what there was left of it; it was shredded and slick with grease that had leaked from somewhere. My stockings were torn, my shoes ruined.

I heard nothing, except for a few night birds twittering somewhere.

There were lights toward the right down below. I grabbed my purse and keys and began to move gingerly toward them, no mean feat given my broken heels and injured ribs. I needed to find a phone. Of course, it was then I remembered the flashlight I'd left in the garage and meant to stash in my glove compartment. I could hardly see. There was only a half-moon to guide me. I made my cautious way downhill, terrified of twisting or even breaking an ankle, clutching bush by bush for leverage and remembering, with horror, that coyotes wandered in these hills. Thank goodness, I thought, near hysteria, that it wasn't the night before garbage pickup, when all the trash cans would have been out and coyotes would have been scavenging on every hill and every sidewalk in the city.

I almost tripped. Idiot, pay attention to where you're walking.

Once I got back down to the road, which I imagine took an excruciating twenty minutes, I could see ahead of me that there were houses lining both sides of the canyon. A half mile farther and I might have crashed into one of the many expensive homes in this canyon.

I trudged down the street. The first lights I came to, I dragged myself up the circular driveway of a large two-story Tudor-style house and rang the bell, then had the sudden thought, Who would open their doors to anyone in the dark of night?

But thankfully the porch lights flashed on and a face peered out at me through the louvered side window.

"Please help me, I've had an accident. I crashed my car," I sounded pathetic and I didn't care.

I, personally, would never have opened up a door to anyone looking as frenzied as me, thinking it would be a scam with a robber-partner-in-crime ready to leap out from a bush and rush the soon-to-be victims. Oh, that imagination of mine, but that's what makes a good writer, thought I, while praying for help.

Maybe it was my slinky-though-messy cocktail dress that assured them. Thieves didn't dress this well.

The young twenty-something clean-cut man who answered the door wore a sweatshirt and Levi's, no socks.

His sweatshirt had the Fox Studios logo on it.

Thank god! A *lantsman*—a member of the clan—he must be in the biz.

And his pretty young wife (or girlfriend) appeared. She, too, was sweatshirted and barefoot. "Come in, come in, your poor thing."

The first words coming out of my mouth after "Thanks for saving my life," were, "Fox? I'm starting a staff job at Fox. *Peyton Place*—of course you know the show."

"Really? We're in postproduction on that show, and others on the lot," my savior added.

It was all good from then on. They gave me a huge bath towel to wrap around my shaking body and led me to their book-filled den, where the fireplace blazed and the TV played the new series *Hogan's Heroes*. They sat me down in an inviting, fluffy-pillowed wing chair and offered me a martini and popcorn.

I nodded and pointed at the TV set. "I've met Al Ruddy, the producer," said Miss Name-Dropper, this out-of-control Chatty Cathy who didn't know when to shut up.

"Well, so have we," agreed my host happily.

Party. Party. Party. We sipped our drinks and exchanged work credits and gossiped about all the people in showbiz we knew in common.

I was having such a good time and feeling so at home, I turned in surprise when my rescuer, staring again at my bedraggled dress, asked me if I had been on my way somewhere. Did I need to call anyone? Did I want to call the auto club? Though they offered to drive me home so I wouldn't need to bother with my wounded and abandoned car tonight.

Oh my God. Pieter. I had to call Pieter. Amazingly, I hadn't given him a thought. Oh, the rush of guilt feelings. I blamed it on shock. My hosts indicated their phone. Once I had Pieter on the line, I babbled, not allowing him to get a word in. "I had an accident, no, I'm fine, I really can't get over there tonight. It's impossible. I can't really talk now. I'll call you tomorrow."

I hung up their phone and leaned back in my chair. "Another martini?" I asked, relieved. "And could you add an extra olive?"

I was saved. Saved from falling off a cliff.

Saved. Saved from falling into a marriage with Pieter, a man I really didn't know or love. Saved to stay adrift in my safe little unencumbered world, in a world I could control.

Pieter was gone from my life.

Would there ever be a right man in my life again? Guardian angel, answer me that.

PHONE CATCH-UP WITH JUDY

I Decide to Buy a House, and Judy Has a Big Announcement

April 1965

Hey there." It was my sister calling in. I was at my kitchen table with pad and pen crunching numbers, a job that I didn't enjoy, being hopeless in math.

"Hey to you, too, stranger."

"It's been ages, I know. Been real busy."

"Ditto," Judy concurred.

"What's been going on with you?"

"You talk first."

"Okay. I finally decided to go ahead with it. I'm definitely putting the house up for sale. I found a new and upcoming neighborhood called Sherman Oaks. It's very pretty and near a shopping mall called Fashion Square. My Realtor told me the house prices are still reasonable."

"How much?"

"Thirty-five thousand."

"Gulp. But you said yours might only sell for nineteen thousand. That's a pretty huge jump."

"I know it sounds crazy. But I feel I can swing it. The *Peyton Place* job is a staff writer job . . ."

Judy interrupted. "Staff? No more freelance? You'll be going to work in an office again? I thought you liked freelance so you could be home with the kids more?"

"I have to be realistic. I get paid every week. And it will bring in around two thousand a script. If I write twenty-five of them, that will be fifty thousand a year. That's a fortune to me."

"That's a fortune to anybody." Her voice took on a wistful note.

"I start in two weeks, and I'm excited. This sounds like a fun job. I'll be working in an office with seven other writers."

"Yeah, but how do you know you'll write that many scripts? Or that you'll stay in the job a whole year? Or what if the show gets canceled? What if your contract isn't renewed after a year, then what? And what if you hate working in an office instead of home . . ."

"What if . . . What if? Hey, stop. Guess who you sound like? Our mother, that's who. In fact everything you said, she just said to me when I spoke to her last week."

"I don't know. . . . Sounds like a giant step." Little sister still worrying about me.

"A giant step *up*! The show is a huge success. It's on twice a week, and they're talking about adding a third. That could be 150 scripts divided among seven writers."

"But you're always telling me how insecure your business is."

"I just have faith that it will work out." I did, I really did.

"Boy, you must have someone up there looking after you."

I was tempted to tell her that her dead brother-in-law was looking after me. No, not even my sister would believe that Hank was my inner ghost. "But enough about me. What's your news?"

"Well . . ." Her voice took on a coy lilt.

"Well, what? What are you hiding from me?"

"Maybe it was all those piña coladas on TGIF night around the pool, but—are you ready?—Paul proposed. We're getting married."

"Married!! Wow! Married!" I was practically jumping up and down. "And you let me rave on about houses and money when this is really big news. Tell me!"

"We're getting married December 10. Mark your calendar."

"You lucky stiff."

"You bet I am. And you know what? The first thing I'm going to do is quit my job."

MOVING IN
And Moving Up, and Moving On

Summer 1965
(Kids are 5, 9, and 13)

The Bekins truck, finally empty of my worldly goods, backed down my cement driveway, and I was officially moved into my new Sherman Oaks house. The neighborhood was hailed as the next step up from blue-collar Van Nuys.

The houses on my new street were all built by the same architect, each according to one of four variations of an identical one-story floor plan. Built, as the brochure promised, on slab foundations, the houses featured open area plans— kitchen, living room, family room, all merging into each other, with sliding glass doors leading to generous back patios. The garage actually had a mechanical door opener—no more tugging to get that heavy door open.

Now the inside work had begun. All hands on deck. My trusty, dependable women friends were there for the unpacking of the pots and dishes and cutlery to go with my new, improved kitchen homeowners were meant to adore. Joan was at the ready to deal with the children, helping them unpack boxes in their rooms, hopefully without bloodshed. Keeping them busy and not underfoot.

Judy was at work today. She had promised to come on the weekend, saying she would be in charge of the bathrooms.

My wonderful friends, having performed the many house-moving routines for each other over the years, were experts and well organized. Annette and Ethel, being the shortest, were in charge of ripping off the masking tape to open and empty the kitchen boxes. I rinsed, wiped, and handed over each object to Harriet and Doris, who, being the tallest, were in charge of reaching high shelves.

At the same time, we were swaying to the music on my transistor radio. The Supremes had us boogieing to the likes of "Stop! In the Name of Love."

Annette commented over the loud music, "Did you hear that they're making a TV movie about when Steinem snuck in to work at the Playboy Mansion as a bunny!"

We cheered. Über-macho Hugh Hefner and his Playboy Mansion were the antithesis of the new freedom for women. Gloria Steinem was taking on the male insult of having beautiful young women serving drinks to lascivious club members while wearing round cotton tails attached to the rear of their low-cut, practically indecent bunny costumes.

Ethel joined in with "I read somewhere she's about to start her own woman's magazine."

By now, all of us were reading feminist books and articles, which started for us with Betty Friedan's *The Feminine Mystique* in 1963. We were eagerly following all reports of the dedicated, energetic Gloria Steinem's path.

And my friends were changing their lives because of these new leaders of freedom for women.

Annette had already gone back to college to finish her degree in clinical social work. She intended to work in the field of child adoption.

Ethel was getting involved in local politics, guiding candidates running for office.

Harriet was researching the history of the Jewish pioneers in the old West and intended to write a book about them.

And Doris was still churning out beautiful short stories, having no difficulty selling to the classiest of women's magazines.

Annette summed it up. "It's about time we put our college degrees to some use."

I was so pleased for them. They had taken their avocations and turned them into vocations. I didn't feel so alone anymore.

Ringaling. Ringaling.

We were interrupted by a familiar bell chiming from the street.

In a matter of seconds, my gang was upon me. The strident choir of their voices informed me (as if I didn't know) that the Helms Bakery truck was outside. All three sets of palms opened. "Donuts!"

I shrugged and reached for my purse. "Might as well get some for all of us. Buy a dozen assorted."

Like whirling dervishes, they were out in a flash, naturally slamming the screen door, with Joan calling after them, "Make mine jelly."

I sighed. "I thought I'd escaped the calorie-filled bread truck, but it followed me here. Guess I'll put on another pot of coffee."

My friends stopped what they were doing and grabbed for mugs.

Harriet smiled. "Any excuse to stop working."

When the kitchen was done, with donut in hand and coffee mug in the other, Annette offered up a toast. "Here's to the women's libbers who told us we were not only wives and mothers! That there was a world out there for us to join."

Harriet added, "Amen to that."

My weary women friends left for their homes as the sky darkened, calling out as to when next to get together. I was bone- and muscle-tired. All I wanted was a scalding bubble bath in my new Jacuzzi tub and a glass of Chablis. I might even light a house-warming gift lavender candle. A new decadence for me to revel in, in my upscale house!

Joan was in her own room, unpacking her things.

But first, I checked on the children. In her bedroom, Susie was busily placing her toy horses, pet rocks, and turtle in his little bowl in a line on the windowsill. More important than hanging up clothes.

I peeked in at the boys, sharing their room. What was this? Rick was cutting out cartoon pictures and taping them to a small chest of drawers. My thirteen-year-old was giving my five-year-old instructions.

"Socks," he said pointing to a cartoon image of a pair of socks that he'd just taped to the front of the top drawer.

Gavin pointed to the picture. "Socks," he repeated.

"Good boy. So what do you put in here?"

"My socks?"

"Well done." He gave his small student a big hug.

The little guy was excited. He obviously liked this game. He dropped in a second and third pair of socks, then picked up another picture and pointed. "Shoes." He started to put his sneakers in the next drawer down.

Rick pulled them back out. "No, shoes go in the closet."

Gav was not happy. He turned, agitated, rubbing at his freckles. "In there. In the shoes *drawrer*."

Trouble in paradise. What would his older brother do now?

Rick saw tears forming in his sibling's eyes. "Okay, shoes in shoes *drawrer*," his brother imitated in return.

Gavin beamed and put his shoes back in. Rick taped the picture of the cartoon footwear on its appropriate drawer. I'd been worried that Rick would resent having to share a room with his little brother, but I could see I needn't have been concerned. My son was enjoying the role of being the big brother who knew all about everything.

I left them to it.

PEYTON PLACE

How I Met Women Writers at Last and Learn How to Drink Martinis at Lunch
(Like Guys Do) and Not Fall Down, and Mia Cuts Her Hair

TV LOG LINE: 1965
Peyton Place, ABC
"A Night to Remember"
Rodney and Allison board the family yacht for a romantic evening.
Constance and Stephen Cord discuss her legal problem.
Staff written.
Cast: Ryan O'Neal, Mia Farrow, Dorothy Malone, James Douglas.

Exit the world of freelance and insecurity. Enter an enchanting world of no more wondering when and where the next assignment would pop up. Thanks to my ever-busy agent, Mel, I'd gotten my first job as a staff writer. What could be better than on the already successful TV show *Peyton Place*? Unlike *Dr. Kildare* and the shows I'd done up to now, this meant no freelancers allowed. All scripts were written in-house. A paycheck was guaranteed weekly. I was so looking forward to working with the seven other writers. No more writing at home all alone. A whole new experience awaited me writing with a team.

The TV show was based on a best-selling novel by a housewife turned author, Grace Metalious, and was considered shocking and risqué. She had become famous—or, rather, infamous—for allegedly writing about people in her own New England hometown. Smoldering sex (sort of, for its time) and secrets galore. The book focused on the relationship of a widowed mother and her teenage daughter and how life in a small town affected them. After it was made into a successful movie, it was picked up for this TV series.

The series had already made megastars out of the leads, newcomers Mia Farrow and Ryan O'Neal. Mia Farrow was the daughter of a well-known director, John Farrow, and actress mother, Maureen O'Sullivan. She became newsworthy when she married (briefly) Frank Sinatra. Later, made a big splash when she starred in *Rosemary's Baby*. Then she partnered with Woody Allen and appeared in many of his films.

Ryan O'Neal had started as a boxer and had worked in TV until *Peyton Place* made him a star. He then went on to appear in many films, and was best known for playing the troubled young husband in *Love Story*.

Peyton Place was produced at Twentieth Century Fox, one of the six major Hollywood studios, which was pretty, with grassy lawns, park benches, and historically interesting buildings. We were housed in the picturesque, ivy-covered "Old Writers Building." It looked like a two-story Swiss chalet, with surrounding beautiful gardens and flagstone patios, and had originally been built for the internationally famous child star Shirley Temple in the 1930s. It featured a rabbit warren of little rooms, and was well-known for also housing the legendary writer F. Scott Fitzgerald. Like most buildings and streets on studio lots, it was used as a location set for numerous TV shows and movies.

When I walked into the main office that housed our group, I found my fellow writers waiting to greet me. To my surprise and pleasure, here they were at last—there were women writers on *Peyton Place*. So they did exist after all. Three of them!

I was delighted. Immediately, I learned that Sonya Roberts, a dark-haired, intense intellectual hippie, came from a wealthy family on the East Coast.

Irish, redheaded Peggy Shaw, though tiny, was feisty and sophisticated.

Our third female, tall, gangly Carol Sobieski, was shy and sweet. She lived in a famous architect-built Frank Lloyd Wright house in one of the canyons and was married to a guy who came from a long line of Polish royalty.

Though we were very different in personality and working habits as well as looks, I bonded with these women easily. They seemed as happy to see me as I was to meet them.

It was as if I'd finally found my tribe.

The four guys were Michael Gleason, Lionel (Lee) Siegel, John Wilder, and Jerry Ziegman: a smart, cute bunch; a happy-go-lucky selection.

They and our communal secretary, Wanda, toasted me with wine and cookies, giving me a royal welcome. I felt like the newbie kid in the sandbox and was so happy that my playmates were willing to share their pails and shovels.

I was the oldest at thirty-five. They were all in their twenties. We liked one another, and our job didn't seem like work. We were on a winning show and having the time of our lives. There had been staff writers before us, all male, but this was our time. The show had first aired in September of 1964, and I was part of the staff of 1965 through '67.

Producer Paul Monash, fortyish, dashing, dark-haired, and eloquent, was a talented, clever man whose sly sense of humor had us in stitches a lot of the time. He was many different things depending on his mood: friendly, charming, devious, manipulative, and very much the brains behind the show. If he had one fault, it would be that he convened an obsessive number of meetings where he would hold court endlessly. Afterward, he would send long missives about how his show should be done. He missed his calling: He should have been an actor. He loved to emote.

Unlike Dick Berg, Paul didn't have to test women. It was obvious he liked working with women and was comfortable with us. He took time finding the right ones. He understood that we women gave scripts sensitivity and class, and wrote about women realistically. Finally.

We even had another woman on staff besides the writers: Nina Laemmle, who worked with Dick DeRoy and Del Reisman. These were the story editors who came up with the plots from which we wrote the scripts. They would hand out show outlines, like a deck of cards, and we each would write the script according to the outline. Of course, we had to make sure we didn't repeat anything, so we read each other's drafts. After a while, our writing fell into a group style and we couldn't recognize who wrote what. It was a lot of fun.

Our faithful Wanda had hung a large bulletin board in her outer office where we posted information as to where we'd be at all times so she could find us, especially when Monash wanted us. But we developed a secret code for where we really were. For example, for Michael, "getting a haircut" could translate to watching a few innings at Dodgers Stadium with buddies. For Peggy, "at the dentist" could mean she was going to a shoe sale at the May Company or somewhere else. Like that.

Wanda protected my secret. Rita "out doing research" would always mean that I was taking a nap after that two-martini lunch that Peggy always insisted upon, and Wanda was made to understand it had to be a life-or-death problem before she interrupted lunch or naps.

If sudden script changes were necessary, she would find us and say, "Code red"; that would be the signal for us to get back, fast. The boss wanted us. "Code pink" ranged from an actor demanding a line change to other histrionics on the set. Not to rush, but get back soon.

It was a fateful day when Wanda called us on a double code red, which had the whole gang racing back to deal with the mother problem of them all. Wanda pounded on my locked office door.

"Why are you waking me up? I have another half hour!" I whined.

"Get up, get moving. All hands on deck, now!" Wanda sounded hysterical.

"What's so important that can't wait?"

"It's Mia—she and Frank had a whopper of a fight on their yacht!'

"So what else is new?" I yawned, and rolled over.

"She cut off all her hair 'cause she was so mad at him."

"All her hair?" I jumped up from my couch at that.

Translation: It was rumored that when newlyweds Mia Farrow and husband Frank Sinatra battled, all hell broke loose. (Mia denied it.) This time, it affected the studio. Mia was famous for her long, razor-straight golden hair, copied by teenage fans all over the country. She was so skinny that with her hair chopped off, she almost looked like a boy. Talk about panic and hand wringing! The studio heads were horrified.

What to do? With Monash and our three story people, we quickly invented a car accident. "Poor Allison" was rushed to the hospital for immediate brain surgery and came out of it in a coma, so of course we had to "cut all her hair." (I always wondered why they didn't use a wig?) What a furor.

When the shock died down and the newly shorn Allison was unveiled with a cap of hair cut tight around her head, the loyal teenyboppers of that era cut their hair too. And thus, a new look was born. The style became famous countrywide. That was the effect of the popularity of this show. Ratings were so high—almost unheard of—that our show did go from airing two nights a week to three.

THE CAPTAIN'S PARADISE— EVAN

Cute Meet

Still 1965
(Kids are 5, 9, and 13)

I met Evan on the Fox Studios lot. I finally noticed this nice-looking man, who reminded me of a young Alan Ladd, an actor who made looking shy sexy. We'd passed each other a number of times as I walked to and from staff meetings. He always smiled at me.

One lovely day I decided to eat a brown-bag lunch outdoors, and what better place than the town square that had been built as a standing set for *Peyton Place*. It had a park feeling with freshly mowed grass and its own gazebo. I had already written a number of scenes that took place on this very set.

I was sitting on a park bench when I looked up, and there was this same man looking down at me and grinning. He was about my height, with hair the color of beach sand, pale blue eyes, on the thin side. He carried a brown paper bag too. He asked if he might join me. I shrugged, why not.

Evan told me he was a studio executive, a fancy title, he explained modestly, for troubleshooter; if something went wrong, day or night, they called him. He asked about me and I told him about working with other writers in the Writers Building. Finally, he admitted that he'd been admiring me from afar and was hoping to be introduced to me. Surprised, I asked why.

"Because you're lovely—no, more than that. Beautiful," he said.

At first I thought he was kidding, but he was not. He was bashful and I was hesitant. He continued to pursue me with charm and sweetness. And I thought, such a nice man.

We started seeing each another—well, dating actually. We'd go to lunch often, and always off the lot, as he explained, because if we stayed on the lot, people would come up to their table and bother him, wanting solutions to their problems.

I was being teased by my new women friends, especially nosy Sonya, wondering who I was having all those lunches with. I didn't tell them much; I was being as secretive as he was. It was as if neither of us wanted an intrusion on our privacy.

He would stare at me as if he wanted to absorb every part of me. We'd go to a movie and he'd never look at the screen—he'd only look at me. All he wanted was to be alone with me.

It was heady stuff. And intense. This adoration was hard to resist. Evan told me it was love at first sight. I didn't know how I felt about him, but he was easy to be with, so endearing. Spending time with him was pleasant.

Evan liked my children and they liked him, too. He was entertaining to be with; he became a kid when he was with them. Fun nights involved all of us either playing board games or watching movies on TV and eating popcorn. It had been so long since I'd had such affection. All that mattered to him was me.

We chatted about anything and everything, except that he didn't want to talk about divorce. He hated when men whined about their past mistakes.

The children got used to seeing him around. He was just as comfortable with them as he was with me. He would bring them presents, movie memorabilia from the studio, and they were hooked.

I could see a future with Evan.

NEW NEIGHBORS

And It Does Take a Village

'm home. Mom's home early. Where is everybody?" I called from the hallway. There was no answer. I followed the delicious smell and headed to the kitchen, where my housekeeper, Joan, was busy cooking. Her record player was turned up high.

"Something smells wonderful. What's baking?"

Joan jumped, not having heard me walk in. She threw up her hands. "Saints preserve us. You scared the bejesus outa me."

"Sorry, I did call out. I asked what's for dinner."

Joan lowered the sound on her Celtic music down to what she deemed low and I defined as earsplitting. Having Joan around introduced us to the likes of the Dubliners and the Irish Rovers, among others. "We call it a veggie roll. Dinner at seven," she replied in her usual easygoing manner.

"What's in it?"

"Peppery beef, leek, carrots, bacon, sausages, eggs, tomatoes, and mushrooms."

"Uh-oh, you know how they feel about veggies."

"Don't worry. I'm pushing the protein and carbs part."

"Good thinking. The house is too quiet. Where are my darlings?"

"Rick is at the library. Susie's hauled the little one off for a walk. She's on a quest. No worries—she promised never to let go of his hand."

"Really?" We'd only been here a month. It had taken a while to get settled in. Getting the children registered in their new schools. Buying new furniture for the extra rooms and a real patio this time, needing lawn furniture. Informing family and friends of the new address. All while getting my head wrapped around a new job. I had zero time to meet any of my neighbors. Now my nine-year-old was walking these streets with my five-year-old. I began to feel uneasy.

As if on cue, the phone rang. When I answered, a friendly woman's voice said, "The answer is yes."

I was amused. "What's the question?"

"Your daughter was over here. She's been knocking on every door in search of a playmate for her beloved brother. I'm Sara Kay. I live right around the corner and my husband, Jack, and I welcome you to the neighborhood. And yes, we have children. We have Cathy, who is Sue's age and David, whom, I hear, matches the age of your older son. Sorry, no babes of five."

"Well, thanks for the neighborhood update."

"They've had quite a few Toll House cookies and the obligatory milk to go with it. Hope it won't ruin their appetite for dinner."

"But they're not at your house now?"

"No, they're probably at Betty's. The Simons. They're located about eight houses down the street from you. Most of the neighborhood kids like playing over there, especially since they have a gully behind their house that gives children endless hours of safe fantasy play. They do have a child your little one's age, Andy, and also a daughter, Hillary, Sue's age. I hear your traveling tots have also interviewed the Grayers, who have three girls. Your daughter is quite the coordinator."

"I'm not surprised. I'm looking forward to meeting you. And all the others, as well. Thank you for calling."

"See you soon."

We both hung up.

The front door opened. Susie and Gavin came running in, beaming, with smeared, chocolate-covered faces, all excited. Babbling about new friends and "hundreds" of toys and chocolate chip cookies.

I had gotten lucky. This neighborhood was going to be good for my children. I would soon meet these remarkable, intelligent women, two of whom would become lifelong friends.

Susie tried to peer into the oven window. "What's for dinner?" she demanded suspiciously of Joan.

Joan answered with studied casualness. "A pie with yummy meat and potatoes."

"Good," she answered, "as long as they don't got veggies."

They devoured it.

I DIDN'T KNOW IT THEN, that these golden days would not last forever. This was a generation of houses with front doors left unlocked. Cars still had keys in their ignitions. Children could play outside from dawn to dusk and parents didn't worry. Mothers up and down our streets looked out for everyone's children. If a Band-Aid was needed, any home would do the applying. The little adventurers would arrive home just in time for dinner, scruffy from a day of vigorous and joyous play.

Decades later, there would be the expression "It takes a village." That's what we all enjoyed in those early sixties before the world tilted off its axis and there would never be such innocence again.

EVAN—PART TWO

Even the Kids Love Evan, and So Do the Cat and Dog

Weeks later

The inevitable happened, one night, long after the children were asleep: Evan took me to bed, the first man since Hank to do so. He was a kind and gentle lover, and he made me feel warm and safe. Everything about him exuded kindness. But I felt myself holding back. I was not able to give my all. I felt as if I was cheating on my dead husband.

I asked why we never went to his place. I teased him. Was he such a terrible housekeeper, he was ashamed to take me there?

Reluctantly, he drove me to his apartment, one of those dreary rent-by-the-month fly-by-night-type places. He'd been intending to shop for someplace better, but he never had the time. And besides, my home was so much nicer, wasn't it? He strongly added that he didn't like the idea of my leaving the kids alone at night, even though I had a live-in housekeeper.

Because of his job, he worked crazy hours. Quite often after dinner, he'd have to return to the lot and fix some problem or other. Then he'd sometimes leave my bed in the middle of the night. Some weekends, he'd be away on location. Whenever he'd come back, he'd amuse me with spicy anecdotes about the troublesome celebrities.

I asked him, "Don't you get tired of only being with me? Wouldn't you like to invite some of your friends over for dinner?"

"Maybe later," he agreed, "when the blush is off our 'honeymoon.'" He caressed my hair, whispering, "Though with me, this honeymoon might last forever."

One night, when I was home alone, there was a prowler sneaking around the house. I saw a hooded figure looking in my windows. I called the police, but by the time they got there, they didn't find anyone.

When I reported it to Evan, the next day, he paled, then became overwrought. Next day he brought me a loaded gun, which shocked me; I didn't want such a thing in my house. He insisted we go out into the countryside, where he taught me how to shoot. He taught Ricky as well, as his amazed siblings watched. They thought it was exciting, just like in the movies.

Maybe he should move in? He told me he would die if anything ever happened to me. Was he the one I'd been waiting for?

THE LADIES WHO LUNCH

Sonya, Peggy, Carol, and Me, and the Japanese Tourists Visit and Catch Us Off Guard

W e four were having lunch in the Polo Lounge, a restaurant in the Beverly Hills Hotel. The famous hotel was known as the Pink Palace, I guess because it was huge and pink. Since the 1920s, for world royalty and movie star royalty, this was the place to stay.

Marlene Dietrich once came down to breakfast wearing slacks, so the management changed the dress code. Katharine Hepburn jumped fully clothed into the swimming pool after playing tennis. Liz Taylor stayed at the hotel with six of her eight husbands. Such were the legends.

And big deals were made at their sumptuous breakfasts.

The dining room was spacious and the huge windows made it airy and beautiful. This was a room in which to stare and be stared at. Periodically, a bellboy, dressed in a costume of red and black with a black pillbox hat with attached string tucked under his chin to secure it, would enter. This iconic Little Johnny, copied after a cigarette slogan of the time ("Call for Philip Morris," for those who devour trivia), would walk through the restaurant paging some VIP who was wanted on the phone. When located, a phone was brought to the table and plugged into the jack to be answered by the big shot. Of course, the diners glanced up to see who had received an important call. Sometimes celebrity wannabes would pay the bellboy to walk around announcing their name, pretending innocent surprise at having been found.

This was several light-years before the game-changing world of cell phones and smartphones et al.

Peggy was big on lunchtime martinis. Her motto was you weren't really a writer unless you were a drinker. She would gleefully list the famous writer drunks, neglecting to mention that most of them had died because of drink. Peggy easily downed three. Sonya grimaced her way bravely through two. I played with one, disliking the taste. Just licking the rims of the glass got me high. Carol never followed what other people urged her to do. She stuck with water.

I brought up the subject of women writers. I asked Peg how she got into the business.

"Easy. I married in. I married a writer. Lou Shaw. When the marriage was over, I went out on my own."

Sonya said her story was similar. She and her husband, Juarez, had a nice run writing together. "But suddenly he was getting called for action flicks, so I tried for shows that featured women. And Paul Monash was actually looking for women writers."

And Carol was next. I asked her how she got into TV.

"I enjoy writing scripts, so this is the route I've taken."

So two of us had come into the business on arms of husbands. I had entered reluctantly. Carol, the youngest and purest of us, hadn't needed a male to help her get there. She was the most self-assured young woman I'd ever met.

"What do you want out of this business?" I asked my new friends, braving another teeny sip, desperately craving the nap that would follow.

Peggy kept sipping. "I want to marry up into wealth. I'm looking for the next husband, but this one has to be better connected than Lou."

Sonya wanted success, as did Juarez. "I came from a rich family, and rich didn't do it for me. Ambition was what drove me."

Carol just wanted to write forever.

And funnily, my turn when asked, I didn't know my own answer to this question. I suddenly had this image of the wacky comedian Jimmy Durante singing, "Did ya ever get the feeling you wanted to go and you wanted to stay. . . ."

"A penny for your thoughts," Sonya said, poking me.

I hadn't realized I'd drifted off.

"Come on, what's his name? You used to go to lunch with *us* all the time. . . ."

"Am I that obvious? He's just a guy. . . ."

It was time to get back to the studio and I was glad the subject was dropped.

BEING YOUNG and frisky, we high-spirited writers did lots of wacky things in between writing. My favorite memory:

Peggy, the most mischievous, of us, would start like this: "Hey, ladies. Big sale at Neiman Marcus. Bathing suits, twenty percent off."

The cowardly wimp, me, said, "We can't. We have to write the Betty-Anderson-confession-to-Rodney-Harrington scene about being pregnant with his child! It's due tomorrow."

Peggy's usual co-instigator, Sonya, continued the pitch. "We can knock that out in twenty minutes, tops. When we get back."

Carol suggested, "I can stay and get it started. You girls go out and shop."

Peggy and Sonya insisted. Lady Musketeers, all or none. She had to come with us.

The boys, all too eager to be left to their own devices, egged us on. Michael assured us they'd be delighted to get on the scene immediately and promised it would be done before we returned.

Needless to say, as always, Peggy had her way. Fifteen minutes later, we girls were all at our "business managers," according to Wanda's big board. In reality, we were gaily trooping through the vacation-wear section of the well-known department store.

Of course, when we returned, the guys, who had done no writing at all but had played poker, wanted a preview.

"Why not?" Peggy agreed.

Shrugs all around. In for a penny, in for a pound. We raced off to change.

With that, the guys went to our conference room and kept clapping and stamping their feet egging us on.

Giggling and playful, Peggy and Sonya and shy Carol and dubious I made a grand entrance as we sashayed in. With our new designer bathing suits on, plus sunglasses, flip-flops and straw sun hats, we climbed onto our big conference table and modeled them in a parody of Miss America contests. The pretend-leering guys accompanied this sassy parade with more clapping, stomping, and whistling strip-tease music. John and Lionel (Lee) threw dollar bills at us. Michael threw coins to be funny. Jerry, who insisted he was always broke, turned out his pockets to show his pathetic lint.

However, it turned out that William Self, the executive in charge of all TV production at Fox Studios, had decided to gratify a large group of touring Japanese visitors by stopping in our building to visit the writers of their favorite show.

Apparently they'd already toured the set and met the actors. Our turn next. We could hear them just outside our conference door.

"And next, on to our brilliant writers." Repeated in Japanese by their interpreter. With that, William Self opened the door.

Caught! Mr. Self looked apoplectic. Japanese eyes opened wide. Wanda, standing behind them, was signaling a warning to us. Too late.

We froze—we girls still in sexy poses on the table, and the boys enthusiastically in midclap.

But those "brilliant" minds prevailed. Michael, the quickest of us, explained that we were acting out a new scene for an upcoming episode.

John, getting it, jumped in. "It features our women characters Allison and Betty Anderson and Rita Jacks, and their best girlfriends. A scene where they gossip about the men in their life."

Sonya couldn't resist and ad-libbed, "They all went to the beach."

Peg capped it. "A birthday party for Allison."

Carol and I watched, impressed, these vivid imaginations at work. They were all such good liars.

The Japanese guests were enthralled by our beautiful bodies as we continued to "write" the scene. We dissed Stephen Cord, booed Betty Anderson, and sang "Happy Birthday" to Allison, and the interpreter giggled as she translated. Our visitors, wanting to show their solidarity, clapped along with the boys. At the finale, they bowed. We bowed back.

Stern glances from William Self; oh boy, were we in trouble. Heads would roll. But, later, we learned through the grapevine, aka a grinning Paul Monash, that the Japanese visitors had enjoyed our part of the tour best. Whew.

On-screen it was time for the big moment we'd been building to for months. Allison and Rodney were going to finally have their big love scene on the Harringtons' family yacht. Tension was building all over the country. Showbiz journalists were recording the upsurge of excitement amongst all the fans. Ratings climbed.

Since each writer already had his or her week's script assigned, it was my turn to write that episode. I was given the love scene. And I followed our outline.

This is how the scene played. Rodney and Allison were all alone on the yacht. A beautiful starry night. The two of them stared deeply into each other's eyes for a long moment. They sipped champagne, and then Rodney took Allison's hand and led her belowdecks. That was it! Fade out.

Wow! Saucy stuff. Imaginations ran wild at what must have happened below deck. Huge ratings. Gasps that shook the teenybopper world.

That was the sixties idea of hot and heavy. Imagine how that scene would have been played today—especially on Showtime.

EVAN—PART THREE

Things Are Heating Up

A month later

I told Evan my friends were bursting with curiosity to meet him. I was planning a dinner party for the following Saturday night. Evan said that it was fine with him, but I sensed hesitation. I began to wonder if he was being too possessive.

The dinner party was going full blast, but Evan was delayed out of town, and finally, very late, he called in with bad news. Rain and mud on location were giving him more trouble than he expected. He'd try to be home by 2 a.m., but he wasn't sure. He was apologetic and hoped I'd give his regrets to my friends.

I was so disappointed.

My friend Annette joked about it. "Maybe he's avoiding us because we're not good enough for him." Everyone laughed.

I insisted he wasn't avoiding them, but I wished I sounded more convincing.

One Sunday, Evan informed me he wanted to give up his apartment, since he was never there anyway.

I was hesitant about his moving in, but I didn't know why. Maybe it was because it hadn't been presented with any discussion of future plans. And I still wasn't sure about my feelings. Why was part of me resisting? Why? Because whenever I tried to look at Evan's face, I could imagine Hank looking at me reproachfully. I said, No, not yet.

EVAN—PART FOUR

Then They All Fall Down

Weeks later

was sprinting from the parking lot toward my office, late for a staff meeting, and I was looking neither right nor left, but in spite of my hurrying, I turned as something caught my eye.

I saw in my peripheral vision a man, woman, and child standing in front of the studio administration building. The woman was holding onto a child with one hand; with the other hand, she was gesturing at the man's face. I stopped, curious.

The woman was shouting, clearly angry, invading his space. He was cowering, his head rearing back, trying to avoid her nearness, her vitriol.

What was going on? It wasn't a scene being shot. No cameras. It couldn't be about business; the girl, around the age of nine, was crying. I couldn't hear the words, but the meaning was clear.

It was personal. A girlfriend? No, more than that, much more. This was a wife shouting at her husband with their child watching, timorously. A wife—there was no doubt, owing to her possessiveness of this man.

Not just any man—my man. It was Evan.

I gasped.

Evan, sensing being watched, turned and saw me. From the look of shock on his face that gave him away, I knew I'd guessed right. His blue, blue eyes were pleading. He looked as gray and grim as death.

The wife, aware of his attention wavering, turned. She saw me on the path with the appalled expression on my face, and knew. She whipped around and slapped her husband.

A crowd was beginning to form. I ran and didn't stop until I arrived inside my office building.

I locked myself in my office, having instructed our Wanda to inform the other writers that I had a blinding migraine headache and needed to lie down for a while.

Oh God. Oh God. How was it possible? It had all been a lie. Every moment with him a damned lie. A fantasy. A folie á deux, a madness for two.

Like billiard balls clicking into the deep pockets, everything started to fall into place. On the nights he'd come home late from work, he had to have gone home to his own house first; he'd have dinner with her, then find an excuse to leave and have late dinner with me.

He'd do the same at breakfast. If he slept at my house, he'd eat breakfast at 6 a.m., then run home, slip into bed, get up, and have breakfast with her.

He'd have sex with me. And then go home and do the same with her? Of course he would. Oh . . . oh . . . oh . . .

I reached for the in-house studio telephone book and looked up his name and job description. Why hadn't I thought of doing this before? But then again, why would I? In those days, who checked up on potential boyfriends?

I found the listing and there he was, a man with a simple managerial position, a job that had regular hours. There were no problem-solving situations, just a crazed man running from woman to woman. How did he ever keep us straight and not make a mistake, not calling one of us by the wrong name?

I couldn't stay at work a moment longer. I staggered out of my office, saying I was ill, which was no longer a lie, and must go home. My fellow writers were solicitous. They'd cover for me. "Feel better," they called after me.

In the car the same words rang over and over in my head. I knew it. Too idyllic, too perfect! Nothing could be that perfect.

I arrived at Evan's dingy rental apartment building and found the manager. No surprise when I learned the manager rented it to him the day Evan and I first had lunch, and I cringed at the landlord's cynical remark about how his "tenant" never once lived in this place. "So what con was he playing, lady?"

On my way home, I remembered the British movie in the 1950s starring Alec Guinness playing a bigamist captain of a ferryboat who traveled nightly between two "wives," in two ports. *The Captain's Paradise* was a delightfully funny movie. Would I ever think of this episode in my life as amusing?

Oh God, how was I going to tell my children that Evan wouldn't be around anymore? What would they say? Or ask? How could I make clear what I could hardly understand myself?

But five-year-old Gavin suggested a reason. "Did Evan die, Mommy, like Daddy?"

Hank's ghost still resided in our home and in our hearts.

For one long week after the revelation, Evan appeared nightly at my door, at 7 p.m. sharp, obviously right after his usual work shift. I imagined his wife holding him on a short leash. He knocked and rang the bell over and over again, calling out to me to let him explain.

But I never opened the door.

Finally, he gave up.

An Aside

I remained on *Peyton Place* for two years. By then, Evan had turned into a bad dream. I dated some men, but none worth mentioning.

Then, with my contract ending, I bid my writer friends so long as I left to go back to the world of freelance.

All told, there were 514 episodes in five seasons before the series ended. At its peak, the years I was there, it had sixty million viewers, a record for nighttime television.

What happened to these *Peyton Place* writers? Michael Gleason and John Wilder went on to successful writer-producing careers. Michael had a hit cocreating *Remington Steele*, which launched the career of Pierce Brosnan, and John produced the popular miniseries *Centennial*. Peggy eventually married again and divorced again and moved to New York. Sonya and Juarez Roberts quit the biz and went to live in Northern California. Carol wrote many fine TV shows and eventually went into writing feature films.

But what came up next for me after *Peyton Place*, I could not have predicted. What a change of pace.

THE DOCTORS

In Which I Entered the Odd World of Daytime TV—It Was Like Inhabiting
Another World, Pun Intended

New York City
(Kids are 7, 11, and 15)

TV LOG LINE: June 1967
The Doctors, NBC
The lives and loves of doctors and nurses in a big-city hospital.
Althea and Matt spend the day alone.
Head writer: Rita Lakin.
Cast: Elizabeth Hubbard, James Pritchard.

Another job possibility popped up—an unusual one, from a New York producer named Orin Tovrov, of a daytime drama called *The Doctors*. He came to L.A. and held a cattle call, inviting probably every WGA TV writer he could locate, intent on hiring a new head writer for his show.

Free drinks and appetizers at the posh Beverly Hills Hotel? A lot of freeloading writers showed up. Why not? I went for want of anything better to do that evening. I did my usual search for women. Nope. None were at this impromptu gathering.

Of course, like every other writer there, I firmly intended to turn the job down. Especially since Tovrov seemed like some character out of an over-the-top Russian novel. Wild black bird's-nest hair, bad teeth. Long Moscow-type woolen coat and scarf. In L.A. heat?

Then I thought, wait a minute. New York? My favorite city, my hometown. A six-week paid-for stay in New York to get used to the show, then head back to L.A. to complete the contract? Good salary. Writing a daytime soap would be easy-peasy.

The lightbulb flashed giving me an *aha* moment. I hadn't seen my folks in way too long a time. I could bring the grandchildren to stay with Grandma and Grandpa in the Bronx—my folks would be over-the-moon thrilled. What better way to show my kids the city I loved? Not only that, but since school wasn't quite over yet, they'd get to attend New York City schools, the ones their own mom had gone to. The young ones would get to go to PS 93 and the oldest would go to James Monroe High School. They'd get a kick out of that. I'd see them evenings after school and on the weekends.

More planning. Spending time with my New York relatives. See my old school friends again. Museums. Theaters. Central Park. A whole city filled with delights.

Judy told me she wanted to visit Mom and Dad, too, but she and her husband, Paul, were traveling around the country in their RV. She'd get to New York but didn't know when.

I knew none of the other Hollywood writers would take the job. Their snobbish attitude was, if you were a nighttime writer, why would you go backward careerwise, writing for one-dimensional daytime soap operas? You wouldn't. I had no competition. I took the job. Tovrov was deliriously happy at my acceptance. I should have wondered why.

What's that Robert Burns poem about the best-laid plans?

SINCE KNOWING I needed to be close to the studio, I sublet a New York apartment from a darling, petite new actress, Barbara Minkus, who was going on tour with the successful musical *Funny Girl*. I was looking forward to seeing the original with Barbra Streisand while I was in the city. Especially since the play had been written by Isobel Lennart, a true female pioneer woman writer.

Thirty years later, Barbara Minkus would come back into my life when she starred in a musical comedy I cowrote. It was the true life story of an amazing pioneer businesswoman who started a Jewish resort hotel in the Catskills in the thirties. We called it *Saturday Night at Grossingers*, and Barbara played Mrs. Jennie Grossinger.

The apartment seemed a perfect work location. The *Doctors* office was literally around the corner, in the Wellington Hotel, a block away from Carnegie Hall and close to the heart of the theater district. Also in the city were revivals of *Fiddler on the Roof* and *My Fair Lady* and *West Side Story*; so many plays I longed to see. I could hardly wait.

The studio apartment was tiny and plain. It had only one window, and that faced the air shaft. Oh, well. Not that it mattered. I'd be too busy writing and sightseeing and visiting and enjoying New York. Why worry about a view?

Oh, was I wrong.

So there I was, my first meeting at the show's office in the Wellington Hotel. I guess New York workplaces were plainer than in L.A. His office was, to put it mildly, shabby, and I don't mean shabby-chic, I mean ugly. And the hotel itself was kind of old, worn out, and threadbare.

Orin Tovrov gleefully spelled out the job for me. *The Doctors*, like all soaps, was on five afternoons a week. Which meant producing a half-hour script every day. Which meant there had to be a quick turnover of scripts. The deal agreed upon was that I would be the head writer, which meant overseeing a staff of my own, and I'd also write scripts. I asked about how many writers would be working under me.

There was much too long a pause. "You are it. For now," sneaky Tovrov informed me. "Until you pick writers you want to write for you. I will, of course, look, too," spoke the liar.

Okay! Innocent me liked the sound of that. By now, I knew a number of women who were writing fiction. This was a good way to get them actual jobs where they'd be paid for their talent. And soaps would be an easy learning job. Writing for daytime was almost simplistic. Thirty pages of slow-moving storylines. The trick was to make it always seem fresh.

With great eagerness I told the women I knew to send examples of their work. They were all good writers. Of course I offered the work to Doris first, but her attitude was still *No sirree*, never would she have any part of TV. She was still on course selling her short stories.

And so my job officially began. First, I supposedly had to catch up on all the plots, from every episode that had aired in the last four years. But there wasn't enough time. I had to come up with the new story lines fast. I had to learn the ever-changing schedule. Certain actors could only work certain days. Every week was a writing challenge to use the right actors in the right scripts on the right days. And then I had to figure out where to place other regulars who were "under five" actors. That meant these characters could only speak under five lines. More would cost the production extra money. Daytime soaps, as it turned out, had an overwhelming, mind-blowing number of details and logistics to juggle. I'd had no idea. It was a massive undertaking. Nighttime TV was a piece of cake in comparison.

There was hardly time to breathe. I'd have to write these five daytime shows fast, by the seat of my pants. Tovrov and the head director, Rick Edelstein, would inform me when I was too close to already taped story lines, and I'd have to come up with something else fast! Easygoing Rick directed half the shows. He was New York smart, sophisticated, and, I could sense, ambitious. He was good-looking, and actresses liked him a lot. Over the weeks, when I might run into Edelstein briefly, he always seemed to be watching me oddly as if he had something on his mind.

IN THE SIX WEEKS, did I ever have time for my little family or even get to my parents' apartment? See friends and other members of my family? Go to any of the shows I'd picked out? Even take in one movie? Take my kids to Central Park or anywhere else? How about just go for a walk? No. All I had was work and a view of that damned air shaft.

Every writer I suggested that Orin hire was turned down by him as not good enough, and he informed me he was having no luck finding anyone either. I wanted to debate him and plead my case for my chosen writers, but Tovrov had no time to waste.

I felt like a whirling dervish. I couldn't even think about anything but grinding out all the half-hour episodes day after day, working seven days a week with no other writers appearing on the horizon. Six weeks zipped by incredibly fast. I watched my shows on Barbara's ten-inch TV set while I gobbled down my lunch. I fell into bed at night, frustrated and exhausted.

Thank goodness the famous Carnegie Delicatessen was two doors away from my building. For six weeks, they delivered breakfast, lunch, and dinner. I certainly had no time to cook. I couldn't even walk downstairs to eat in their restaurant. What about exercise? Hah! No time for anything but work.

Occasionally, when I felt I'd go crazy if I didn't get out of that tiny apartment, I'd walk the few blocks to the sets in the NBC building to watch Edelstein direct. Within five minutes, Tovrov would appear, still with the wool scarf around his neck, scowling, tapping on his watch, so I'd leave and dash back to my prison cell.

I managed a bit of time with family when we needed to cast a little boy for a short scene. I suggested my youngest, who at seven was still covered with lots of cute freckles, to play the part of a patient for a pediatric story. Tovrov said yes, and so the family took the subway from the Bronx and finally got to see me and the studio where the show was taped. Gavin was adorable. He let the actor/doctor Terry Kiser "examine" him. He sat so still, he didn't need a second "take." What a pro.

After it was over, the kids were eager to do something else, since they were already in the city. My mother was nodding her agreement. Maybe go to Central Park, which was a few blocks away. How about Radio City Music Hall, which was located in this same NBC building, to see the Rockettes? Go roller-skating in Rockefeller Center, right around the corner?

I kept shaking my head sadly. No, I couldn't. No, I wish I had the time. No. My next day's deadline loomed ahead. I couldn't leave. They were bitterly disappointed, as I was too. I almost cried when they left to go home. I missed them terribly because of the impossible schedule on this show I was beginning to resent.

It took me two weeks to write a half-hour episode. Not fast enough. I got it down so I could dash one off in one week. Unheard of. I kept calling Tovrov. Find me some writers! He didn't bother to return my calls.

The weather was getting warmer and my apartment had no air-conditioning. I was suffocating and writing in my underwear.

By the fourth week, I was dictating into to a tape recorder that I'd bought in Times Square on a twenty-minute break. It took me three hours to dictate a new show. By the sixth week, I could dictate one in an hour! No sane person could have accomplished this impossible task.

I didn't even have time to replay what I had dictated. By the time I gasped out the last few lines, the typist was already at the door, waiting to grab the tapes. I was utterly wiped out.

Finally, the unfeasible six weeks were over. Time to take my family home and write the show from there.

A few days before I left, I got a late-night phone call from Rick Edelstein. Sounding furtive, the director told me to meet him the next morning in Central Park. Early, before we were due at work. He had something important to discuss.

SEATED ON A BENCH, in shorts and a T-shirt, Rick looked in all directions in order to make sure Tovrov or any of his flunkies weren't around. I felt like I was in a spy thriller. Moms with strollers and avid bikers went by, and energized stickball games were being played in a nearby field. Cops on horseback clickety-clacked down the dirt path. The sounds from transistor radios filled the air. I could smell the chestnuts from nearby vendors. The day was gorgeous. The park was filling up, but I was paying attention to Rick. Here's how it went down:

ME: I can't believe I'm going back to L.A. and we haven't had a chance to get together before.

RICK: That's because Tovrov made sure we didn't talk. He gave me orders to stay away from you.

ME: Why? What do you mean?

RICK: Don't you think it was odd he didn't like your writer choices and couldn't find any here?

ME: Frankly, I never had the time to even think about it.

RICK: There were plenty of capable daytime writers around here who'd kill to get work. He never intended to hire anyone else.

ME: (*shocked*) But why? That sounds counterproductive.

RICK: He went to L.A. to nab a nighttime writer because this show was in the toilet. It was minutes away from being canceled. He needed better writing and he also knew it would be tough getting a nighttime writer to do it. We all were amazed that he got anyone. Especially you. With all those great credits. Tovrov couldn't believe his luck.

ME: Swell. I only agreed because I wanted a paid few weeks in New York to have a good time with my family and friends.

RICK: (*practically sneering*) And how did that work out?

ME: You know perfectly well. I never made it out of that damned sweatshop apartment.

RICK: Got that right.

ME: I still don't understand.

RICK: If you'd had five seconds to breathe and read the trades, you would have noticed that the ratings soared once your scripts went on. The show is nearly up to number one! The entire staff was thrilled. Especially the actors. At last they had good dialogue.

ME: You're kidding. I knew from nothing.

RICK: Remember that show you wrote to save the production money? You came up with the idea of Althea and Matt staying home and shutting off the phone? You wrote a two-character play, and using one set. It was sensational.

ME: (*amazed*) Thanks.

RICK: You saved his devious Russian ass.

ME: That SOB. I want out.

RICK: You can't. You have to fulfill your two-year contract.

ME: (*indignant*) I'll fix his wagon. I'll write crappy.

RICK: (*laughing*) No, you won't.

ME: I'll finish out the year, but I'm not going to write all those second-year scripts by myself, no way. I have to find someone else to write. And I'll insist Tovrov accept that person. Trouble is—I'll never have time to train him or her, and who could I find who'd know the show immediately?

RICK: (*short pause*) Me.

For a long moment, I stared at Rick Edelstein. This was why he had called this secret meeting. He was hiring himself. He laid out a plan. The lightbulb flashed on. A way out! Then we shook hands. And that's how we devised a kind of partnership that had never been done before (or since) in daytime.

Here's what we came up with. From L.A., I would finish my year's contract. By then I would have written two hundred and sixty shows by myself (*gasp!*). Then Rick and I would share the second year. The advertisers, who owned and controlled the show, accepted it. Tovrov had no choice but to allow it. Our unusual working pattern even made the trades.

Headline in *Variety*:

> **These "Doctors" Soaper Scribes Deal Out Scripts Like Cards**
>
> . . . Working entirely through the mail . . . Miss Lakin and Edelstein have worked out an arrangement that gives them each 16 weeks off during the year. She and Edelstein formed a partnership splitting the $100,000 salary. Arrangement works because they are both fast writers . . .

When the second year ended, I quit. I never looked back. Nor did I ever watch any more of my shows. *The Doctors* eventually died. And I never heard anything about Tovrov again.

EVEN THOUGH my children loved being with Grandma and Grandpa (though Grandma made the scrambled eggs too runny), they hated my old schools and the mean teachers. Ditto their classmates with funny (Bronx) accents. So much for infusing New York culture. When not in school, they sat in Grandma's living room and watched TV. My little guy drove them crazy with Dean Martin's rendition of "Everybody Loves Somebody Sometime," which he played on the hi-fi all day, singing and using a hairbrush as his microphone.

As I was leaving, my mom whispered to me that I had been right—things were changing in the neighborhood, and not for the better, and they were thinking of moving away. I had been reading about a mass departure of people leaving New York and heading down to Florida. But hard to believe my family would be joining that exodus, departing their native, much-loved city.

"Dad would leave his old buddies and old haunts?"

"No, he's against it, but Aunt Rose, Aunt Ann, and I have a plan to convince him."

I smirked. "Lots of luck convincing Dad. Keep me informed."

My children sulked during the whole trip home, about this boring nonadventure, and were justifiably angry with me. We hadn't gone to any of the places I'd promised. I swore I'd never do that to them again. And I meant it. Lesson learned.

Valuable writing lesson learned as well. I now knew that, if I had to, I could knock out any script in record time. That was to serve me well many years later.

SUMMER CAMP

The Kids Are Away and the Mouse Will Play

Summer 1967
(Kids are 7, 11, and 14)

Finally, home sweet home. Away from New York and away from that heat and humidity. The eager three were busily putting away their East Coast clothes, still clean thanks to Grandma's last-minute ministrations. Then they called friends to say, Hey, we're back!

I thumbed through the mail that had piled up. Mostly ads and organizations asking for money. Joan, per my instructions, had sent me the important pieces.

It was lovely to be home again. No more air shaft view. Or traffic noise. Or the sounds of garbage trucks at 5 a.m.

I glanced over at the answering machine and decided to check my newest messages. Number one was from Doris. "Call back now!" Number two was strident: "I mean right this minute!" And three and four, the same. My first thought: Something was wrong. But, no, her voice was high and abrupt as it usually was when she left messages.

When she picked up the phone, she sounded as if she were doing three things at the same time. Doris was not one for small talk. "About time you called."

"What's going on?"

"Pack the kids' summer clothes. We're sending Nancy and Gail away to camp for four weeks, and yours are signed up as well."

"No welcome home? How was the trip back? No wanting to hear the newest gossip on my *Doctors* job?"

"Later. No time for that. While you were away I met some lovely people who run a children's summer camp in Taylorsville, up in Northern California. I saw their home movies of what it's like and it looked promising. I also followed up, talking to parents who recommended them highly. I've done all the research. The girls are excited to go with your kids."

"Thanks for including us. What's involved? Are we planning for August?"

"No, they leave in two weeks, immediately after school lets out, and you better hurry and make the plane reservations to Reno before it fills up. It's a small puddle-jumper with not many seats."

"You're telling me this now and they leave in two weeks? Why didn't you call me in New York so I'd have time to prepare? And where the hell is Taylorsville?"

"It's about a three-hour ride from the airport. Once picked up, I hear that the kids get to ride in the back of the truck and sing lots of songs. They'll love it. Trust me, this is good. Look in your mailbox. I left the brochures."

"Moving a little fast for me, Dor. Don't clothes for camp need labels and that kind of stuff?"

"Yes, health certificates, permission slips, and all that jazz. Joan can help you with that. You're lucky Bobby Watson and his wife, Doris, yes, another Doris, say they have room for your two. Call them immediately."

"But we only just got back from being away. I really ought to check with the kids to see if they're even interested."

"Check fast. And think about you having four weeks all to yourself. G' bye. Gotta go. Heading for the mall; the girls insist they need new bathing suits."

I looked through my rejected-mail pile again and there it was. "Welcome to Walking G Ranch and Summer Camp."

My darlings sat on the floor of the playroom, legs crossed, eagerly listening as I read them the brochure. "Water-skiing on Lake Antelope, swimming under Indian Falls on the Feather River . . . Ping-Pong . . . badminton . . . hiking . . . horseback riding . . . homemade ice cream . . . skit night . . . the Fourth of July costume parade." It did sound like fun.

"Anybody interested?"

Rick and Sue jumped up with a chorus of yeahs!

Maybe they liked the idea of being on their own as well.

"But what about me?" Gavin wailed, too young to leave home.

HOORAY! I couldn't believe it. They were out of the house. Gavin was happily delivered to a daily kindergarten-age summer camp nearby. Was it unmotherly to be thrilled that my children were gone for four golden weeks? I didn't care—I felt half guilt, half delight. I had promised them something special when we got home from New York, and this bonanza dropped into my lap. Now I could work peacefully on what was left of what I owed Orin Tovrov without one of them leaning over my desk, hand on hip, saying, in that disapproving tone, "You're thinking. Right? That means you're working. Right? That means I can't ask you a lot of questions? Right?"

Peaceful.

I could clean closets.

I could control the TV and watch summer reruns of the *I Love Lucy* shows with the amazingly funny Lucille Ball.

I could go to the movies in the afternoon and I could see something that didn't emerge from a comic book. Grown-ups talking about grown-up things.

After reading an article in the trades, I was looking forward to the opening of the movie *In the Heat of the Night*, starring Rod Steiger and Sidney Poitier. It sounded like a groundbreaking story. And the script had been written by Stirling Silliphant, Yes, the same guy who, years ago, rewrote "Shattered Glass." It was no surprise to me that Stirling would someday be a big-name feature film screenwriter.

I could sleep late on the weekends and not have to carpool to baseball games and ballet lessons and piano lessons.

I could walk around the house in my undies.

I might even go on a date if someone asked me.

The house was so empty. I missed my kiddies already.

RICK WROTE DAILY; his notes were basic. He asked for money to buy more secret candy at the local grocery, on days that Bobby drove them into town. Sweets were naturally forbidden at camp. Susie was having too much fun to write more than a couple of brief cards.

I didn't find out until later that Bobby Watson had originally been a high school PE teacher who lost one leg in a sports accident. He drove the camp pickup truck, filled with all our children, using his prosthetic leg on the clutch to engage the gears! (I'm so glad I didn't know.) He was an inspiration to all of them, still a gifted athlete, showing that having a handicap should not stop one from living a full life.

Years later, my children listed the Walking G Camp high up on their list of the best experiences in their lives. Gavin joined them when he was older.

Bobby and Doris, summer after summer, made their camp experiences memorable, filled with learning and joyfulness. They were part of the "it takes a village" people who made my children's lives forever meaningful.

ALFREDO

I Meet a Man, Mysteriously, and Ask, "What's It All About, Alfie?"

1968
Home and producer's office
Chasen's restaurant at night
(Kids are 8, 12, and 16)

was out searching for a new assignment once again. Even though I was looking forward to something new, I wasn't in too much of a hurry. I needed a rest from that crazy *Doctors* experience.

I don't recall where or how I met this movie producer. I don't even remember his name, but what does stick in my mind was having an appointment in this man's office in a posh section of Beverly Hills.

I wore my typical work outfit, a brown skirt, matching jacket, light-colored rayon blouse, and low heels. I wasn't much into any of the 1960s creations. Go-go boots? Miniskirts? Not for me.

It was a large, well-appointed office with dark walnut paneling. There were the usual plaques on the walls, but I never got close enough to see or inspect the producer's credentials in the dimly lit room. The lighting was just two floor lamps. One beside his desk and one at the far corner of the room next to a couch.

Maybe this producer had eye problems and was bothered by light. He was seated at his desk when I entered. I wasn't offered coffee or water. He appeared well dressed. I think he was about fifty. There were no papers on his desk. I don't know why, but I was instantly uncomfortable.

"So, what movie ideas have you come to pitch to me?"

I started my storytelling, but he didn't seem to be paying attention. I saw his eyes darting back and forth toward the other floor lamp.

At one point I managed to take a quick peek, wondering what was attracting his interest. To my surprise there was a man sitting on a couch in the shadows. I couldn't see him clearly. How peculiar. The producer didn't acknowledge the man being there.

I rambled on but I knew it was a waste of time.

The producer abruptly looked at his watch and stood up. "Sorry," he said, abruptly, "I have another meeting. Come up with some more ideas."

How rude, I thought.

He came around the desk and walked me quickly to the outer door.

I would have said something to his secretary about another appointment, but she was no longer there. Just as well. Why should I bother coming back? This was a dud.

When I walked outside, my eyes hurt in the dazzling sunshine. I was still puzzled.

I stood there for a moment, thinking about what had just happened, or rather what hadn't happened. Why had he bothered meeting with me? Well, that was bizarre.

A glance at my watch made me realize it was almost time for the kids to get home from school. I left the rarified air of Beverly Hills and headed back to the Valley.

When I turned the key and opened the front door, I could hear my phone ringing.

I hurried to answer and to my surprise, a deep male voice said, "I was the man sitting in the corner under the lamplight. Would you have dinner with me tonight?"

Huh?

"Please. I know this sounds odd. But I'm harmless. I promise."

I have no idea why I said okay. Perhaps because he caught me off guard and it was easier just to say yes rather than get into a discussion with a total stranger. Maybe I was curious to see who had been hidden in the corner. And ask why he was there. In the 1960s we weren't as paranoid about strangers as we are now.

Had it been a real meeting I attended or was the whole thing a setup? Surely not to meet me? Gee, if he wanted to meet me, there were less dramatic and elaborate ways.

Not that I was interested in meeting a new man. Not yet. Besides, the Evan fiasco would put anyone off of dating.

I told Mystery Man to honk when he got to my house and I would come out. I didn't want to go through introductions with my children. They'd ask all their usual nosy-kid questions.

He honked. Exactly 6 p.m., as he'd promised. I walked out. Oh my. There was a black shiny Rolls-Royce and a man standing next to it.

Behind me I felt the kids and Joan peeking out the living room window. They were plenty curious and so was I.

What I saw, standing there holding the Rolls door open, was a much older man. Maybe sixtyish, which to me at thirty-seven seemed almost old. He was portly, with hair that was wavy deep brown, but with gray at the temples. His suit looked expensive. His face was deeply tanned. He wasn't bad looking for his age. Probably still went to the gym. Color him distinguished.

He helped me into the car and off we went.

What had I gotten myself into?

I looked back and saw my little tribe grinning and waving.

New York City, c. 1940s. Here I am with Mom and Dad and kid sister, Judy.

RUTH FIELDING
IN
MOVING PICTURES

ALICE B· EMERSON

My first inspiration.

New York City, June 17, 1950.
I marry my wonderful Hank.

Lake George, New York,
1950. On our honeymoon.

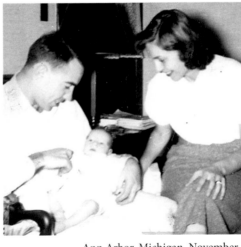

Ann Arbor, Michigan, November
1952. With firstborn, Howard Eric.
Daddy is studying at the university.

Ann Arbor, Michigan, c. 1954. Mama gets kissed by Howard, now nicknamed Ricky.

Van Nuys, California, 1956. Our first home. Daddy playing with Ricky.

Sherman Oaks, California, 1962. My three children, now including Susan and Gavin.

Lake Arrowhead, California, c. 1966.
Family vacations. We love traveling.

Sherman Oaks, California, 1966. A cheerful family portrait.
Ricky wants to be called Howard once more.

MANHUNT

WORLD'S MOST POPULAR CRIME-FICTION MAGAZINE

OCTOBER, 1962
35 CENTS

JAMES A. DUNN

MICHAEL ZUROY

RICHARD DEMING

CHARLES SLOAN

BRYCE WALTON

R. W. LAKIN

JOHN KNOX

VERY STORY NEW!

My first writing sale in 1962—$12.00! Notice the
initials—no women writers, a man's profession only!

At home, burning the midnight oil.
Remember typewriters? I miss the
"ping" at the end of the line.

Peyton Place, 1965. *Left to right:* Dick De Roy, Sonya Roberts, Michael Gleason, Nina Laemmle, Peggy Shaw, Lee Siegel, Paul Monash, me, Carol Sobieski, Paul's secretary Celia, and Del Reisman. Official creative team photo. Finally, there are other women writers! Notice how women dress for work in those days.

Return to Peyton Place, c. 1980s, PR shot. I'm with Barbara Parkins and Dorothy Malone, reunited again. We're discussing women in TV at a press conference.

Mod Squad, 1969. *Left to right:* Clarence Williams III, Michael Cole, Peggy Lipton, and Tige Andrews. "One white. One blonde. One black!" The '60s ad being politically incorrect.

EDGAR ALLAN POE
SPECIAL
AWARD
presented to
Rita Lakin
for her teleplay
In This Corner—Sol Alpert
by Mystery Writers of America

Mod Squad, 1970. An important award. But where is my statue? Ask H.B.

Mod Squad, c. 1971. With Aaron Spelling. He tells me to always stand near the man in power.

Sherman Oaks, California, c. 1970.
On our patio by the swimming pool.

Tel Aviv, Israel, c. 1970s. With my sister,
Judy, at our hotel after sightseeing.

"Where are we going?" I asked.

"Chasen's. If that's all right with you?"

I'd heard about that restaurant. Exclusive and fancy.

Back over the canyons into Beverly Hills again.

"Dave and Maude are dear friends."

Of course they would be. I guessed he was referring to the owners of the restaurant, which was well-known for being a movie star hangout. I leaned back to enjoy the amazing car. It practically purred.

"Ahem," I started. "Since you already know my name, might this be a good time to ask who you are?"

He smiled and patted my hand. "The long or shorter version?"

"Your choice."

"Alfredo Francesco Vincenzo Angelo di Salvo. Or you may call me Al."

Thank God he didn't expect me to address him by the entire list.

"I hope you hold nothing against Italians."

That sounded like a double entendre. I changed the subject. I couldn't resist asking: "That story conference today was really about meeting me?" I had this sudden thought. "I was brought there so you could look me over?"

"You could say that."

I had to admit he had a soothing voice.

"I guess I must have passed the test." I thought of Dick Berg testing me on my tolerance for foul language before he would hire me. What was this test for? I was beginning to have an idea.

"Yes, you did."

I was about to ask how he knew about me in the first place, but we had arrived at Chasen's. Alfredo Francesco, etc., etc. parked his Rolls in the adjoining lot. Obviously nobody touched that car; the waiting valet attendants knew better.

Sure enough, Dave and Maude Chasen hurried over to greet him at the entrance. So my Alfredo was definitely a VIP.

As Dave walked us through the restaurant to our table, I spotted some famed actors. There was Jack Webb from *Dragnet*. And Warren Beatty, having just finished the fabulous *Bonnie and Clyde*. With some gorgeous woman.

And was that Sinatra two booths away? Wow! He was obviously no longer with Mia Farrow. I squinted, trying to determine whether that was Ava Gardner hanging onto Frankie's neck.

The diners were dressed to kill. I sure must have dazzled them with my go-to-story-meeting ensemble from that morning; I hadn't thought to change. Who knew I'd be at one of the most celebrated restaurants in the city. And makeup. Why hadn't I, at least, put some lipstick on?

Dave sat us in what must have been Alfredo Francesco Vincenzo Angelo's personal booth in the far back. My God, it even had a curtain! I didn't let my mind dwell on what must have gone on when it was drawn. But thankfully, Al left it open.

The evening went by pleasantly enough. Al was exceedingly polite. And quite solicitous. I drank a lot of white wine—Al informed me it was pinot grigio. All I remember is being asked many questions about me, my kids, and my dreams, hopes, and desires, along with gorging on a huge broiled-lobster dinner.

When Al took me home, he kissed my hand and said, "Good night. I had a lovely time. May I call again?"

"Sure," I said dashing into my house as quickly as I could. I didn't want to linger. I was puzzled about the whole weird day. Hopefully I'd never hear from him again. He certainly wasn't my type and was definitely too old.

I realized he hadn't said one word about himself all evening.

I'd felt something odd when I'd pulled my house keys out of my purse. I looked inside to find a pair of nylon stockings. And a one-hundred-dollar bill! Huh?

ALFREDO—PART TWO

With an Offer I Couldn't Refuse?

Next morning
Home

I t was 9 a.m. and I'd already had a busy morning. I'd taken my unreliable car into the shop again, and it wouldn't be ready till noon. One of the mechanics had driven me home, and I was to call to get a ride back when it was done.

I was finally drinking my morning coffee and thinking that I had no choice. It was necessary to see Al again. To give him back his stockings and his money. Who puts those things in a woman's purse anyhow? Weird. What was that all about? And how was I going to find him? I needed to call that producer again, but I doubted whether he'd be in his office on Saturday.

The phone rang. And guess who? It was Al, calling to invite me to lunch. Persistent, wasn't he. I didn't want another date, but I did need to return his "gifts." After a moment I came up with an idea, so I told him I was busy. If he wanted to see me, he could do me a favor and drive me to my garage to pick up my car and we could have lunch while we waited. The garage said my car would be ready about noon. My plan was to slip him his "gifts" when I had a chance. I was sure hanging around a low-rent garage would bore him and he'd leave soon.

"That sounds like fun," Al said. "What time should I pick you up?"

Unbelievable!

HIS IDEA of a relaxed daytime outfit was another pricey suit, but without the vest and no tie. My idea of what to wear on a day of errands was tan slacks and a matching blouse and sneakers. I certainly didn't want to dress up to impress Al.

My boys, who had been outside shooting hoops and admiring his Rolls-Royce, insisted they wanted to come too. I was about to say no, but Al was delighted and invited them along for lunch as well. So we all climbed into the luxury car. The boys were dumbstruck. Since this wasn't my lemon of a car, which they happily trashed whenever we drove anywhere, they sat rigid and still—unheard of—breathing shallowly lest they did anything wrong. Something about the Rolls-Royce made them behave differently. Too bad they didn't have the same respect for my little Chevy Corvair. Not a peep out of them the whole trip.

The garage was in a small strip mall. BILL'S AUTO PARTS—WE CAN FIX ANY-THING THAT MOVES was next to a newly ubiquitous McDonald's. The kids excitedly begged to have lunch there. Al seconded the motion. That was a surprise.

We certainly made a splash when we drove into Bill's shabby parking lot. Remembering Al's attention to his car last night (was it only last night?), I wondered what he'd do here in this questionable Van Nuys neighborhood. Stores had eight-foot-high chain-link fences, which did not bode well concerning safety. His was an automobile crying out to be stripped, stolen, or vandalized. Al seemed unfazed as he parked alongside a rickety fence now partnered with various junker cars and trucks.

Lunch at McDonald's went well. Once again, Al amazed me. He seemed to savor his cheeseburger as much as he did last night's lobster. I couldn't swallow their food, so I sipped the awful coffee.

Rick and Gavin decided that they wanted to eat at their own table; grown-ups were boring. They moved two tables away from us and giggled. I didn't know whether they were trying to give us privacy or do what I usually chastised them for, eating only one bite of the Big Mac, which they really didn't like, and then devouring the skinny French fries with too much ketchup. And downing the greasy mess with a vanilla shake.

It was now or never. I discreetly pulled out the stockings package and the hundred bucks and shoved them under the table and into his hands. "What were you thinking? Why would you give me this?"

He looked at me questioningly. "Why not?"

I pushed my tepid coffee away.

"It was a gift to a lovely lady," he said mildly.

"What for? You don't know me."

He smiled. "I'd like to. I have a proposal to offer you."

A what? What was he up to now?

"After you drop your car and the children, may I take you for a ride this afternoon around Beverly Hills or even Bel Air if you prefer? Pick a house that you and the children would like. I'll buy it for you. Of course, I'll put it in your own name. And you do need a better car," he said, disparaging my faithless, newly repaired Chevy, which now sat pathetically next to his Rolls. "The other part of my package deal . . ." An even bigger smile.

". . . We'll go to a lawyer of your choice. He'll write up a contract. Also included will be money put away for each of your children to attend college. The money will be held in trust and allowed to grow. You already have a son getting close to that time." And here he emitted a small, self-satisfied chuckle. He sat back against the orange plastic seat, pleased with his presentation.

For a few moments I just sputtered. When I could speak again I asked, "And then what?" As if I hadn't figured out what that might be.

He was happy to answer. "All I ask is to visit you once in a while. I promise not to bother you too often. Perhaps only once a week. Of course, for the sake of the children, I won't stay all night . . ."

"Stop," I managed to get out of my quivering mouth. "Are you kidding?"

He looked hurt. "I know you have a medium-price house and I also know what you earn and I think you deserve much more."

I guess I sure talked a lot on all that pinot grigio last night. I stood up. "Al," I said choking on the words, "thank you very much, but I can't accept."

He got up too. "I understand. You want to think about it."

"No. I can't. I won't. Please don't call again and please leave now."

He stared at me for a few moments, trying to decide whether I was just playing hard to get. Was he debating whether to throw in an Olympic-size swimming pool?

He took my hand in his. "Thank you. I enjoyed our petite lunch."

With that, Alfredo Francesco Vincenzo Angelo di Salvo left my life.

The boys complained. They had wanted to ride back home in the rich car.

WHEN I THOUGHT about it later, I was incensed. That damn "producer" had been a pimp! I went to the library, on a hunch. I wanted to look up Al's name. Somehow I knew he'd be listed somewhere. Of course, there weren't any computers at that time. I went to the research section.

And there he was. Like a cliché, he was New York Mafia, street name Fredo al Diablo. Good grief! His territory was the meatpacking district below Hell's Kitchen. "Fredo" had served a five-year sentence in a federal prison. After which he retired to California.

I wondered how many houses he'd bought for how many women.

I had to laugh. I never realized I was a femme fatale.

I promised myself to buy a better car. My Corvair's time had come.

An Aside

Many years later
CBS office

I met a lovely young woman who was a CBS programmer at the Fairfax Avenue office in West Hollywood. By the 1980s I was well-known enough that I could pitch series ideas to produce on my own. And by that time, women executives finally had jobs on a ground-floor level. We were chatting merrily along as we tossed out stories about growing up in New York before we discussed potential TV projects. Another member of the came-from-New York club. And we did the usual identifying litany. Where did you grow up? What neighborhood? What school did you go to? When did you leave? When did you come to California? Why? And so on.

So there I sat with the network exec enjoying playing "Can You Top This" yet again, as it played out with the woman I met long ago, the mysterious Lee. It always went the same way.

"I went to Hunter College," said I.

"I went to NYU," said she.

"We were so poor, we lived in the East Bronx," I admitted.

"*We* were so poor, we lived in Hell's Kitchen," she countered.

And suddenly, as the expression goes, the penny dropped. I thought she looked familiar, even though I'd never met her before. I had this appointment with Ms. Francesca di Salvo! Oh my! No wonder she seemed familiar. She looked like her father!

Before I could stop myself, I blurted, "Do you have a relative named Alfredo di Salvo?

Francesca froze. It was as if the blood drained from her face.

I knew I'd blundered, as the words had jumped out with a mind of their own. Me and my big mouth. The New York shtick had loosened my tongue and swept away normal caution.

The friendly smile disappeared. She asked, with ice in her voice, "Were you one of *his* women?"

I whispered, "No. I was . . . once introduced to him . . ."

She tried to hold back tears. "He destroyed our family. My poor mother. All our friends were aware of the women he was keeping all over Beverly Hills. Where we lived! Can you imagine what she felt? The shame?"

"I'm sorry," I said.

Our meeting ended abruptly. Francesca suddenly had a migraine.

I was not surprised when she never called me back. I felt terrible for having brought it up. Sometimes the past should be left where it was. Far away and long ago.

FRIENDSHIP

We Girls Go Jogging, and I Get Teased

A week later
Beverly Hills

We were jogging around a fancy dirt track (an oxymoron?) in Coldwater Canyon, my friends and I. It was in a high-profile area and women, heavily made up and stylishly coifed, dressed in the latest in jogging clothes, pranced around and about us.

Our being here came about because we'd made a pact a while ago to do fast walking at least twice a week in the name of health and beauty.

I'd missed six weeks of this exercise plan when I was cooped up in New York. I didn't count as health-giving the three flights of stairs I had to schlep up to my sublet while in the city.

I stopped, stretched, and groaned. My back was aching from being out of condition. It didn't help that it was windy up here in the canyon and my sweating was beginning to chill me. Besides, I never was one for keeping fit. I had finally quit smoking, but my breathing had already suffered. Right now I just wanted to get home and soak in a hot tub.

"Keep up, keep up," Annette shouted from behind me. "We still have another twenty minutes."

"OMDB," I whispered to myself, then whined, "I have to finish my *Doctors* script, so don't nag."

Ethel snickered and stopped next to me, running in place. "Your choice, babe. You could have had it way easier."

Hands on hips, I took her on. "And just how was I supposed to do that?"

Annette, getting her drift, stopped also and joined in, her voice dripping with sarcasm. "You could have chosen any house in Beverly Hills or Bel Air. Servants. Money. Never have to cook or clean or even work again. And a hot older man offering knowledgeable sex. Yum, yum. You missed a golden opportunity."

Doris then pulled up abruptly and leaned against the nearest tree, using the short break in order to light one of her many cigarettes. She still refused to quit. "College money put away for all three kids. How could you resist?"

I squirmed. "I shouldn't have told you about Alfredo. You'll never let me forget it, will you?"

Harriet added, "What, and take away our chance to hear real Hollywood dirt?"

"And besides, I didn't need his old money. I made a hundred grand last year and I'll double it this year. So there!" I couldn't believe how childish I sounded. Funny, it felt good saying that. Is that how men feel when they boast about their salaries?

The four laughed at me.

"Come on. I mean it. I have a deadline to meet." I started to turn away from them.

"Big deal. I have a client coming over in an hour." Annette was enmeshed in her job as a social worker in a Westside adoption agency, a wonderfully meaningful job.

"And I have to reread our latest draft," said Harriet, referring to the historical reference book she and her husband, Fred, were working on.

"And you know how busy it always is around now," added Ethel. Ethel was embroiled in running the election campaign of City Councilman James Corman. Politics had always intrigued her.

"Go ahead," I said to Doris. "Join the gang and brag about how busy you are, too."

I smiled inwardly. My woman friends were all in the workplace now, and it was exciting. They were out of the house and into doing what they loved. And all their choices involved them in positive, life-confirming activities.

Doris didn't chime in about her latest short-story project. So unlike her.

"So, who's next?" Annette asked. "After Pieter the ice-man and Evan the fantasy man and Alfie the gangster, what will you do for an encore?"

I sighed. "I'm thinking of giving up on men forever. Obviously I attract all the wrong types. I'll never meet Mr. Right."

"Maybe you invite men you instinctively know are wrong for you so you don't have to commit," spoke my friend the psychologist–social worker, never one to beat around the bush, giving me a one-minute therapy session.

All my friends were still married, and happily, as far as I could guess, and I felt it was my destiny; I'd always be the odd woman out.

I started moving out of their range of criticism. "I'm leaving now so you can talk about me all you want behind my back. Be my guest."

I dashed off the field.

"Truth hurts," Annette called after me.

"That's cheating," I heard Harriet yell, "Get back here and finish your walk."

I HURRIED INTO MY HOUSE, intent on getting to my Jacuzzi tub, quickly, before the kids got home from school, when Joan called after me.

"Wait, you had a phone call."

I was already at the door. "Please hold that for me until I get out of my bath."

"He said it was important."

I stopped midway. "Who? What 'he?'"

She met me in the hallway brandishing a slip of paper. "A Mr. Chudler, said it's about tonight."

I shrugged. The name sounded familiar. But surely it could wait.

She read from her note. "He's the principal of Gavin's Sherman Oaks Elementary School."

Oops. Now I recalled the name. Did that reflect on how little I knew about my child's life? I'd never met or spoken to the man. Why had he called? Surely my perfect, darling boy couldn't be in trouble? Visions of scenarios popped into my head. He pushed a kid on the playground? He stole someone's lunch? He said a bad word? None of these were possible. Oh no, he got sick! My baby was lying on a nurse's couch? While I was out jogging? But wait, he said something about tonight? That didn't make sense.

I dialed the number that Joan had given me and sat down, in case the news was bad. Joan went to get me a glass of water. Did she think I was going to faint?

Mr. Albert Chudler answered immediately and thanked me for my prompt response.

I held my breath. Tell me already.

"I only realized this today or I wouldn't have left it for the last minute. Tonight is the special early dinner and health education film. It's a little late to get a permission note for Gavin to attend"—and here I heard a sound like a chuckle—"but he won't need it if I'm the one who brings him."

My heart went back to normal pounding. This was about dinner and a movie? "You want to know if he has my permission? Yes, sure."

Another chuckle? "I'm being dense here. You see, because the film and lecture are about sex education, we'd decided to use that sensitive subject as a special event. To make the boys more comfortable, they are being accompanied by their fathers."

He stopped, letting it sink in. Yes, it certainly did sink in. My little boy had no father.

"I hope you won't think me forward, but I hoped you'd allow me to be your wonderful son's surrogate for the evening."

I couldn't speak for a moment. I was choked up and I did need the glass of water. Joan worriedly hovered over me. I managed a smile and a wave, so she left me, relieved.

"Yes, Mr. Chudler. Yes. Of course. Thank you."

"Good. I'll pick him up at five. Looking forward to meeting you."

I sat there for a while, forgetting my bath, thinking about the kindness of this man I'd never met.

THE PRINCIPAL of the school who came to pick up my son was in his forties, slightly bald and slightly chubby and with the sweetest smile and kindest brown eyes I'd ever seen.

Of course Gavin refused to tell me anything about the evening. Especially not one word about the "movie." He did admit there was a lot of giggling. But he assured me he behaved and didn't giggle and that Mr. Chudler was a lot of fun.

Another angel. I might not have a man in my life, but I had a wealth of people who contributed selflessly, knowingly or not, helping me get through my life as a mother without a father figure for my children.

Another member of my "village."

AND THE BEAT GOES ON

Another Year Passes By, and the "Relationships" Are Piling Up

1969

Then There Was a Man Named Ira

I met Ira at a party at my agent's house. It was a housewarming, and Ira was his neighbor. What a great guy—we hit it off right away and started dating. He was good-looking, in a boyish, charming way. He made me laugh and was easy to be with. We absolutely, positively liked each other. Had fun together. He passed the usual litmus test—my tots approved of him. He was a salesman, and I had to admit it bothered me that intellectual conversation was limited.

He was gentle. He was kind. Being with him made the day brighter and the night warmer. So what was the other fly in the ointment? He had three children and an ex-wife. And they were trouble. Their kids were seriously messed up; ditto the ex.

It shouldn't have mattered, since they all lived in another state and Ira seemed removed. He never brought any of whatever he may have been dealing with into our home. But it troubled me that he couldn't help his own kids. And although they were elsewhere, once we'd marry, they'd enter the family circle somehow. I truly believed you didn't just marry the man; you inherited his family as well.

Having three kids of my own was responsibility enough. With six, you get trouble. I felt mean-spirited, but it was too problematic for me.

Color him with too much baggage, and color me cowardly.

I talked myself out of him and I missed him when he was gone.

Dan

I met him through mutual friends just after his beloved wife died. I felt as if I was there to guide him through his grief, having been there myself. And I know I helped him and I know he was grateful, but it was too soon for him to think of a replacement.

So he was not ready. 'Bye, Dan, sweet man. I wished him well.

Max

This guy was something else. He picked me up at a screening of a TV pilot at the Writers Guild Theater. He was one of the show's writers. Smart, sardonic, quick-witted. A glib and clever talent, a definite challenge. He had some quirks. Some?

High IQ came with its own sort of baggage. It was imperative he call his mother at 6 a.m. every day. She would die if he didn't? Is that what he thought? His phone calls were keeping her alive?

He went to his psychiatrist three times a week.

"Why?" I once asked, surprised.

"Because I need a paid friend," was his answer.

To his credit, he was good to my kids, with whom he was registered as "weird." And to his further credit, he was very kind to me.

He was complicated, fanatically political, highly opinionated, verbose, and never boring, but sometimes strange. So maybe a guy could be too intellectual. I knew in his heart of hearts, he was a confirmed bachelor.

Thanks for the roller-coaster ride, Max, but I'm getting off here.

THERE WAS ALSO a married man to whom I was highly attracted, but I sent him back to his wife because although the attraction was mutual, he could find no reason to leave her. Oh, virtuous me.

And a parade of others too uninteresting to relate.

I managed to find flaws in each, still not ready to admit the problem was me. Me. Me, not ready, even after all these years.

In a moment of silliness and dissatisfaction, I once made a list of what qualities and interests my perfect man must have. I figured if someone came along and matched my checklist 100 percent, he'd surely be the one.

He had to love children (number one on the list.) Be handsome enough, craggy would do. A great cook (since I was not), decidedly intelligent, (a college grad would be nice). Great sense of humor. (Like mine, ha-ha). Love all the arts. Theater, dance, music, etc., etc., and, of course, the classic cliché of long walks on the beach, loves to travel, loves reading, loves deep-sea fishing (I was sure that would be a deal breaker). Good family background (insuring no mob connections, no deadbeat family members, and no mean mothers-in-law). I wasn't going to make this easy.

Believe it or not, he actually came along. My perfect man, a dashing college professor. He rated 100 percent on my wish list.

How did that turn out? Sigh. There was no chemistry. No physical attraction. He had a pencil-thin mustache, which utterly annoyed me. Nothing. Nada. Bye-bye.

My children had a mother, but at the rate I was going in my unerring quest to find them a father, my two sons would be old enough to be fathers themselves by then.

THE BARBECUE

Introducing Harvey Fishman, Quiz Kid; Excuse Me, Harve Bennett, Producer

1969
A neighborhood barbecue
(Kids are 9, 13, and 17)

I met Harve Bennett, one of the producers of *Mod Squad*, at a party. It was a typical Sunday afternoon family barbecue in my neighborhood at the house of my neighbors and friends, Bobbi and Alan Holtzman.

Think suburbs, Little League games, brownie bake-offs, Saturday shopping for home supplies at Builders Emporium. The dress code, shorts and T-shirts, super casual. That was the easygoing style of weekend living.

When we pushed our way through the Holtzman gate with me carrying my contributed plate of potato salad in hand, Susie immediately raced off to find her friends. Gavin, of one mind, headed straight for the food.

Bobbi greeted me eagerly. She couldn't wait to tell me that any moment now we were going to have an actual TV producer dropping in. "No big deal for you," she said, smiling. "You see them all the time."

She informed me they'd met Harve Bennett at the little theater group for whom Bobbi directed plays. The group was an outlet for her creative juice; her adoring pediatrician husband, Alan, helped out building sets on his days off.

"Harve showed up for my production of *Lysistrata*. Afterward he came up to me and said nice things about my directing."

Alan put an arm around his wife's waist. "Bennett was impressed with how well Bobbi modernized the play about women and war."

Bobbi beamed. "In my excitement I tossed out an invitation to our backyard shindig, but I never dreamed he'd agree to come. Do you know him?"

"No, but the name sounds familiar."

After dropping that tidbit, with my potato salad now in her hand, Bobbi hurried off to continue her hostess rounds. Alan smiled and went back to tend the barbecue.

I walked over to where Sara and Jack Kay were standing at the punch bowl. Hugs followed; we'd become close friends in these four years since the legendary day my daughter took her little brother searching for friends in our new neighborhood. Jack worked in publishing and Sara once announced to me she wanted only to be a happy wife and mother and the chance to read every book ever written. And Jack professed a desire to travel all over the world. What was my fantasy, they asked me?

I didn't have an answer. I was just letting my life unfold.

"Have you seen our boys?" I asked. "Rick raced out this morning saying he and David had a meeting."

We all three smiled at that. Our seventeen-year-old sons, close buddies, had come up with a business they'd invented. It was a car rally club, in which kids who had drivers' licenses joined, paid a fee, and were given an interesting driving course to follow that the boys designed. The boys manned the checkpoints and awarded trophies to the winners of the ones who finished first. It was like a scavenger hunt on wheels.

Jack grinned. "Already entrepreneurs. I'm thinking of retiring and letting my son support us."

We laughed. They were smart kids with rich imaginations and were always coming up with clever ideas to astound us. I wasn't surprised when David went on years later to teach mathematics at UCLA. And my high-IQ kid went into the screenwriting business, like his mom. But more of that later.

I looked around to check on the kids. Susie was sitting with the three daughters of Ellie and Bill Grayer, working on their communal patchwork quilt. When Susie spent time at the Grayers', there were always crafts projects going on. I waved at Ellie, who was giving them instructions. She waved back. Ellie was a psychiatrist and Bill an engineer.

How lucky I was to have such kind, intelligent neighbors for friends.

Gavin was still at the long trestle table indulging. My youngest son, labeled lovingly by his siblings as the slowest eater in the West, was nibbling at a corncob, studiously eating the corn one kernel at a time.

A while later, there was a murmur of voices. I looked around, assuming the celebrity guest had arrived.

We were all dressed casually, and he was dressed casually too. Our casual came from Sears catalogs. His, probably from Rodeo Drive.

He was with his wife, Jane. Tall and willowy, she seemed shy and nice.

Bobbi was flustered, worried that the little tykes splashing in the plastic pool would misbehave. With one watchful eye on them and her arm through Harve's, she piloted her special guest around, introducing him to all the curious onlookers.

He was quite a good-looker, oozing confidence. Tall, tan, and wore a *Mod Squad* baseball cap.

Alan and I, flipping burgers, chatting about local stuff, glanced at the visiting dignitary. He whispered to me, "I heard somewhere that his real name is Harvey Fishman. He was actually one of the original Quiz Kids."

Wow, not only was he successful, good-looking, and such a good dresser; he was also smart. That earlier *Quiz Kids* show featured children from all over the country with high IQs to compete against one another.

Just as I was happily scarfing down my burger, I heard a honeyed voice behind me.

"I'm told you're a very good writer."

I turned. Caught with a mouth full of juicy meat, Dijon mustard, lettuce, and dill pickle, I chewed fast and nodded.

"I'm Harve Bennett." He introduced himself as if he weren't aware that everyone now knew who he was and was staring at him, ears bent, listening in on his every word.

After I swallowed, I managed to shake hands, hoping mustard didn't get onto his expensive-looking lightweight pale-blue silk jacket, a perfect match to his sparkling blue eyes.

I tried to formulate something sophisticated enough to say, but before I could get a word out, he asked, "What shows have you worked on?"

"*Dr. Kildare. Peyton Place,*" I said, modestly.

Harve nodded. "Nice. Classy. David Victor, Paul Monash. Major hitters."

"Yes, lovely men, both of them. They were very nice to me. . . ."

Harve interrupted. "Working on anything new?"

What I was working on was a bit of gristle stuck in my teeth, but I played the game. "I'm in between, as we writers are wont to say." Something about him made me fall into pseudo-Hollywood talk.

"How about that! I'd call it perfect timing. How would you like a job on my show? I've been looking for a story editor. Do you know the show?"

He whipped out a card from his pocket and handed it to me. "Call Monday and we'll talk."

With that he walked off. "Janie," he called to his wife, "we must be moving along."

He quickly extricated her from the cheese-laden sideboard where she was discussing recipes with a group of housewives.

"Aaron's expecting us. We mustn't keep the head honcho waiting."

A quick round of goodbyes and so-nice-to-have-met-you's and the VIP guest was gone. I looked at my watch. He'd only been here for twenty minutes.

Poof. Shoulders relaxed. Conversations returned to holidays, sports, and children.

It was as if the air changed in the backyard.

Bobbi and Alan rushed over to me, grinning. "Wow," Alan said. "Did you take the job? Congratulations."

"Not so fast. I don't have it yet." I didn't want to show how excited I was, in case I didn't get it.

"Don't worry, he'll hire you," my neighborhood champion insisted. "He knows talent when he sees it."

How cultured Harve Bennett was. How smart. How elegant. And he wanted me to work for him! I was in awe.

Had Harve not dropped in at this party and had I not been there at that time, I would not have been offered my next job. Kismet? Lucky happenstance? Never look a gift horse, etc. No way would I turn down that job. It was an important career jump. Story editor on *Mod Squad*, another hit show. Wow. I surprised myself. I no longer thought of myself as working in order to support my kids. I liked the writing. And it had been fun working on staff at *Peyton Place*, but I suddenly realized I wanted to know more about how television worked. In this new job, I'd be inside. I'd finally have a chance to learn the technical side.

Yes, I'd have a career. I liked the idea of having a career.

THE MOD SQUAD

Meeting the One and Only Aaron Spelling, and the Girl, the Guy, and the Brother

A few weeks later
Paramount Studios

The first day on my new job, I was introduced to Aaron Spelling, the show's executive producer and boss of us all. I had no idea this man would become an important part of my life, weaving in and out of the years. He may have been toothpick skinny, not too tall, with pale blond hair, and even a pale face, but he came across as a dynamo. He was already on his way to becoming one of the biggest movers and shakers in the business.

We shook hands. He smiled and it was such a shy smile. There was once a bashful boy before he'd turned into this powerful man. I could detect the vestiges of the language and manners of a Southern childhood. He had a teasing gleam in his eyes as if to say he knew the punch line to the joke, and he wasn't telling the joke. He came across as low-key, dressed simply (but expensively), a pipe almost always in his mouth.

What he lacked in physical stature, he made up in office space. His office was immense and exquisitely appointed. All his showbiz creds were part of a major show-and-tell filling the walls, especially featuring glossies of the glamorous actors from all his shows. He surrounded himself with beautiful images. I admit I was impressed. In the pecking order in the aviary, executive producers had the fanciest feathers.

"About time we had a good-looking woman on deck" was his welcoming remark. Notice, he didn't say, *About time we had a woman writer, one with a female sensibility.* Of the many times in the future that Aaron and I would work together, his attitudes about women as depicted in film would clash with mine. We were on a constant yet gentle battlefield. He always treated women gallantly in real life, but on film there was eternally the undercurrent of women as dismissible sex objects, first and foremost.

I didn't see too much of him at first. Then I met the stars.

They seemed like nice kids. Peggy Lipton, Michael Cole, Clarence Williams III, known respectively as "Julie," "Pete," and "Linc," the lead characters in a series about hippie teenagers becoming undercover cops. The show premise was that these three troubled kids were given a choice: Go to prison or help the police catch young criminals. And in the sixties the company could still get away with an ad that touted, "One white. One blonde. One black!"

But instant fame soon overwhelmed them—it was too soon and too much. And since it was the changing sixties, it was necessary to be au courant. Theirs was an uncomfortable role—it wasn't cool in those days for young people to be considered working for the "fuzz."

They were trying so hard to be "hip," half the time they behaved as if they really weren't there. When you watched them on-screen, they would be hanging onto each other with Pete always in the middle, looking as if they had to hold him up. They *were* holding him up. Pete was usually nursing a hangover (from late-night partying?) And Linc, feeling he had to represent all blacks so they wouldn't think of him playing a snitch, wore a huge Afro and shades, which he never took off, day or night, be he in caves or in showers.

My benefactor, Harve Bennett—formerly Harvey Fishman, the Quiz Kid, as I liked to think of him in full phrase—was my immediate boss. He was busy, busy, busy with all the production details for each show.

I was kept busy too. Reading and writing comments on the ever-flowing barrage of material from hopefuls wanting to get a writer's credit on this successful show. Not only did I get to read sample scripts sent in by agents, but I was able to hire writers and sit in on their story conferences. I gave notes for each of their drafts and then, finally, I edited their final drafts until the project was ready to shoot. Heady stuff for the new career girl.

And during the times when I wasn't busy with my story edits, that was when my education truly began. I would sit on the set for hours. I studied the actors and the way they were directed and photographed. I was fascinated by how directors chose which shots to print. Sometimes it took many, many takes before the director decided he'd caught the best performance, the right emotion, the one he felt was the best choice of film.

I sat in on the dailies in our screening rooms with the producers and directors and watched the film of the previous day's shooting and listened to their comments. Leslie Green, head film editor, made me welcome in his dim work cubby, and I saw how he processed the film and how scenes were cut together. Though the script had started with the dialogue and directors, and then the camera took over, in the end, it was the editors who put it all together, who had the power to make or break a film.

I loved learning about what got to go on the screen and why. It was exhilarating.

A month later

So when did I get to work with busy Harve? After hours, when he had time for me. When I should have gone home like the rest of the staff. This created real problems for me, because it meant I'd hardly see my children. All I had of them was the frantic morning rush, they to make it in time for the first bell, me to be on time for work. It was hard not being there when they'd eat dinner, when I'd usually listen to them talk about their days at school, basking in their successes, commiserating with their worries. Not being there for the ritual of bedtime, story time, and choosing the next day's outfits. They needed me!

And that's when I saw another side of Harve Bennett. He could sit for half an hour agonizing over finding one perfect bit of dialogue while I squirmed and anxiously sneaked looks at my watch.

I was uptight. I mean, this was *Mod Squad*, for God's sake! Not *War and Peace*. Did it really matter what the character Pete said, since Michael Cole garbled most of the words? Julie, the colt-like blonde, constantly whispered. I needed to be home.

And why bother with hours of these minuscule changes for Linc? We wrote carefully chosen dialogue, and Clarence Williams would rewrite every word with his breathless prose; a whole sentence could translate into one word—*solid*. Or *cool*.

He was a one-guy voice of the sixties. "Can ya dig it, man?" "Far out." And anybody in authority was "the man." Those were his favorites.

Nevertheless, Harve rewrote scripts and rewrote and rewrote them again, to his idea of perfection. And I fidgeted and suffered for it later with grumpy kids, who paid me back with passive-aggressive behavior at home. Despite my strict orders, I could imagine them spitefully eating rocky road ice cream with chocolate syrup and whipped cream and watching forbidden TV way after their bedtimes. *Take that! for being away, Mama!*

The last straw came one night a month later; there was a late phone call. It was a fireman from the Sherman Oaks fire department. Calling from my house! It seemed that my busy daughter, Sue, was making candles, and the wax had set the curtains in her bedroom on fire.

I gasped, horrified. But the fireman reassured me, saying everything was under control. My housekeeper was calming the frightened children. However, he assumed I'd leave for home immediately. I assured him I would.

I grabbed my jacket and turned to Harve, who was still hunched over the pages of the next script. The man never wanted to go home. Poor wife Jane—little did any of us know her married days were numbered.

"Did you hear?" I asked.

He didn't look up. He nodded. "On page thirty-two"—of a sixty-page script due the following day but which would be late because of his vacillations—"Linc tells Julie she has to hide her fears of being killed by the gang of drug dealers. We need to show her apprehension."

Julie? That brought to mind Dorothy Parker's famous line about Katharine Hepburn: "She runs the gamut of emotions from A to B." Why bother?

He patted my chair, indicating that I return to work. I was having trouble with my anxiety. I sat back down. And after a few minutes, finally realizing I was no longer able to concentrate on a word he was saying, I said, "I have to go home."

"What for? The fire's under control."

"You're kidding, right?"

"The housekeeper is home with them."

"But their mother isn't!" I stared at him, dumbfounded. "My children could have been killed!"

Still not looking at me: "I need a comment from Linc here."

I wanted to smack him. "They could have been fried!"

"You think Julie would decide not to go out until Linc convinces her? But that would add another page and we're long now."

My voice, low and ominous: "Little charred bodies lying on my kitchen floor."

He looked up finally, puzzled. "What's Linc doing in the kitchen?"

I walked out and insisted I never work late again. Harve got the message and from then on we worked during regular hours, and I was home for dinner. It was the first time I ever stood up for myself, not realizing this was one of the early tenets of women's lib.

EVEN THOUGH I remained busy editing other writers' work, I finally found time to write a script of my own. I came up with an idea that I felt was different. I called it "In This Corner, Sol Alpert."

The story took place in a run-down apartment building in a poor neighborhood owned by a slum landlord. The beleaguered tenants, with Sol Alpert as their spokesperson, knew our hero kids and begged them to help. People were getting hurt in the unsafe building and the landlord refused to make repairs. The kids tried, without any luck, to appeal to the landlord. He would do nothing. The courts could do nothing. There was no way to force the rich man to do the right thing. But our ever-awesome threesome (i.e., the brilliant writer) found the unique way and justice triumphed.

I was totally pleased with the script. So was Harve.

WORDS, WORDS, WORDS

My First Production Meeting — You Don't Wanna Know

1969 continued
Mod Squad *conference room*

Aaron Spelling taught me the most important lesson I ever learned in Hollywood.

He summoned me one day and told me to grab a copy of my script and to hurry over to the conference room. This was the second time he'd actually spoken to me since I climbed on board (his expression).

Why? What was going on?

It was the production meeting for my script "In This Corner, Sol Alpert."

Aaron informed me that it was about time I learned how to take a final draft and turn it into a shooting script.

I was thrilled. I knew that for each episode there was a production meeting with Aaron, the executive producer; Harve, the creative producer; and the guest director for the upcoming episode. I'd never been invited before. This was really big, being included. It never dawned on me that of course I should be invited to my own script production meeting.

I eagerly rushed into the huge conference room clutching my script, a pen, and a pad. The room was already crowded with people drinking coffee, chatting, and settling in. I saw a chair right next to the back door. Sitting myself down, I waited quietly.

At the far end of the room, at the front edge of the long rectangular table, the three top men were gathered: Aaron, Harve, and the director of my episode, Robert Michael Lewis.

Looking around, I recognized most of the team from hanging around on the set. Nearest to the big three, starting at the left angle of the table, sat the production manager, who was in charge of the entire crew. This included every department head. Seated next to him, and also under his jurisdiction, were the assistant director and the script supervisor. Then the cameraman, in charge of his own crew. Set design and decoration. Art director. Sound. Props. Makeup and hair.

Transportation started the right angle away from the big three. Wardrobe. Location manager. Then the film editor and the music supervisor.

With an open script of mine for one and all.

Probably about two hundred people worked under this small elite group.

From my constantly asking questions, I knew their job descriptions. Now I was going to see them in action.

It was heady stuff. All of them dedicated to turning pages of my script into a living, breathing film. I could barely hide my eagerness.

The director, recently a film editor on the show, now graduated to directing, Robert Michael Lewis, was in charge of the meeting. Each week's episode of *Mod Squad* had a different director, and this week it was his turn.

I didn't pay much attention to him, nor did he seem to notice me.

Aaron might have been the executive producer and Harve the line and creative producer, but when the director came on board, he had final say. The director's decisions were law. This, I learned, was standard for every series on TV and all feature films as well.

As we were about to start, Aaron waved to me to come over. I hurried to his side.

Harve and Bob Lewis were busy talking to some of the crew.

Aaron pulled me close and whispered, "What are you doing sitting in the back, near the door?"

I shrugged. "I didn't want to get in anyone's way."

"Listen to me carefully, pretty lady, and remember what I tell you. Always sit next to the seat of power. Always." With that, Aaron stood up and pulled another chair over. And literally sat me down right next to him and patted me on the cheek.

Wow. The three most important people in the room and I was now the fourth. The seats of power. See how insignificant and insecure a woman writer felt back then?

I was thrilled. And I never forgot his advice. Thereafter, I never missed a production meeting for any one of the shows I ever wrote; I always sat up front in the power seat.

The director, Bob Lewis, called the meeting to order. We all opened our scripts to page one.

Jack, the production manager, announced. "Production number 31004-039."

I wondered about my dialogue. How would they handle that? Were they going to ask me to read? Did they act out the parts? I sat straight up in anticipation.

Bob Lewis started by addressing the sound guy, Jeff. "The teaser. We'll be beginning with the door buzzer and pounding."

The sound guy responded, "Got it. Question: Didn't we establish three shows ago that the door buzzer was no longer working?"

For a few minutes, there was a busy discussion of fixed or not fixed. I twiddled my thumbs. Finally established. Buzzer now working.

Jeff was satisfied. "Didn't want the buzzer and the TV not working at the same time."

Lewis continued on. "That brings us up to that TV set. We'll need the static."

"I'm on it," Jeff said.

"Wardrobe," Lewis called.

Ann answered. "They're going out for dinner. Chinese. How dressy for Julie?"

Harve suggested, "Not too dressed up. A tad better than her usual tie-dye stuff. Jeans with a nice white blouse."

Ann waved as she wrote it down.

Lewis now addressed the prop guy, Al. "The usual snacks for watching TV. Potato chips and dip. No beer."

Laughter around the room. Aaron turned to me, explaining, "Those devious kids played us a trick. We gave them soda pop last time and they filled the bottles with Mexican beer. They had themselves a ring-ding party."

"Very funny," added Harve sarcastically. "In the next scene they were going to a funeral and they were expected to be mourning a friend. And they played it laughing, dead drunk."

Al called out, "Done deal on chips and dip. And sodas."

Back to my script. I grimaced. We were still on the top two description paragraphs of the first page. No wonder these meetings took four hours. At last, here came the dialogue.

Suddenly I sat up.

Lewis was flipping the pages, the others turning with him as he commented, "Words . . . words . . . words . . ."

What? What did he say? Did he just skip two pages of dialogue?

Lewis went on. "Page three. Transportation." Santos looked up. "For the exterior, we need Sol's truck in front of his store. An ugly dinged brown preferred. As beat-up as possible."

Wait just one minute! What happened to Julie saying after the knock on the door, "Okay! Come on in"?

I was about to comment when Aaron glanced at me and ran his finger over his lips, the sign meaning *Keep it zipped and be quiet*. I reined in my frustration.

Santos nodded. "Check. I've also got you six old ND cars."

That was it? My dialogue? "Words . . . Words . . . words . . . ?" Dialogue that I had struggled over? (Well, not so much in the stars' speeches. They couldn't handle too many syllables.) I was shaken. The heart of my play, ignored.

Lewis droned on, facing the art director. "Lance, get me the sketches for Sol's sign over his store. Preferably old, hard to read, yet we should be able to make out 'TV Repair.'"

Lance made his notes.

"Casting, Alpert, Brown, and Rodriguez. Twenty atmosphere. Dressed down."

I translated in my head. The characters, Sol Alpert, Brown, and Rodriguez were the three actors in this scene. *Atmosphere* was the name for any people hanging around the street where Sol's store was located. Dressed down meant these were poor people.

Aaron spoke. "I like Marvin Kaplan for Sol. I like the way he plays sympathetic."

The casting woman, Ellie, commented. "He'll do it. I'm also looking at Noam Pitlik for Simon."

Aaron stayed pleased.

I was numb. That was it? Endless discussions of trucks and buzzers and tie-dye?

This was what scripts were for? I had never questioned before why they were in so specific a form. Now I understood. In fiction, words were king. It was just the writer and the printed page. In theater, no one dared change a word without the playwright's permission.

Movie and TV scripts had nothing to do with an art form; they were merely a blueprint for the crew. To them the dialogue was inconsequential. That wasn't their concern. Words were for the actors. A whole different department.

On and on it went. A lesson in humility. More words . . . words . . . words.

In my film, of the hundreds of people who would work on the crew, it was possible that none of them would have read a single word! They had to focus on their many own complicated, specific tasks.

Aaron saw the pained expression on my face. He had started out first as an actor and then as a writer, and he could guess my thoughts. He grinned, leaned over, and whispered, "We writers get no respect."

All of the department heads came over afterward and congratulated me. It was gonna be a *helluva* good show. The nuts-and-bolts crew told me so.

Bob Lewis hurried off first. All the others dashed off to wherever they had to be. I was rushing too. I'd never expected the meeting would run so long. Harve caught up to me. "You late for a lunch date? Me too."

Keeping pace with me, he added, "Good meeting."

"Sure was," I said, moving crisply down the outside steps.

He smiled. "How did you like being at the head of the production table?"

"I liked it real fine."

"Listen, it's time to add the credits. And I was thinking—we both worked really hard on "In This Corner." How do you feel about me adding my name as cowriter?"

I was startled. As well as young and inexperienced. And stupid. I should have said, *That's your job, editing.* This was my creation alone. But we were both in a hurry and I was intimidated.

I didn't think it would matter.

I hesitated and then said, "Okay . . ."

I was able to say no to him when it concerned my kids, but not for myself. At the door, we parted. Harve rushed off in a different direction. Late for what lunch date? Harve never went out for lunch.

THE NEW WRITERS

I Get to Choose Women to Write for Our Show, and the Men Are Perplexed

Still 1969
My office

I was up to my neck in rewrites when there was a timid knock on my door. And there stood Charlie, Richard, and Herbie, the three assistants to the line and creative producers.

"What's up, guys?" I asked, my mind still on the script in front of me. My office was small; scripts were in piles. On my desk, on the only other chair, on the floor. My walls were covered with memos. Some day I hoped to decorate, maybe with curtains and paintings. Even family photos, my kids' artwork, but I never seemed to find the time.

These three somewhat burly guys filled the entire space. There was no room for them to sit down. They stood bunched together.

Richard started. "We need, maybe, a favor?"

Herbie followed quickly. "We could use some fresh blood. Need a couple, three, four new writers."

And Charlie was the closer. "You get to those writer meetings, know anyone you could suggest?"

Ka-ching! I had a brainstorm. "You know, I do have some suggestions. I'm acquainted with a few talented women writers. How's that grab you?"

There were a few moments of delayed reaction. The guys looked from one to the other. A scratch on one head. A shrug from one shoulder. A lopsided grimace from the third.

Herbie said, "Why not? As long as you can vouch for them."

Hooray.

I called Sonya Roberts, from my *Peyton Place* days, and filled her in about calling Peg Shaw and Carol Sobieski as well. She jumped at it. "Sure, we'd be interested. I also met another gal recently, Joanna Lee, a terrific talent."

I was delighted. "I'll send in all four of your names," I told Sonya. "And I'll see you when you get an appointment."

We chatted happily for a few moments, both of us apologetic for not keeping in touch and not finding time to go to lunch like we used to.

Sonya said, "But that's a good thing; we're all busy. Don't laugh, I just finished a *Mission Impossible*. Me, who's a pacifist, writing about spies. The guy who created it, Bruce Geller, is hot stuff."

I smiled. "Yeah, I'll bet Juarez doesn't think so. Is he jealous?" Juarez was what I'd call a macho guy.

"My hubby's fine with him. Whenever they get together, the two of them have fun talking about shows filled with blowing things up."

"And Peggy? What's she up to?"

"Peggy had a development deal at MGM to come up some new series ideas. But you know how long it takes for answers from the networks, especially for women. She's still waiting. And Carol is receiving the attention she deserves. She may be getting an offer to write a feature film soon, and I know she'll be fabulous."

No doubt about it. We all knew Carol would go the farthest. She was the most dedicated of us all.

"Your timing is good. We're all available now."

A FEW WEEKS WENT BY. The three guys were back. Same place, my office. Same nervousness. Here's how it went down. With words, words, words.

Herbie stammered. "Uh, Rita, we followed up and we made four appointments. . . ."

He stopped short.

"And?"

Richard jumped in. These guys were like the Three Musketeers. Or maybe three blind mice. "And before they arrive, we need your advice."

Nods of agreement from all three.

"About what?"

Herbie, pausing first: "About the women. How do we treat them?"

"Treat them? What are you talking about?"

Now Charlie took his turn. "Well, they're women." Anxious pause. "They're different."

"And what am I, chopped liver?"

Richard: "You . . . you're a writer. . . ."

"Yes. Thank you. And you treat me like a writer."

Herbie: "You're like one of the guys. . . ."

Getting sarcastic now. "Oh, really? What's that supposed to mean?"

Richard: "It's a compliment. You never nag."

Herbie added quickly, "And you never use your feminine wiles."

I leaned back in my chair and squinted at them. "Oh, no, you never get those wily feminine wiles from me."

Charlie, serving the coup de grâce. "And you never cry to get your way."

Shaking my head in disbelief, I commented, "And just you wait, 'Enry 'Iggins."

I felt like singing the lines from *My Fair Lady*, "And why can't a woman be more like a man?" I hated to think what their home lives were like. I snickered. Poor darlings. They must be cruelly treated by those nagging wives who used wiles and crying to get what they wanted.

Herbie again: "You know what we're trying to say. Your writing is great. You do the job without complaints. You're a professional."

Charlie: "We trust you."

I couldn't believe these guys. "And the women coming in are professionals too, so treat them as you treat me."

They seemed relieved. Meeting over. They tippy-toed through the piles of scripts and left. I had to laugh. These big guys, afraid to meet women?

But then again, this was new ground we were breaking. They didn't know how to deal with women in the workplace. But why were they so antsy? We women knew our roles. Weak and submissive, that's what.

WE WAITED, the three staff members and I. I was dressed, as I typically was, in a simple comfortable beige dress and a cardigan sweater, with low heels. I'm making this point on purpose: This describes my basic work uniform.

And in walked our very first woman writer candidate. Not one of my three friends. The fourth woman they'd suggested. The one I hadn't met yet.

Joanna Lee was nearly five foot ten, but was taller in her stiletto high heels. *Statuesque* would describe her. She had startling pinkish-red hair and she wore a short, short skirt and a tight red sweater under which I guessed she wore one of those new-style push-up bras that accentuated her chest. Layers of makeup. When she crossed her long, curvy legs, I glanced at the men, who were trying not to gawk. Charlie uttered a low moan. They turned to me and I knew that inside they were groaning . . . thinking, Yeah, sure, treat them like writers.

Oh, Joanna, I wish you hadn't been first one in; what have you done? Wearing one of those miniskirts that are part of the rapidly changing fashions? Scandalous. They're going to see you as sexy, a definite distraction; they'll think you're tough and threatening.

AS IT TURNED OUT, Joanna was a fine writer, gave us a good script, and had a successful career ahead. But maybe the guys were right to worry. Maybe Joanna was only the tip of the iceberg of the many women about to invade their cherished space.

After they met Carol, Sonya, and Peggy (dressed prim and proper), it dawned on the guys that we were all different from one another. These women had talent.

The men were pleasantly surprised, treated us with respect, and even started dressing a little better.

And that's when the lightbulb went on in my head. I had another reason to stay in this business I'd accidentally fallen into. I'd tried it with *The Doctors* but had failed because I let myself be browbeaten. I was in a position to open doors or crack the glass ceiling, as it was being called, and bring talented women in.

And maybe someday, I might actually get Aaron to agree to have women written as real people instead of caricature male fantasy objects.

At the moment, that seemed an impossible goal.

THE PARTY

The Price of Fame

Two weeks later
Home, and then Hollywood
(Kids are 9, 13, and 17)

I was busy rushing around the house, getting dressed for a party, putting on my makeup, then hurrying in and out of the kitchen. I needed to check on the children's dinner that would be waiting for them when they got hungry. So I only caught snatches of their conversation from around the kitchen table.

Rick asked, "Come on, already, who do you like in the first? We're talking daily double and exacta."

Susie raised her hand as if still in school. But maybe that made sense, since her older brother was the teacher in this game of make-believe sports and high finance. "I pick Golden Slipper because it reminds me of Cinderella."

Rick made the notation in his racing form that he'd picked up that morning at the local drugstore. "And who in the second race do you want for the exacta?"

"I don't know yet. But who's that jockey I can never say right, the one who always wins?"

"Lafitte Pincay."

"That's the one. I pick any horse he's on. I bet two dollars."

Rick nodded. "Good thinking."

I stood there attaching my earrings and listening. I loved how they made their choices of possible winners.

Gavin was using his favorite method, that of closing his eyes and sticking a fork into the newspaper sports section that listed the next day's entries and choosing the one name ripped by the paper.

Susie gave him a shove. "Stop doing that. Your horses never win."

He shoved back. "I don't care, I like it this way."

I smiled. My dad was the culprit who had instilled in Rick the gambling bug. Just as he did with me when I growing up. His way of bonding with children was to take them to the racetrack. My mother would yell at him, "Take them to a movie instead!" She was sure that her grandchildren would become hooked gamblers like him. Poor Dad, accused by her of being an addict, when all he ever bet was two bucks at a time, maybe forty dollars a day, when he really splurged.

Truth was, those trips to the racetrack gave me some of my favorite memories of my father. And they did the same for Rick.

And, chip off the old block, my dad's grandson was as good a handicapper as his grandpa. Rick proudly listed the amounts he "won" day by day on a chart on his bedroom door. He had turned this sport into a favorite game of math for the two younger ones, who loved this daily "handicapping."

Rick asked Gav, "So, did you make your choice yet?"

Gavin pouted. "Don't rush me. Everybody always rushes me. I'm picking Nibbles."

My older son commented gently, as he always did with his little brother, "I don't think he has much of a chance. He's 40-1."

"Well, I don't care."

As I set the table for them, I asked Rick who he was betting on.

He said, forehead creased in thought, "Pink Pigeon looks good to me; he came in to place last week only two lengths behind, and his morning workout looks promising, but Grandpa says gray horses never win so I'm not sure. . . ."

I smiled. This kid definitely had his grandpa's genes.

Gavin glanced up at me as I stooped to give him a good-night kiss. "When is Grandma and Grandpa gonna come visit us again?"

Susie agreed. "Or maybe we can go back to New York and see them." She added ominously, "And maybe this time you'll take us places."

I moved quickly past my guilt and changed the subject. "Well, Grandpa has retired and Grandma wants to move to Florida, so I'm waiting to hear their decision."

"Yay," cheered Gavin, then added, "So he doesn't have to plumb any more."

I smiled at his made-up grammar. "Yes, he doesn't have to be a plumber any-more."

"Yay," his sister agreed. "And maybe if they move we could go to Marineland."

Rick laughed and said, "Yay, and Grandpa would like Hialeah Park. It has a fancy track, with flamingos parading around."

But I wondered if my mom could ever talk him into leaving New York.

They were having so much fun, and for a few moments I was tempted to stay home and join them. And then I thought, I did the best I could, and hoped my children loved me in spite of it.

I kissed the littlest two, hugged Rick, and told them I was leaving but wouldn't be back late. None of them looked up at me, but they did wave as I left.

I had been invited to a party in Hollywood, and I was already lost.

I worked in what people *thought of* as Hollywood, which was not actually in Hollywood at all, but studios spread all over Los Angeles.

Tourists came to *this* Hollywood, not knowing any better, thinking it was the real thing because a fifty-foot-high huge lettered sign on a hill told them so. It's fairly common knowledge now that the HOLLYWOOD sign was erected in 1922, originally reading HOLLYWOODLAND, which was an ad for a housing development.

Years later the LAND dropped off. Eventually the sign became known as the icon for Hollywood.

Then there were the cross streets of Hollywood and Vine. Tourists thought this intersection, which included Grauman's Chinese Theatre with its famous star footprints, was proof.

Truth was, this part of Hollywood was the home of sleazy bars and porno shops and tourist traps. In the hills behind it were houses built years before the glitz moved west to Beverly Hills, Bel Air, and Malibu.

Many of the studio workers lived up these winding hills in Cracker Jack box–like homes.

L.A. was full of cul-de-sacs, those streets that became sudden dead ends, and I kept entering one after another by mistake and backing out, needing to try a different route, mindful I'd be arriving late.

I probably wouldn't have attended this party, but I had committed. It was a balmy night and pleasant to be out. Not sure how one dressed for Seymour's friends, I'd put on a black rayon blouse and black-and-white polka-dotted skirt, and wore heels.

I'd met Seymour on the *Mod Squad* set. About forty. A big, easygoing guy, reminding me of a friendly, bulky teddy bear, who always had a kind word to say. He was a gaffer, an electrician, who helped light the set according to the needs of the cameraman.

I'd walked past him one Friday as he was handing out directions to his house. He turned to me and, on the spur of the moment, invited me as well. What was the occasion? No reason other than a TGIF party. Party was casual. The invitation involved another acronym—BYOB. Bring your own bottle. Also some chips and dip.

And I'd said, "Sure, why not." Seymour was a nice guy.

Finally I found his house. It was small, needing painting, from what I could tell in the dimming of daylight. A few scraggly cacti drooped near the front door. I could hear the Beatles, playing loud. Seymour answered my knocking and welcomed me.

"Am I late?" I apologized. "Those cul-de-sacs . . ."

"Nah, anytime is the right time."

As I walked through the living room, I instantly knew I'd made a mistake. It wasn't the fact that the house had few pieces of furniture, most of it obviously second-hand. Nor that the walls were covered with tattered movie posters. Nor that the lighting was weird—colors flashed wildly (Seymour once mentioned something called strobe lights). The house had some kind of aura that I instantly picked up on. It seemed dreary and sad.

Seymour really meant it when he said casual. He was dressed in Bermuda shorts, a Lakers basketball team jersey, and flip-flops. On his huge body, the ensemble wasn't too appetizing. He took me through to the kitchen and called out to the partygoers in passing, "Hey, troops, say hi to Rita Lakin."

A chorus of hi's followed me across the room. There were maybe twenty people gathered, all around age thirty or so. All standing with drinks in their hands. I recognized one of the hairdressers from the show. Skeleton skinny, bouffant hairdo, a lot of makeup; at that moment lighting a cigarette with the butt of the one she had in her mouth.

The kitchen was like the living room. Sparse. A cracked gray Formica dinette table. Two plain chairs painted brown. On the table there were a few bottles of cheap bottle-capped wine and some potato chips. I deposited my contributions. The Kelvinator fridge made a lot of noise. I laughed as I looked at the old refrigerator door. Seymour had Scotch-taped a huge poster on it, of the overweight Kate Smith, the singer, a well-known radio star whose claim to fame was her rendition of "God Bless America."

Seymour explained. "When I'm tempted to eat, I just look at Kate and I change my mind."

I smiled, but I was feeling uncomfortable.

With a water glass hardly filled with a drop of wine, I followed Seymour back into the living room. He strolled with me as I looked around.

A guy in sailor-style bell-bottoms and a tee that read DEFY AUTHORITY said to a couple on the ratty-looking couch, "Who needed the damn scut job anyway? I wasn't about to put up with that talentless director's crap."

Another guy in jeans was wearing a sweatshirt that read BADASS. He was talking to two young women who listened avidly, both also wearing T-shirts. One reading MAKE LOVE, NOT WAR, and the other decorated with a peace sign and dove.

He complained. "They said I wasn't the right type for the part. What a load of bull. They hated my reading. I know they did. I'm lousy with cold readings. I was perfect for the part."

I looked at Seymour questioningly.

He shrugged. "Sorry. I forgot to tell you our theme is wearing a favorite tee with a message that reflects the times we're living in."

Wouldn't have mattered. I didn't own any. I couldn't imagine why people would want to wear clothing with free advertisements or political opinions on them.

We moved on and I picked up on the conversation from the group with the hairdresser, whose shirt message was HAIR TODAY, GONE TOMORROW.

A tiny guy with a marijuana plant sketch on his tee was gesturing wildly to make his point. "To survive in this phony-baloney town, you gotta pick your mafia to get in. The gay mafia, the Jewish mafia, or the Mafia mafia. A straight white Christian doesn't have a chance in hell. I kid you not."

This next group had a woman in tie-dye reporting, "Hey, I was willing to climb on the casting couch, but he didn't want me—he wanted my boyfriend."

The marijuana plant guy who had commented on the mafia influence concluded his riff loudly for all to hear. "So, who do ya hafta fuck to get out of this business?"

The guests shook with laughter.

A frizzy-haired woman all in black; tights and sweatshirt, black ballet slippers, doing a bad imitation of Audrey Hepburn, holding a glass of red wine, drunkenly shouted out to me, "Hey, are you who I think you are? The story editor on *Mod Squad*?"

I turned, startled. Her anorexic-seeming husband was equally swathed in black, including a black beret. His expression mirrored hers—rage.

What was this?

The room came to a screeching halt.

Frizzy Hair pointed. "Yeah, you with the la-de-da polka dots. Who died and made you God?"

Her husband joined in. "You didn't even have the decency to write a note, just our script sent back in our SASE."

She almost spit. "You think we can't write the same crap you do? You think you're better than us?"

I felt bad for them. Rejection is always hard to take. But what was I to do? Explain that various people read the massive amounts of scripts that came in? That I probably hadn't even seen their work? And that even if I had read theirs and turned them down, I must have had a good reason. But why should I have to defend myself to some drunks?

She wasn't finished. "Next time remember our names. Phyllis and Larry Fink." She spat, "Bitch!"

With that, she rushed over to me and threw the rest of her red wine in my face.

For a moment, there was a stunned silence. Then the group applauded.

They *applauded*? They agreed with what she was saying and doing? What kind of people were these? Filled with so much animosity.

Embarrassed, poor Seymour rushed over and pulled me into the kitchen as the guests silently watched us go.

At the sink he handed me a towel and I wiped my face and blouse. I was glad I disliked that outfit.

"I'm sorry," he said. "The Finks always drink too much. Maybe too much weed."

"Why did they do that?" I was furious.

He took the stained cloth and rinsed it and wrung it out and handed it back to me. "I shouldn't have invited you. You don't belong in this group. You're up the ladder where they desperately want to be but can't get to, and they resent you."

"But that's so crazy. I'm a plumber's daughter from the Bronx, for heaven's sake! I'm no snob."

"When they see you, you remind them of their failure."

I was shaking. "Seymour, I've got to get out of here. But I won't go through that room again."

Seymour led me to the back pantry door. He spoke softly, his face sorrowful. "Like those lyrics from *West Side Story*, I guess you have to stick to your own kind."

I looked at him, but he wouldn't meet my eyes. With a last glance at the absurd Kate Smith poster, I grabbed my purse and walked out.

I ran down the dark, unlit side of his house, momentarily catching myself as I almost tripped over a sprinkler head, until I reached my car. For a few minutes, I sat with the motor running, trying to comprehend what had just happened.

I was shaking. Would she have dared to throw that wine had I been a man?

Was that true? When you climbed to a higher plateau, you should never look to see who's behind you? You didn't dare look back? In case someone else was breathing down your neck? I didn't want to think that way.

From then on, when I went on the set and Seymour saw me, he turned away.

I thought about another party going on that same night. One of Aaron Spelling's Friday after-work soirees. I'd heard stories about the champagne and fancy canapés. Lots of insider talk. Butlers serving. More than booze? I didn't know much about drugs, but there were rumors. There would be a massive working the room, kissing up to Aaron, trying to make deals. I was never invited. Maybe I wasn't up high enough on *their* ladders. Or was Aaron protecting me?

I didn't think I'd fit in there, either. I wouldn't know how to play that game.

Where did I fit? Would I ever?

All I wanted to do was hurry home, quickly change into dry clothes, and hear about the rest of the horses my kids had picked. Maybe I would be in time for the tenth race so I could make some of my own picks. Maybe I'd find a horse named Stick-to-Your-Own-Kind. A sure winner.

"IN THIS CORNER, SOL ALPERT"

In This Corner, Me: A Stolen Prize, and the End of an Era

TV LOG LINE: December 16, 1969
The Mod Squad, ABC
"In This Corner, Sol Alpert"
Sol Alpert, living in a below-standard apartment building,
fights his own cousin, a slumlord, into making changes.
Executive producer: Aaron Spelling. Producer: Harve Bennett.
Director: Robert Michael Lewis. Script: Rita Lakin, Harve Bennett.
Cast: Peggy Lipton, Michael Cole, Clarence Williams III, Marvin Kaplan, Noam Pitlik.

Well, it did matter that I allowed Harve to put his name on my script. It turned out to be the most recognized and talked about show I ever wrote. The show got rave responses, far above those garnered by the usual *Mod Squad* episodes. It caught the attention of reviewers throughout the country. Not only TV reviewers but literate commentators on the American scene about how meaningful this story was. Robert L. Shayon of *The Saturday Review of Literature* wrote a full-page article on January 24 (my birthday—and what a present that was) describing how powerful the story was and said I was (along with Harve, unfortunately) "to be congratulated for carrying off a risky exercise in useful entertainment with good taste and fairness. They balanced dramaturgy and moral responsibility in sensitively handling a social problem without feeding the fires of ethnic stereotyping. . . ."

Wow! What a difference in tone and intelligence from what the local TV reviewers spewed out. The article continued on in this literate vein. For the first time, I was aware of feeling proud of my work.

It was nominated for an Emmy, that special award given each year by the Television Academy in which writers voted for the best-written work of the year. "In This Corner" didn't win. A fellow writer whispered to me later that I would have won if Harve's name hadn't been on it. He wasn't liked by other writers.

Never mind, I thought, what's done is done. Well, it wasn't quite done. One Monday morning, weeks later, Harve arrived and handed me an envelope. "Guess what came for you," he said, smiling.

I opened it. It was a certificate from some organization called the Mystery

Writers of America, with headquarters in New York. And that I'd won a prize called an "Edgar" for "In This Corner, Sol Alpert." I had no idea who or what this was. I hadn't even realized that my script would be considered a mystery. I started to ask Harve about it but he quickly shrugged me off; we had work to do.

I hung the certificate up in my office at home and thought no more about it. For over forty years.

$$\approx$$

An Aside

Present time
San Francisco

In 1998, after I gave up writing scripts, I began writing novels. Mystery novels, to be precise. I am a proud member of that very same Mystery Writers of America.

I had some of my San Francisco writer friends over to my house one day, and they saw my certificate and were impressed.

"You really won that that award?" said one.

"Yes," I said, "in 1970. When I lived in L.A. and was still working in Hollywood."

"Did you have a great time at the fabulous black-tie awards banquet in New York? I'm so jealous," said another.

I frown. An awards banquet? With people winning and getting applause? "No, I never got such an invitation. I never knew about that."

"And where's your statue?" A third.

I was starting to sizzle. "Statue? There was a statue?"

"Of Edgar Allan Poe. That's why it's called the 'Edgar.'"

Slow learner that I am, I finally put it together. Harve had purposely timed it and caught me off guard when he asked to put his name on my script. He knew how good it was. I now am well aware of how prestigious and coveted that award is. How happy and grateful writers are when they win the Edgar, that award named for Edgar Allan Poe. It's a great honor.

Harve must have received our gilt-edged invitations from the MWA office and never told me. He probably flew free, first class, to New York and went to the banquet. He got to hear our names called. And picked up our two certificates. And kept my statue! I can imagine him saying into the mike, "Sorry, Miss Lakin couldn't make it."

On Monday morning, he handed me my certificate and quickly got us to work, I now realized, so I wouldn't ask any questions.

Harvey Fishman, shame on you. I guess I'll never get back my statue.

Did I work with Harve Bennett after *Mod Squad*? No. Did he sink into oblivion? No. He had a long, successful career producing many TV movies and miniseries. Who said crime doesn't pay?

I LOST MY INNOCENCE, as did most of the country during those last ten years of the 1960s. A murdered president and a slain civil rights leader, Martin Luther King. A dreadful, unwinnable war. Drugs slowly becoming the wave of the future.

In the last year, 1969, Richard Nixon became president, Woodstock attracted 350,000 rock-and-rollers, and 250,000 people marched on Washington to protest the Vietnam War. Hey, even the Beatles broke up.

Major changes were affecting our country. Television, as yet, was not reflecting the changes on our streets and in our politics. Benign top shows like *The Brady Bunch*, *Hee Haw*, and *Love, American Style* were still far behind the times, even as we, the people, became more sophisticated, and maybe more paranoid.

Gloria Steinem did publish her magazine and changed all our feminine perceptions when she said we were no longer to be labeled *Miss* or *Mrs.* We were *Ms.* now.

And so ended the 1960s.

My INTERVIEWER, *Chelsea, was practically jumping up and down in her chair. "Hey, wait a minute! Not so fast. Weren't you angry at Bennett? He stole your statue."*

"You bet I was. But what was I supposed to do forty years after the fact?"

"But you should never have let him put his name on that script."

"It wouldn't even have entered my mind to fight back. He was my boss and I was just a lowly woman."

As for me and my evolving career: I wondered, How did I give myself permission to push forward, when many times all of me wanted to hide and cry? Maybe not all of me. There was this strong pull: The demands of my children and the caring of friends and family said, You have no choice, you are needed. And so, I was. I had to go on.

The seventies brought a personal surprise I wasn't expecting. Lights. Camera. Action. Enter Robert Michael Lewis.

End of Part One.

Part Two

THE SEVENTIES

AN UNEXPECTED CHANCE MEETING

Hello Again, Bob

Late 1970
Paramount Studios

Hi there, Rita Lakin. Wait up."

Someone was calling out to me as I was heading at a fast pace toward Aaron Spelling's new office. The voice interrupted my musing. I wondered if Aaron's new executive producer's digs would be as fancy as they were on *Mod Squad*. I turned. For a moment, I wasn't sure who the man in jeans, a light-blue windbreaker, and sneakers was, but then it came to me. Robert Michael Lewis, from *Mod Squad*, who had directed my "Sol Alpert."

I waited until he caught up. He greeted me with a wide, friendly grin, I smiled back. "Remember me? Bob Lewis."

"I do."

"We never had a chance to chat at the production meeting, but I kept thinking you'd show up on the set, or at least at the dailies once I started shooting."

"Well, I guess I was busy." Thanks to Harve Bennett for making sure of that, I thought, bitterly. While he had been constantly on the set and present at all the dailies, he kept me in my office, wasting time, reading unsolicited manuscripts, most of them deadly dull, with none of them having a monkey's chance of being bought.

"I was hoping to tell you in person how much I admired your script and what a break it was for me."

I was pleasantly surprised. "Really?"

"Okay, if I walk along with you?"

"Sure, why not?" I answered nonchalantly. I started up again and he matched my pace.

"I was a film editor for years and Aaron finally gave me my break and let me direct. I was honored to be able to direct that amazing piece of work. "

His voice was boyishly earnest and respectful. How nice. I was warming up to him, flattered by his eagerness. I found myself looking closely at Bob for the first time, summing him up. Medium height, slight of build, dark curly hair, glittering eyes. My impression was that he was probably a dynamo at his job. I would guess he was near my age but slightly younger.

Bob said, "I'm heading for Harve's office. I assume you are, too?"

"No, not really." Not ever again, if I could help it was my icy, unspoken thought.

I sneaked a look at my watch, not wanting to be late, yet not wanting to be rude. Besides, the sky was threatening a storm, and I hoped not to get caught in it. Rainy season in L.A. was about to make its yearly dramatic entrance, and it could get dicey, fast.

"I'm directing my eighth episode," Bob said proudly. "And more to come."

I was impressed. "That's quite an achievement."

I picked up my pace, at the same time my mind was running through my story ideas, trying to polish them before I had to present them to Aaron.

"Yeah, it is. But it's become 'same old, same old,' I'm starting to look elsewhere. My agent told me about a new show, *McMillan & Wife*, starring Rock Hudson. Thought I'd give that a shot, pick up a few episodes there. Where are *you* off to?"

"Aaron Spelling's office. I have an appointment in fifteen minutes."

Bob looked puzzled, as if that didn't compute. "Writing another one for the *Squad*? Wait a minute. I thought Aaron moved off the show and was doing something somewhere else."

"He is. He's into producing those new weekly movies for TV. The ones they're calling MOWs."

Did I imagine it? Bob's smile faded. No, here it came back again, maybe a little too brightly? "Yes, I heard that's the next big thing. Movies, huh, that's exciting. So, you're going to get to write one of the very first ones? Lucky you."

"Don't I wish. I have some ideas to pitch. I hope he'll like one."

"Oh, he will. I always thought you were Aaron's favorite." He laughed, as if he was joking, but his eyes belied the fact.

I didn't know what to say to that, and I was glad we reached the familiar beige building where I'd spent nearly two years. Bob stopped; it was his destination.

"Well, it was nice seeing you again," I said, as a closing comment. I was about to move on, when Bob reached out for my arm and held on tightly.

"It would be even nicer seeing you again and . . . again. May I call you?"

His touch seemed electric; his expression was no longer casual. Suddenly, I reared backward, flustered, feeling my face redden.

His dark eyes seemed piercing, and I had the ridiculous thought that he was staring deep inside me.

I found myself stuttering. "I guess so . . ." I was unexpectedly aware of the menthol in his aftershave. I felt myself breathless and unsure, trying to sound lighter than I felt.

He let go of my arm.

When I could breathe once more, I gathered myself together and hurried down the path without any further goodbye.

Curiosity had me toss a backward glance as I was about to turn the corner. I could see Bob, now standing in the building's adjoining phone booth, seemingly talking agitatedly on some call. Was I imagining it? He was pounding one hand against the glass?

What had just happened?

WOMEN IN CHAINS

The MOW and Aaron: Moving Up in the Biz

Five minutes later
Aaron's new office

Suddenly, somehow, in the mysterious workings of the biz, I'd become bankable and was being offered bigger and better writing assignments. I had no idea that I was now at a peak of success in this world, at the top of my game. There was a not-so-secret A-list for the so-called hot writers, yet I had no clue that I was on it.

Even after ten years I still didn't recognize the truth about myself. I was unwaveringly only reactive. I never chased after an assignment; each one I did came to me. And I took whatever was offered. I had no ego. Nor ambition. I was forever ambivalent. I didn't take advantage of opportunities. And here I was, a successful woman in spite of myself.

Enter the lucrative world of movies made for TV, the Movie of the Week. These two-hour ABC television specials were in heavy demand. They were receiving special publicity and were considered a big deal. They attracted big-name writers, directors, and actors. And they paid top money. And I was being invited in.

So when I got a personal call from good old Aaron Spelling, I was pleased and surprised. Aaron was glad to see me again, and I was glad to see him. And yes, his office *was* even bigger and better than the monster one he'd had on *Mod Squad*. It took ten minutes to walk from the door to his desk. Kidding—it just seemed like it.

It was there I met his new partner, Doug Cramer. Doug Cramer didn't say much, but he was quite an impressive presence. Extremely good-looking, *GQ*-dressed, and, from what I'd heard about him, a collector of fine art and an intellectual. I thought this time I might get to write about something classier than undercover teenagers who spoke in one-syllable words.

Well, maybe not. Of all the sharp ideas I presented at this meeting, they glommed onto my least favorite premise, one I threw in last, if all else failed.

My pitch went like this: A female parole officer is concerned by stories of abuse to some of her parolees who've ended up back in prison and sustained serious wounds like concussions and broken limbs. A few women have even died of mysterious injuries. A prison guard is suspected. Nobody is talking.

My parole officer heroine finds a way to secretly go undercover as a prisoner to investigate. Only one person knows the truth, her coworker friend in her parole office. Her friend begs her not to do this dangerous thing, but our heroine is determined.

The story builds to her being trapped by the dangerous, sadistic guard as, at the same time, her friend in the office dies. There is no one who knows where she is and no one can help her escape. Now *she* is in danger of being killed.

"Well done," said Aaron. "I like it." Doug merely nodded.

Knowing how to work the pitch game, I quickly became animated about this now viable project. "Thanks. May I say something? About casting?"

Aaron smiled sweetly, always the charmer. "Of course, honey, for you, anything you want. You're *my* heroine."

First Bob Lewis. Now Aaron. This was my day for blushing. I still had cachet for "Sol Alpert." I climbed on my soapbox and pleaded, "This kind of story is tricky. It's way too easy to fall into the cliché trap. You know—prison guard. Masochist. Scary. Threatening. A lot of sneering and wringing of the hands. And subsequently laughable." I shook my head at that.

Aaron nodded his head in agreement. "We wouldn't want laughable."

Doug was reminding me of a museum statue. I couldn't believe anyone could sit so still.

I kept on. "We should go against type. For example, even though she's a fine actress, Ida Lupino would be absolutely wrong for this part. I mean she's already played the cruel warden in something called *Women's Prison*. Brrr," I said, shaking my shoulders. "Talk about on-the-nose casting."

Aaron, to be amusing, imitated my shrug.

Doug finally spoke. "Who would you have instead?"

I rhapsodized on how I wanted to write the prisoners and jailers with true psychological reasons, showing how and why they'd become the people they were.

Doug and Aaron dutifully let me rant on.

When the meeting was over, I felt good. I was glad I'd spoken up. I was beginning to feel comfortable expressing my own opinions when writing about women.

So that was the meeting "I took" with Aaron. ("Taking" a meeting was a commonplace ungrammatical and widely used expression. But maybe correct because one went into battles in meetings and hoped to "take" the win.)

When I left Aaron's office, I thought about my encounter with Bob Lewis, wondering if he would call, and if I wanted him to.

It poured all the way home. Was that an omen?

≈

TV LOG LINE: January 26, 1972
Movie of the Week, ABC
Women in Chains
A parole officer places herself in prison undercover to determine
what has happened to inmates, only to find herself in danger.
Executive producers: Doug Cramer and Aaron Spelling.
Producer: Edward K. Milkis. Director: Bernie L. Kowalski. Teleplay: Rita Lakin.
Cast: Ida Lupino, Lois Nettleton, Jessica Walton.

Late 1971

ONCE THE SCRIPT was done and approved and all was well in my new little world, casting of the actors began. Popular Lois Nettleton would play the parole officer. Her coworker, Penny Fuller.

And guess who they hired to play the psycho guard? Of course, Ida Lupino. Despite all my arguments.

Naturally, I raced into Aaron's office again. I begged him to reconsider. "No. No. You promised."

"But Ida is a friend and such a lovely actress." Aaron sweet-talking me again. Smoothing troubled waters. The Southerner did not cotton to conflict.

Aaron smiled a lot and promised he'd see what he could do. But he was always like that. I remembered from *Mod Squad* that he hated upsetting people and tended to promise to give what one demanded, with absolutely no intention of keeping his word.

So it was no surprise that he didn't listen to me.

Our battle lines were drawn. I always wanted to dig deeper into character, and Aaron went for the glitter and fantasy. If you looked closely, my suffering woman inmates looked pretty good with all that stage makeup and careful hairdos.

All through his years producing show after show, Aaron gave men and women viewers what he was sure they wanted. Fantasies for both—what men wanted women to be and what women imagined they wanted to be, too, in order to please men.

Aaron wasn't interested in my reality.

Paramount screening room

WHEN I FINALLY SAW the show a year before it aired, I shuddered. Aaron and the elegant and sophisticated Cramer went for exactly what I was afraid of—every tired prison cliché imaginable. Women cat-fighting down and dirty, with hair-pulling and name-calling. With Ida Lupino chewing up the cell walls, playing the guard totally nutso, replaying the exact same part she'd had in that earlier potboiler movie.

Bernie Kowalski, a lovely man, was too good a director. He photographed all the grit and violence, and the show felt downright creepy.

EIGHT YEARS LATER, in 1980, the incredibly talented and utterly gorgeous Robert Redford did a feature film of a male version of a true story of a prison warden who went undercover. *Brubaker*. Need I say it was done brilliantly and without a cliché in sight?

HEY, WHAT DID I KNOW? Kevin Thomas, *L.A. Times* reviewer, congratulated me for "creating some fat parts for a group of gifted actors," and he found Ida Lupino "chilling."

My first TV movie, one that made me cringe, remained the highest rated number one show on the weekly Nielsen rating list (beating out about forty other shows) and held that title for five years.

(FYI: Nielsen media research has been used since 1950 in TV. The company put boxes into 25,000 homes and recorded the viewing habits of each member of the family. Whether it really is accurate, I have no idea, but they are still in business. And their reports determine which shows live or die.)

Being on the A-list might have meant getting better and better movie assignments. But I still didn't have much power. I didn't know it could have been mine had I demanded it. Since there were few women getting these jobs, I assumed I had to zip up and be grateful.

Aaron Spelling was in and out of my career all throughout the years. In a funny way he was my mentor, trying to help me learn the ropes. He wasn't conscious of playing that role, nor did I realize I was his mentee. Yet, at the same time, concerning women characters in his shows, he was my bête noire, literally the bane of my existence. What interesting relationships we had in Hollywood.

NOW IT BEGINS

Coffee with Bob

Early 1971
Solley's Deli

Bob waved as I walked into the popular local deli. I usually smiled when I passed the owner's motto pasted on the wall behind the first counter: IF I GET TO LIVE MY LIFE OVER, LET ME LIVE IT OVER A DELI. It was lunch-hour crowded. Noisy with conversation and clanking dishes. Was it the pungent smell of pastrami that greeted me? Got me salivating, but I had insisted this was only a "meet for coffee." Bob already had a cup in front of him.

I squeezed into the chair opposite and struggled out of my warm winter jacket.

"Thanks for meeting me. I mean, since I was already in your neighborhood . . ."

I laughed. "You were? What studio is in Van Nuys?"

He blushed, caught in his little fabrication. "Could I say visiting my dentist?"

"Really?"

"No, my dentist is in Santa Monica. Kidding. Just wanted to meet up with you again."

The waitress came by with the massive, plastic four-page menu. When I said, "Just coffee," she went sullen and gave the look that grumbled, *For that, you're taking up a table when it's so busy?*

She hustled off and I explained, "She's always that way. Has a heart of gold, really. So, okay, what's the agenda for this meet?"

"I came to ask you if maybe you'd like to go to a movie with me."

I could tell he was turning on the charm and it was flattering. "We could go to a screening. At your Writers Guild Theater, or mine at the Directors Guild. Your choice of movie? I hear Jane Fonda is supposed to be great in *Klute*."

My coffee arrived with the expected resentful *klunk* and slight spill.

"Sounds good. Would your wife like to come along?"

Bob, startled, blushed again. It was charmingly boyish.

He couldn't know I'd survived the married Evan with the fake apartment. I wasn't about to repeat another version of *Captain's Paradise*, dinner with me and breakfast with her and sleeping with both. "Come on, you checked me out and I asked about you. You do have a wife."

I watched as he played with his leather folder with WEEKLY PLANNER embossed on it in gold lettering. Unbuckling and buckling its clasp.

"Let me explain."

I shrugged. "As long as it's not 'She doesn't understand me,' or the more current 'We have an open marriage.' No, thanks."

Bob took a sip of his now-cold coffee and grimaced. "It's complicated."

"It always is." I leaned back, pushing myself slightly away from the table.

Our waitress, ever watchful Miss Charm School, came over and did a quick coffee refill, leaving the check, to remind us we had already overstayed our welcome.

Bob leaned in toward me. "Look, the marriage is over."

"Why?"

"My wife is a lovely woman. We just outgrew each other. We've already talked to lawyers." He looked directly into my eyes and held me in a trancelike state.

I crossed my arms, as I wondered how true this was. "But, of course, you're still living at home? Read the book, saw the play, waiting for the movie."

Assuming he'd blown his chance, he fumbled inside his wallet and threw down a couple of bills on the little ceramic plate holding the check. "I have a son."

"Oh . . . ?"

"I need time."

The expression on the face of the man sitting opposite me melted into anguish. His head dropped down, leaning onto his chest. He was having trouble breathing, barely able to speak. "I can't just walk out on him. I need to help him prepare for the change. Make him understand he's not to blame."

"How old is he?" I asked softly.

"Eleven." His hands were shaking.

I reached over and took his hands in mine. That seemed to calm them. "I have an eleven-year-old also."

He lifted his head and smiled gratefully.

He had me at "I have a son."

That evening
At home, my bedroom

COFFEE WITH BOB that morning had aroused something in me, and my mind was reeling, thoughts tumbling, body tossing and turning in my always empty bed.

Last year had already been a big one for me. With my career charging ahead at full throttle, I was offered more jobs than I could take on. I'd already made over $200,000, my all-time high, doing projects I enjoyed. That was huge money in those days. I felt secure.

But I had to admit it: My private life was as dry as the Agua Caliente desert surrounding Palm Springs. All these years of holding back, never admitting missing anything, believing the kind of love that once existed with Hank could never come again. Burying the feelings. So I'd lived a life, as I would describe it, on two cylinders, thinking that was enough.

I counted my blessings.

And my pleasures: The clatter of the typewriter keys at night, the dainty ping at the end of the line. The joy in the words I wrote. The kindness of the men I worked with and for. The satisfaction in any job well done. I truly convinced myself that the work filled the vacuum.

My children on any given day. The sweetness of their little selves. Watching them grow and unfold into special people. The hugging and holding. The unconditional love. That was enough, I believed.

A meaningful life.

And yet . . . and yet on only those two cylinders.

Today, I was attracted to a man. I don't know why. He admitted getting divorced, already a failed marriage. Wasn't that a red flag? But he had revealed true feelings about his son, and I was touched. I knew I was going to become involved with him.

So Bob entered my life. It would never be the same again.

DEATH TAKES A HOLIDAY

My Kids Get to Visit a Set, and an Actor Flees

TV LOG LINE: October 23, 1971
Death Takes a Holiday, ABC
Death takes a human form to discover why people fear him.
Producer: George Eckstein. Director: Robert Butler. Teleplay: Rita Lakin,
from a play by Alberto Casella.
Cast: Melvyn Douglas, Myrna Loy, Yvette Mimieux, Monte Markham.

Three months earlier
(Kids are 11, 15, and 19)

It was my first time back at Universal Studios and lo and behold, I ran into my old secretary buddy, Melody, near one of the elevators in the Black Tower. I was coming off and she was about to get in. Once we recognized each other, we hugged like two lost sisters elated to be reunited again. I stared at her, mild young secretary evolved into this smartly dressed, grown-up woman.

She caught me up with her news. She was now working for top dog Lew Wasserman, way high up in the penthouse of the Black Tower. She had literally worked her secretarial self up to the summit. I was impressed. She'd made it big-time in her own working world.

"Guess what?" She flashed her rings. "I'm also married."

"Congratulations," I said, with amusement, "but obviously not to Cary Grant," remembering her girlhood crush.

"I did date him once. He was divine."

I pretended to look envious. "Wow, I'm in awe of you. So, if not a movie star . . . ?"

"Close enough," she answered. "Rich and handsome."

We both laughed, recalling her suggestion to me years back.

"And you?" she asked. "Still married to the writing?"

That stopped me short for a moment. "I guess so."

"Whatever turns you on." With that she waved and got into the elevator that I had left behind.

I HAD GRADUATED to eating lunch in the VIP room of the commissary. But I did that only to impress visiting friends. When I ate alone, I was happy to be back in the cafeteria section and schmooze with the worker bees. Then it was time to meet my new producer.

George Eckstein at Universal Studios offered me *Death Takes a Holiday*. I was definitely attracted to doing an adaptation.

This MOW was intriguing and—finally—classy. The plot line I was given was that Death takes on a human form in order to find out why humans cling so desperately to life. He falls in love with a beautiful young mortal woman. What attracted me was that it was a play about ideas—at last, something intelligent to adapt. In one amazing scene the character Death has an argument with the woman's father about the terrifying effects that would occur if people stopped dying all over the world.

The project already had a long provenance. The original was an Italian play called *La Morte* by Alberto Casella, produced in 1930.

In 1934 it was a movie with Fredric March, an Oscar-winning star, and leading lady Evelyn Venable. Then in 1937, it was produced starring March again, on the *Lux Radio Theatre* (Lux being a popular soap at the time), costarring his wife, actress Frances Eldridge. These projects kept to the original, where all characters were royalty.

I suggested to George that we invent an American version of "royalty," a family such as the Kennedys. Eckstein liked the idea.

The actor Monte Markham was to play Death, and Melvyn Douglas and Myrna Loy played the wealthy parents of Yvette Mimieux, the love interest for the unexpected stranger who comes upon them. Maureen Reagan, real daughter of actor and eventual president Ronald Reagan, played another of the daughters.

One morning
My house
(Kids are 11, 15, and 19)

I DECIDED TO VISIT the set. Melvyn Douglas and Myrna Loy in a movie of mine! Wow! These two were Hollywood royalty. Douglas, with forty years' experience, had won an Academy Award for *Hud*. And Myrna Loy, who had started in silent films, became a beloved character in the Nick and Nora Charles series, appearing with the dashing William Powell.

I wanted to be able to watch these icons at work in person.

But before I could make my escape from the house, I heard my gang bickering. My son Howard was home on summer vacation from Antioch College. Howard? By now he decided he no longer fit his childhood nickname and wanted to use his legal first name, which was Howard. Ricky had come from his middle name, Eric.

Howard explained it drove him crazy in school because the teachers always used his first name and his friends the nickname. So now it was Howard, officially a nineteen-year-old grown-up, attending college.

My other two were gung-ho about going somewhere; they were bored. Howard suggested going to Dodgers Stadium for one of the last ball games of the season. The suggestion was vetoed by their sister, who wanted to go bowling. She threatened a temper tantrum.

"Baseball!" Gavin stiffened, not wanting to give in, taking his brother's side.

"Bowling!" Sue thrashing her arms about.

"Baseball!" Gavin said even louder.

"Bowling!"

Howard tried strong intervention. "You guys keep this up, we go nowhere."

And that's when I had my idea and stepped in. By now, growing up in a showbiz atmosphere, my children were beginning to assume that the business was glamorous and something to be coveted.

I recalled Gavin becoming a celebrity of his fifth-grade classroom because his mom worked on that hip *Mod Squad*. In fact, the class had "acted out" a script from the show (donated by Mom). Both teachers and classmates had enjoyed the performance, which made Gav even more popular.

My children had no awareness of how hard I worked or how difficult the workplace was—or how precarious, with its potential for disappointment, loose morality, booze, and drugs.

I intended to change that misconception once and for all.

"Hey, guys, I'm off to the studio. How would you like to visit the set?"

The words had hardly tripped off of my lips when all three dashed for the garage and leapt into my Mercedes.

Yes, I owned a Mercedes. A white convertible. I bought it secondhand, a five-year-old model, on a whim one day. My friend Doris goaded me that since I was still in that degrading TV business, I might as well behave like the rest of them. She had just bought a new Volkswagen, though she and Larry could afford any car they wanted by now. But no snobs, they. So, on a silly dare and to spite her with one-upmanship, I bought the Mercedes from a producer on the Universal lot who was selling, because he was upgrading to a Jaguar. (Doris's comment: "See what I mean!")

I hadn't expected my family's response to the car: They went batty over it. They boasted to their friends that they owned a Benz. Which made me the favorite carpool parent for all events. The neighborhood kids begged to ride in it. I was tempted to turn around and sell it, but frankly, I liked it too. So, little by little, I could see that my kids were creeping their way up to becoming spoiled Hollywood brats.

Today, I was going to nip those preconceptions of easy money, easy work, easy pleasure in the bud. I was going to make them hate showbiz.

In the Mercedes
On the way to the studio

NEED I SAY how excited they were? The two younger ones were jumping up and down on my leather upholstery. Switching and changing seats. In this era before seat belts were a law, they'd climb, back and forth over the headrests, only stopping when I threatened to drive back home.

Howard attempted to keep them occupied with questions. "Okay, gang, so wadda ya wanna be when you grow up?"

Gavin offered, "I could be a movie star. I had experience. Wasn't I a star on *The Doctors*? Even though I didn't have words, I got to nod."

Sue added, "I could be a ballerina and star in ballet movies."

Cynically, I asked Howard as well, "I assume you want to be in movies too?"

"Not really," he said. And just before I could congratulate myself on his maturity, he added, "I just want to date starlets."

"Not after today," I muttered under my breath.

"Rules," I announced as we reached the main gate of Universal Studios. "You must be very, very quiet. No talking, no moving around. You have to make yourself invisible or the director will have you thrown off the set. Agreed?"

Of course they agreed—they'd agree to anything.

I WASN'T about to let them know how thrilled I was, enjoying Douglas and Loy in action. The scene I'd written in which Douglas tries to tell his wife that their daughter must die nearly had me in tears.

And the kids were glued to their chairs, eyes popping, smiles wide, hardly breathing, loving the experience.

This was not what I'd been hoping for.

Suddenly, in the midst of this highly emotional scene, red lights flashed and bells went off and the shot was ruined. Someone had breached the set. All eyes watched as the door opened and a group of wide-eyed casually dressed people trailed after a young man, chatting noisily and happily to each another.

The director, Robert Butler, shouted, "What the hell are you doing here?"

It took a few moments to realize what had happened. A Universal tour guide, in shiny uniform, now horrified, stuttered, "I guess I got lost." His stutter got worse.

"I was taking my group to visit Rock Hudson's fake dressing room. . . ."

Butler's voice was ominously low. "And since when do you open a stage door when the red light flashes?"

He mumbled, "I thought I was still on the tour lot and no shows shoot there, and I thought the bells were like, a . . . sound effect. . . ."

How they got past the gates of the mega-theme park and ended up on the studio's real back lot, we'll never know.

The AD (assistant director) started rounding up the confused tourists like roaming cattle, moving them back toward the exit. "Out . . . Out . . . Out . . ."

They hustled, all the while gaping at the real stuff, their Instamatics clicking, and were quickly gone. For a moment it was quiet, and then suddenly, Melvyn Douglas picked himself up out of his rocking chair on the set and moved off the stage.

He was enraged. "That's it! I'm going home. Now."

He grabbed his jacket and script off his canvas folding chair with his name on it, and he too was gone.

(Douglas didn't mention that his "home" was in New York City, not Los Angeles. They had a hard time getting him back to finish the picture.)

And I felt somewhat guilty over the irony of it: So much for having had my tiny part in getting that theme park built.

Nobody moved after Melvyn Douglas left. Nobody said a word. Then all hell broke loose. Myrna Loy, looking startled, hurriedly headed for her dressing room.

Butler conferred with the script girl, the AD, and the cameraman. It was hastily decided that they would shoot a different scene that used the same set, but they needed to redress it and relight.

We could hear Butler tell his AD, "Get me Yvette. And Tell Myrna to stand by. Tell them what new scene we'll shoot."

People were running in all directions. The tension was palpable.

"That was exciting," Howard said eagerly.

"Wow!" added the two other wannabes. "This is fun."

They surrounded me. "We can go home now," Howard suggested. "We can still go bowling or something, maybe catch a movie."

I gritted my teeth. "Not yet. Sit back down and stay out of the way."

Yvette Mimieux walked onto the set, wearing short shorts and a tight T-shirt, her hair in curlers, and when she sashayed sexily over to her chair, Howard sighed with pleasure. He happily took one look at the leggy, pretty young blond actress and put his arm around my shoulder. "I'm glad you made us stay, Mom. You think she'll give me her phone number?"

I didn't say it, but I thought it: Just you wait.

"Shhh," I told my darlings.

It took a long time before things were ready for the next scene. Lighting had to be changed, props moved, makeup repaired, hair combed; endless small clusters of workers were engaged in decision making, and on and on. . . . Probably more than an hour went by. I purposely left my troops alone and walked around and chatted with Bob Butler for a few minutes. I empathized with him about the craziness of what had just happened. I knew a few others and I hung out with them too, always keeping an eye on my troop.

They were wiggling on their chairs, a good sign. To them, nothing was happening—people just kept moving around.

Food was brought onto the set and the crew grazed the table in between working. My now-suffering kids' eyes lit up. They were hungry and thirsty. I brought them over bottles of water. "The food is only for the crew," lied mean Mommy.

More numbing time passed. Finally, they started shooting. Slowly, slowly. I was delighted. Take after take after take until the director and/or the cameraman was satisfied. It seemed endless.

My kids were leaning on one another, eyes glazing over. They were exhausted. Finally, I took them out of their misery. "Time to go home," I said brightly.

In the Mercedes, with evening coming on, the air chilling us since the top was still down, my anesthetized kids avowed a loss of interest in showbiz.

Howard sighed. "I never thought watching a starlet could be so boring."

Sue muttered, burrowing down in her seat attempting to get warm, "I've never been so bored. Never."

Gavin summed up his experience. "Boring, boring, boring. I guess I'll stick to being a baseball player," my Little Leaguer mumbled, half asleep.

"Mom," Howard whispered, not wanting to disturb his sleepy siblings, "that guy Bob keeps calling and then you go into long hush-hush conversations. Are you dating him?"

A muffled voice popped up. Gavin, with one eye opened, reported, "She sure is. A lot."

Howard was surprised. "Then how come I haven't met him?"

"Honey, you're home from college for only a short while. I wanted to spend all my time with you. Bob can wait."

"Is he someone serious?"

"We'll see, and that's all I'll say on that subject."

THIS MOVIE had been a calm experience, thanks to producer George Eckstein, a real gentleman. And the reviewers were good—one even called my show "a rare and eloquent treat" (I seemed to have a fan in *L.A. Times* writer Kevin Thomas), even though there were complaints about the good-looking blond Monte Markham: Death being played as a "beach boy"!

I thought my script would be the last of the *Death* adaptations, but no. . . .

In 1998, Brad Pitt played the lead in *Meet Joe Black*, a feature film, also a Universal Studios production. New title. Same plot. Anthony Hopkins played the rich daddy. Though I don't know why they left out its most intriguing scene—that of the day no one in the world dies.

And finally, there was a Broadway musical in 2011, written by Maury Yeston, Peter Stone, and Thomas Meehan, all well-known theater people. This team went back to the original Alberto Casella's *La Morte*.

So what started as a play went to radio twice, became a TV movie (mine), then a feature film, and finally a Broadway musical. That's what I call a nice run.

It's gone full circle. Maybe the musical was the end of *Death*, but who knows where it might pop up again and in what venue.

I had the pleasure of working on a class project at last.

It had been thrilling to watch such icons as Melvyn Douglas and Myrna Loy. My only regret: I wish I could have met Anthony Hopkins!

HAPPY DAYS ARE HERE AGAIN

Bob Moves In

Early 1972

B ob moved in with us in February, and how can I describe it? For six months it was like living in a warm cocoon, soft around the edges. We loved. We slept. We ate. We listened to music. Bob had a beautiful voice, as I discovered when he sang along with the love songs on the stereo. Couples historically tend to pick one song and call it "their" favorite song. Well, we enjoyed a new singer, Lori Lieberman: With her velvet voice, she crooned "Killing Me Softly with His Song."

We watched TV and had fun dissing all the other writers and directors. We hung out with the two children, my preteen and teen, and heard what they considered harrowing tales of their school lives. They seemed easy with Bob and we laughed a lot. Howard was still busy away at college. Even the family cat and dog seemed content. They would lie at our feet when we were sprawled out on the couch.

We talked about work and discussed a future plan. Someday we would work for ourselves, as a team, coming up with our own series ideas and movies. Projects we'd enjoy working on.

"And I have the perfect name for our new company, RL Square."

Bob got it. We had the same initials. "A done deal."

"We won't have to please anyone but ourselves."

"Dream on," said Bob, the realist.

I snuggled in closer to him, feeling warm and loved.

IT WAS TIME for our children to get together. I was looking forward to meeting Bob's only child, his son, Mark, who was Gavin's age. Bob reported that the boy was now okay about his dad moving out.

Howard was still away, so Gavin and Sue met Mark one evening in a family-style neighborhood restaurant. Mark seemed a young duplicate of his dad, looked just like him, and had some of Bob's same personality traits I was now aware of. Edgy. Intense. Guarded. He was understandably nervous, having to see the new family his father was living with, but he handled it well.

Gavin, outgoing and open, was Mark's complete opposite in looks and personality. I took one peek at the two boys, eyeing each other suspiciously, not seeing any level of meeting, and I wondered if they could be friends.

The waiter took our orders. My kids, as they'd been trained, ordered from the low end of the price scale, "We'll have hamburgers," they chorused.

"I'll have the filet mignon, medium rare," Mark ordered decisively, another trait similar to Dad. He was obviously used to ordering the most expensive item on the menu.

My children shot me a look that said volumes: *Why was he allowed to eat steak and we weren't?*

I shook my head and that settled it.

Mark was to move in with us later on, and the boys would manage to make it work somehow. Soon they would have more to deal with than just getting along.

But for now, we gathered up into ourselves, Bob fitting effortlessly into our lives. We didn't need anyone or any outside distractions. Bob would repeat aloud continuously, happily, that he had never known such loving comfort, such ease, such acceptance. There were veiled references to a mother who, in her life of discontent, showed only disapproval in Bob and his older brother, Arthur. But that was quickly glossed over.

We lived under a perfect dome of satisfaction.

THE ROOKIES

Round Three with Aaron

August 1971
Yet another new office for Aaron Spelling

After doing my first two MOWs, I itched for other TV movies to do. They were more challenging to write than TV episodes. I felt that since I'd already worked for Aaron Spelling twice, that door was still open. Especially since *Women in Chains* was continuing to show up on top of the charts. I decided to pitch him another movie idea. I had an appointment to meet with him.

Aaron, no longer partnered with Cramer, had yet another new office, now in Century City, an upscale shopping mall. This was my first time meeting him outside of a studio. His office was relatively smaller, as Aaron was, at this point in time, back in the freelance world himself.

When I walked in, he was on the phone. Aaron waved me to a seat and continued his call. He seemed agitated. He spoke low, I assumed to keep his call private. A few minutes later, he hung up and turned to me.

After the usual small talk, he asked about my kids and I filled him in. I asked about his wife, Candy, and their kids. He congratulated me on my film at Universal. Enough small talk: We got down to business.

So what did I have for him? I immediately started my movie pitches, but it was clear he wasn't really listening. He kept looking back at the phone and then at the clock on the wall.

Aaron Spelling looking worried? How odd.

"Aaron," I asked, "is something wrong?"

He shook his head. "No problem. So what did you say your story was about?" He worked on his pipe, tapping down the tobacco.

I started in again, but again it was clear Aaron was jittery.

Then suddenly he interrupted me. "Honey, I do have a problem. ABC wants a new show from me. I've been searching for ideas for months and nothing has interested them." He glanced up toward the clock on the wall. "I have exactly ten more minutes to sell them a show, and then I'm out on the street." He gave me his familiar sweet, shy smile and shrugged. As if this millionaire had anything to worry about.

I thought for a moment, and then opened my mouth, not even knowing what I was going to say. The words that popped out surprised both of us. Where did they come from?

"They loved *Mod Squad*," I said. "Give ABC another one exactly like it, but with a new venue. Instead of undercover kid cops, how about rookie cops? Call it *The Rookies*."

He looked at me; his baby-blue eyes widened, and within seconds he ran for the phone and got the network back on the line. Aaron's voice revealed his excitement. "I've got the show. It's *The Rookies*. About young kids entering the police academy. What they have to go through to make it to be a good cop." He kept nodding at me and I nodded back in cadence.

Picking up the ball, I threw in, babbling, "And it's about the girls they fall in love with, the kids who succeed and the ones who flunk out, and the tough recruiter who makes their lives hell."

He grinned and repeated my exact words.

I guess working on that daytime soap finally came in handy; it had taught me to think fast on my feet. I also remembered my early lesson: When opportunity knocks, be ready to walk in the door. This time, I didn't walk. I had the choice: I leapt.

Aaron continued his pitch: "And I have the creator right here. Yes, the woman who helped make *Mod Squad* a success. Yes, she was the one who wrote the Sol Alpert show that got all those rave reviews. Classy writer. Perfect for the job."

Classy writer. Hah! That was a good one. As if he'd ever let me be that.

There was some more talk and Aaron hung up, his smile wide enough to rearrange his face. He walked over and shook my hand. "Well, partner," he said in his lilting, soft accent, "we just sold us a brand-new TV show. Congratulations. When can you get me an outline?"

My first thought was that this time, there would be no clichés. I'd make sure of it.

All the way down the elevator, I grinned so hard, my jaw hurt. I'd just sold a television series in five seconds that could make me millions!

I'd bet only two people in the TV world would ever know this story. Me. And Aaron Spelling. And Aaron wouldn't tell. Nobody would have believed me if I revealed it. Come up with a series idea in five seconds? It never happens that way. Unheard of.

I thought about it all the way home. This was it. Really, really big-time. My first original created show. Visions of years of unending large residual checks danced in my head. Maybe a five-year first run on TV. Summer reruns. Foreign sales! But the best part was that I could get excited about this project. I would have creative power for the first time. Aaron owed me that.

Instead of the phony, cliché-ridden violent shoot-'em-up cop shows on now, this was a chance to finally do a show on television about real young people going through training. Honest, truthful stories. Show their courageous world. Young men and women cops who truly lived it. I was raring to get into action. First, I would need to get permission to interview kids in training at the police academy.

No one had ever done a series anything like this before. All my friends would be impressed. Crass would *not* win out this time. Class would.

Hah. Yeah, sure.

But right now, I was thrilled.

That night
At home

I MET BOB at the door with a martini in hand. For a moment, I had a tender memory of how my life had been with Hank, with me meeting him at the door after he came home from work. Was it possible that I was going to relive that kind of happiness? It seemed to be headed that way. For once, I didn't find myself making comparisons. Because these men were so different, I didn't feel as if I were cheating on my departed husband.

I'd planned a special celebratory dinner, dressed up for the occasion, candles on the table, pitcher of martinis, Bob's favorite. The kids had easily been talked into spending the evening down the street at the Kays' house, with their friends.

I could hardly wait to tell him the amazing news. What a chance for us to have a lot of money. It could give us the security to do whatever we wanted to do. I had always wanted to travel.

He walked in, clearly in a wonderful mood, and responded to the extra trimmings with delight. Walking behind me, sipping his drink, kissing my neck, he whispered, "How perfect. You must be a mind reader. I was going to call and say, Let's go out and celebrate."

He followed me into the kitchen and watched as I spooned the gravy over the lamb roast in the oven.

For a moment I was startled. Did he already know? Not possible. It had happened only two hours ago. The Hollywood grapevine wasn't that fast. I suddenly had a bad feeling in my stomach.

He was on a high. He had great news. "The producers loved what I did with my first *McMillan* script. Rock Hudson himself asked for me back. They offered me a three-episode deal! Isn't that great?"

I didn't turn around. I could feel myself stiffen. "Great," I mumbled.

On and on. He practically waltzed around the kitchen. "Rock was fabulous to work with. Susan Saint James, well, she's a bit of a character, but your clever boyfriend managed to get a performance out of her.

"Hey, I heard a hilarious joke on the set today. Listen. Mother Teresa was met at the pearly gates by Saint Peter. 'Was there ever something you wanted but couldn't do while you were alive?' Saint Peter asks. Well, Mother answered, 'I *did* want to direct.' Cracked us all up."

How much longer could I just stand there stirring, feeling more and more nervous? "Yeah, funny."

"As if all Hollywood doesn't know being a director gives you all the power and the glory." He grinned at his biblical pun.

I had a flash of Bob the first time I'd seen him, running the production meeting at *Mod Squad*. He was animated, excited. He was in charge. He had that exact power and glory. I suddenly realized just how much Bob needed that.

"So, how was your day?" He finally got around to asking.

And I told him.

When I finished, he quickly turned away. He gave himself a minute and then turned back, pretending calm. "I'm speechless," he said, his tone flat, like some deflated balloon. He managed to choke out a laugh. "That calls for another drink." He refilled his martini glass and downed the contents.

By the time dinner was served and another martini or two later, I was relieved. He was in a better mood, and bandied about how we could spend the money from both our projects. Put away college money for all our kids. Travel around the world. Buy a great big house.

"That is, if Aaron doesn't ruin your script, and we're back to zilch," he predicted.

JIM AND DARLA

The Clock Stops at Midnight

A few weeks later

It was a typical balmy Los Angeles evening, and I was looking forward to meeting officers Jim and Darla at Ben Frank's, a coffee shop on Sunset Boulevard, a favorite cops' hangout.

I was researching how cops work patrol for my first sold series, *The Rookies*. Spelling's office had pulled strings at police headquarters, and that was how I'd gotten Jim and Darla. I hoped I had dressed right for the occasion. Mostly in black as camouflage so as not to be seen when it got dark.

I had completed my research about the academy and had started choosing the characters. Now I wanted some nitty-gritty nighttime action. I carried a list of questions, a notebook in which to sketch my reactions, and a nifty flashlight pen so I could write in the dark.

Were they scared working at night? How did they deal with the endless hours of waiting for something to happen? What was their most dangerous situation? And if they let me, I'd ask about the potential of falling for each another. Could a guy stay faithful to his wife when he spent most of his time with another woman in their police car? A woman whom he had to depend on for his very life? Wow! I was going to be digging into deep stuff never before seen on television.

I walked in and looked around.

There were a few cops sitting at the counter on bar stools and chatting. A couple sat in a booth, so I assumed they were the partners I was supposed to meet.

I strolled over to their booth. Jim seemed tall and Darla seemed shorter. Both had dark hair. Neither was smiling. They downed hamburgers and sucked at the straws of their Cokes. They didn't look up at me, so I couldn't see much of their faces. I guessed them to be in their late twenties.

I was early, seven minutes to ten. Eager, insecure me; I was always early.

"Hi," I said brightly, "I'm your rider for tonight."

They grunted, then ignored me; they weren't pleased to see me. Maybe it was embarrassing to them to drive me around. They might lose face with the other cops. I could respect that.

I wasn't asked to sit down. So after standing there a few minutes looking foolish, I finally said, "Guess I'll wait outside. Get some air." Brilliant dialogue, that.

They neither nodded nor commented, so I slunk out.

They took their time, on purpose. Outside, I was aware of this being a dangerous neighborhood. I wanted to stay in front of the brightly lit coffee shop windows. If I got in trouble I could yell for the cops. Assuming they'd even rescue me.

They obviously hadn't volunteered for this duty.

When Jim and Darla finally came out and climbed into their patrol car, they indicated I should get in the back. Indicated. No words spoken. Dumb, naïve me. I had thought they'd be excited about being interviewed about a new TV show. They did life-and-death things, but to them, I was a lowly nobody. I wished I was home, curled up on the couch, reading or watching TV.

Chilly feeling, being in the back. Separating it from the front was some kind of mesh wiring, and I imagined how perps felt back here. *Perps*—a new word for me. I was learning the jargon. I heard a click. I tried the door. They had locked me in! Now I didn't have to imagine the fear—I felt it. Creepy. Feeling terribly alone. Not knowing what might happen next. Sensing that these cops wouldn't be forthcoming. I could use all these emotions in my script. But I was shivering. I didn't know whether I was cold or nervous being in the heart of things. I could hardly wait for the action to start.

I whipped out my little notepad and my flashlight pen, and got ready for whatever would happen.

"So, Jim, Darla, how long have you been partners?" I leaned nearer to the mesh barrier and started on my list of questions. "What's it like having a partner of the opposite sex?"

Darla was driving, so Jim turned to me. "No talkin'. We have to concentrate. And here's the rules. Do not ever get out of the car when we do. We don't need you in our way endangerin' us."

Swell.

It was a boring night. The two of them whispered, making sure I couldn't hear. There was nothing to see. An hour went by. Now it was dark out. Not many lights on in this neighborhood. The radio crackled and I hoped it was an action call, but I guess not.

I prayed they'd make a bathroom stop, but no such luck, and I was too chicken to ask them. Should have used the facilities at Ben Frank's. I decided not to drink the bottle of water I'd brought.

They stopped once at what looked like some kind of factory. They got out and left me locked in. My dislike meter was rising higher.

By the time they'd got back in, I'd actually dozed off. The slam of their doors woke me up. I wished I'd brought some candy. I glanced at my luminous watch and it was just after midnight. This experiment was a dud. It was about time to return me to my car. Thank goodness.

Suddenly they turned on their sirens and lights and, with tires squealing, they peeled out. It felt as if they were going ninety miles an hour. I held on tight.

"What's happening, what's going on?" No answer. The thrill turned to terror.

They pulled up in front of another dark building. Drawn shades on all barred windows. They jumped out. Jim unlocked my door. "Come on, girlie," he said with obvious sarcasm. "Showtime."

"Follow close behind us," Darla added. "Why did you wear black? We won't be able to see you if there's shooting."

Flunked again. I couldn't do anything right with these two.

Oh my God! Did they say shooting? What was it—a drug bust? Or some dangerous criminals' hideout? Would they have guns too? Would I get killed for a TV show? My poor angels, my last thought would be about my children. I'd promised them I'd never die and leave them.

My guardians of the peace drew their guns and pounded on the front door, pushing their way in, shouting as they ran through a rat's maze of hallways with dozens of closed partitions. Were we in some hotel, but there hadn't been any signs outside.

Darla and Jim shouted louder "Police. Open up!"

And suddenly all the inner doors were flung open. I was nearly knocked down by a small mob of scurrying men racing toward the exit. Men who were totally naked! Some dragging towels to cover their private parts. Skimpy, frayed towels, not much use.

"Run!" called a man who dropped his towel in his attempt to escape.

"Not again, dammit!" screamed another, trying to pull up his pants as he half-hopped to the back door.

Asian women in kimonos added to the cacophony by yelling at the two cops who, in return, yelled back at them.

"Come on, ladies. Everyone out," Darla shouted, waving her flashlight wildly.

I couldn't understand the language but the gestures were clear. The women were furious.

With my back plastered against a wall to keep from getting trampled or killed, whichever came first, I watched, horrified.

Finally, it dawned on me. We had raided a massage parlor!

Then, in fractured English, from one of the young women: "Why you here? You bother us last week. Who pay for night's business?"

Tall Jim patted one of the tiny women on the head. "We missed you, Mariko. So we thought we'd drop in and say hello again." She cursed, I think, in Japanese. He shrugged, turned, and walked out with Darla. I ran after them, utterly embarrassed.

When they reached their patrol car, the two of them slapped each other on the back, choking with laughter. They looked at my confused face and laughed even harder. I climbed into my rear seat again.

"Yeah, some joke, ha-ha," I whimpered.

They immediately drove back to the coffee shop. My door latch clicked open once more. They waited until I got out. They didn't even watch and make sure I got safely into my car. I could hear them still laughing as they drove off.

Cop humor.

I sat in my car, with my doors locked, trying to calm down. No lights anywhere. Ben Frank's was closed and dark.

Grrr. I'd have my revenge. I already had a plan. In one of my upcoming *Rookies* episodes I'd have a "Jim" and "Darla" killed in a shootout. And maybe it would come out in the investigations that they were lovers, cheating on their spouses. That should do it!

There was a knocking on my window. I almost died of a heart attack in fright. But there were Darla and Jim again, looking in on me, smiling cheerfully. They pointed, indicating I should roll down my window. I hesitated but did it. I was furious. They had returned to insult me some more? Not this time.

"What do you want!?" I growled.

Darla grinned. "You should have seen your face."

"We couldn't resist. You were so shocked." Jim added.

"Rightly so!"

"We were just funnin' with you. It's kinda boring out there," Jim said.

"Except on the nights when we almost get killed," Darla agreed.

"We want to 'pologize for scaring you."

I softened a little. "But what about those poor men? You humiliated them. And they could catch pneumonia running outside naked."

Jim shrugged. "Nah, that place gets raided regularly. They're used to it."

Darla giggled. "Those cheapskates should buy bigger towels."

They started to move off. Darla called out, "Good luck with your new show." They waved and tooted me with a short burst of siren. And they were gone.

Off to keep the city safe . . . from crybabies like me?

I had to laugh and remembered my plans to get even. Maybe I'd only maim them.

BITTER NEWS

My Way — Yeah, Sure: Aaron Does an Aaron

Late 1971

I turned in my script and I was pleased with it. For the first time, I'd done research for a project. But in the meetings with Aaron and ABC network execs, when they were questioning everything I wrote, I didn't read between the lines, as I usually did, because I wanted to do it my way. The big shots were tearing apart my first draft—the script didn't have a lot of action. Much too talky. But I waved my banner of truth, nothing but the truth, based on my research, and soldiered on expecting to get my way, as Aaron had promised.

Why was I always surprised when people are consistent? Aaron had never kept his promises to me.

Aaron and the network did a hatchet job on my script. My story was too much about character. Where were the car chases? And the obligatory violence and shoot-'em-up scenes?

I stuck to my guns, pun intended. And they shot from the hip (ditto) and dumped me from my own project. Yes, dumped. They brought in another writer, William Blinn, a respected writer, to do it they way they wanted. He gave them a totally different script; he understood that network notes meant business.

So, there I was; how quickly they forget. Meaning Aaron, who else? The heroine (me) who, in five seconds, had come up with this series idea to save his bacon was then shut out. My baby was thrown out with the bathwater. No invitations to dailies. No lunches at the commissary. No helping pick actors. No visits to the sets. Ever. *Nada.* People must have wondered why my name was on it at all. I'll bet Aaron never mentioned why. As if that magic meeting in a mall office had never happened.

I assumed that Bill Blinn wasn't told that there had been a previous writer on the project. Typical Aaron Spelling subterfuge, crafty Aaron just neglected to mention that to him. Otherwise, Bill probably wouldn't have taken the job. He was used to being first writer on a new project, and I didn't blame him.

Understand why all this Sturm und Drang over who wrote first. The writer who thought up the original idea and wrote the pilot script earned a "Created by" credit, the most valuable bargaining chip one could get. That creator of the series got paid for every single episode that went on the air for as long as the show ran. Plus all the residuals when replayed, possibly all over the world. A big deal if the show was a hit. So that credit mattered. A lot.

Bill thought he'd earned that "Created by" credit. He got "Developed by," instead. Less cachet. Less money. Which was not too shabby either. But that wasn't what Bill thought he signed on for or what he usually received.

To my surprise, Gavin's Little League team was randomly chosen for a scene in the movie. And I hadn't even thought of using my clout to ask for his team. I was pleasantly surprised. But when he showed up, I did pull rank and made sure his freckled face was on-screen.

And not a word from Aaron to me. As if I didn't exist.

"I told you so," said Bob.

EVENTS STEAMING ALONG

Bob Gets a Dream Offer, and We Decide to Buy a House

We wrote off *The Rookies* and made a bet it wouldn't last more than a year or two. Turned out we'd be right. What I got out of it? I made a little money and I was sent a black-and-white still of Gavin playing baseball.

Bob got amazing good news. A swaggering, potbellied businessman, Bernard Gershuny, from Long Island City, New York, who wanted to become a producer, contacted him. He offered Bob a low-budget feature film to direct. This was it: Bob's fantasy coming true.

"Get me out of TV and lift me up into the glorified world of features films with the big boys, where I belong." That was his cry of joy.

Bob remained ecstatic, and I was thrilled for him He was pulled into a whirlwind of casting meetings and location hunting. The film was called *Lapin 360*.

They found two up-and-coming talented actors, Terry Kiser and Peggy Walton. The script was good. It was about a woman who becomes a surrogate mother and then doesn't want to give the baby up. Plenty of heart as well as action. Perfect for Bob. I had never seen him so deliriously happy. All systems were go, and shooting was scheduled to start in a month.

Suddenly, his life's dream was working for him.

Bob announced one morning, "We're on a roll. Let's buy a house. Today. Right now." He practically pulled me out the door, and off we drove, straight to Beverly Hills. We both had been living in much leaner circumstances, but standing in front of the gorgeous Connecticut-style yellow-and-cream brick farmhouse in lovely Coldwater Canyon, we were entranced. Two balconied stories, almost an acre of citrus trees of all permutations (the last owner must have thought he was Luther Burbank) surrounded the house like a fairy-book garden fence. Huge backyard, spacious patio, Olympic-size swimming pool, avocado trees bursting with fruit, a volleyball court, and even an unfinished guesthouse. Wow! (I wondered how we would pick our avocados, twelve feet above us. Answer: We waited until they ripened and fell—splat!—down onto the volleyball court, there to be gathered, bruised yet delicious.)

Bob convinced me we could afford it. "We'll sell your $35,000 house, now maybe worth $50,000, and that will give us enough to buy into this $100,000 dream house." Without Bob, I might have stayed in the Valley, where I was comfortable and happy and living well within my means.

It made me nervous to take on such a large mortgage, but then I thought, with two incomes, we'd be all right. I didn't remember until later that he didn't mention selling his own house, where his soon-to-be-ex-wife still lived.

But Bob had a way of talking me into things.

Happily, we went on a shopping spree, looking for antiques. We loved going to auctions, giggled over winning our bids, and bought great reproductions, as well as the real thing. We owned beautiful things we never could have afforded before. Our house became a showcase. God, we were so happy.

And Bob finally went to work on his dream project.

An Anecdote

My mother came to visit. She would stay a few weeks.

"So, what do you think, Mom?" I had just given her a tour of our new house. She went through all ten rooms, staring, squinting, touching this, examining that. In awe? Mom and Dad's whole apartment would have fit into our master bedroom suite. She never uttered a word. I felt myself getting more and more anxious. So unlike her to be so quiet. Was she concerned about how much we'd spent?

Now we were back, sitting in our vast country kitchen at our nineteenth-century oak Amish-style farmer's table with its sturdy ladder-back chairs, sipping tea from my vintage English bone china set.

"I thought you and your boyfriend made good money," she commented.

"We do. I promise, we still have plenty left over," I said to reassure her.

"Then I don't understand. Why would you buy used furniture?"

Oy. Leave it to my mother to come up with that.

"Don't the children mind sitting on furniture other people sat on? Who knows what diseases people had a hundred years ago, that's still in the cushions."

"Mom, I'm sure everything was sanitized. More tea?"

She reached over and wiggled her finger in one of the gouges in the table. "But furniture with holes in it?"

"That's called 'distressed.'"

My mother was puzzled. "The furniture is made to look unhappy?"

I sighed, remembering a childhood of convoluted conversations like these. "They pound the wood to make it look old and weathered."

"Why would you want bruises when you could have brand-new from Macy's?

She took her last sip, placed her dainty cup in its saucer, and clasped her hands primly in her lap. "I wonder how many hundreds of people drank from this cup. And nobody ever dropped it. A miracle."

I could feel a headache coming on. "Enough about the furniture. How are you?"

"Never mind me. I'm the same. What about you? Is he divorced?"

I noticed my mother never mentioned Bob by name. "Not yet. Those things take a long time."

"I'm not surprised. Breaking up a home is slow."

My back rigidly went up. "I didn't break up his home."

"I didn't say that. I'm talking about *the* breaking it up. Who gets the good dishes? Who wants the cookie jar, Like that."

"Oh." I was bracing myself for the next question I knew she would ask.

"So, you are okay living with a married man?"

Enough. I was getting impatient. "This is L.A. mom, not the East Bronx. Things are more sophisticated here." I was troubled. I'd never seen my mother look at me disappointed.

Mom got up from her chair, picking up the pocketbook she'd been lugging from room to room. Just like Queen Elizabeth, I thought. She pointed a finger at me. "Morals is morals, no matter what coast you live on."

"Mom, please. I'm happy. I'm very happy."

She turned, and over her shoulder she quipped, "You only *think* you're happy."

She always had to have the last word.

It was going to be a rough couple of weeks.

Death Takes a Holiday, 1972. *Left to right:* Melvyn Douglas, Myrna Loy, and Yvette Mimieux. Watching these icons work is a thrill.

Women in Chains, 1972. *Left to right:* Neile Adams, Ida Lupino, Belinda Montgomery, Jessica Walter, and Lois Nettleton. The producers are excited about women beating one another up, I guess, and so are the viewers—big ratings.

The Rookies, 1972. Michael
Ontkean and Gavin Lakin.
To my surprise, my son's team
gets picked for the pilot.

Beverly Hills, c. late '70s. A larger
house, a larger typewriter.

Message to My Daughter, 1973. Bonnie Bedelia and Martin Sheen. Two wonderful actors.

Hey, I'm Alive, 1975. Executive producer Charles Fries, director/producer Lawrence Schiller, actors Edward Asner and Sally Struthers, survivors Helen Klaben and Ralph Flores, and me. Schiller has a party for the two survivors of the plane crash. First time I ever get to meet the real people.

A Sensitive, Passionate Man, 1977. Angie Dickinson and David Janssen. A sad story, beautifully acted.

The Full Slate of
CANDIDATES

Kate Archer qualified for Board candidacy
too late for inclusion here

Brad Radnitz
President

Melville Shavelson
President

Frank Piersen
Vice-President

Phyllis White
Vice-President

Jean R. Butler
Secretary-Treasurer

William Ludwig
Secretary-Treasurer

Hindi Brooks
Board

Allan Burns
Board

Lila Garrett
Board

Irma Kalish
Board

Rita Lakin
Board

Stephen Lord
Board

Ann Marcus
Board

Wendell Mayes
Board

Writers Guild Board of Directors,
1979. Women finally being
treated seriously.

Flamingo Road, 1981. Celebration party.
Left to right: Jeff Freilich, Morgan Fairchild,
Mike Filerman, and me. My story editor,
my producer, and my star. The show is
an audience favorite.

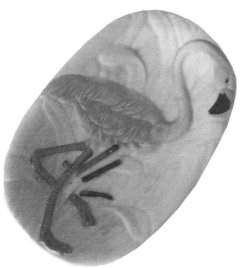

Flamingo Road,
1981. A plethora
of gifts from fans.

Strong Medicine, London, England, 1986. *Top, left to right:* Sam Neill, Dick Van Dyke, Pamela Sue Martin, and Ben Cross. *Bottom, left to right:* Douglas Fairbanks Jr. and Guy Green. Oh, those British actors and those sexy accents.

Strong Medicine, the Lake District, England, c. 1986. Here I am on the set, watching the crew at work.

Strong Medicine, 1987. London. I go to a party with producer Larry Sanitsky and actress Pamela Sue Martin.

Nightingales, 1989. The last picture show for me.

TV Ratings

Here are the ratings for national prime-time television last week (June 27-July 3), as compiled by the A.C. Nielsen Co. Each rating point is said to represent 886,000 homes, or 1% of the 88.6 million U.S. households that have TV.

	Program	Network	Rating
1.	"Nightingales"	NBC	18.9
2.	Night Court	NBC	17.5
3.	Cheers	NBC	17.2
4.	The Cosby Show	NBC	16.6
5.	A Different World	NBC	16.5
6.	L.A. Law	NBC	15.4
7.	Golden Girls	NBC	15.1
8.	ALF	NBC	14.9
9.	Who's the Boss?	ABC	14.0
10.	Hogan Family	NBC	13.8
11.	"Brass"	CBS	13.6
12.	Amen	NBC	13.2
13.	Head of the Class	ABC	13.2
14.	Growing Pains	ABC	12.9
15.	Perfect Strangers (Tue.)	ABC	12.9
16.	Murder, She Wrote	CBS	12.7
17.	Hunter	NBC	12.7
18.	60 Minutes	CBS	12.5
19.	Matlock	NBC	12.4
20.	Newhart	CBS	11.7
21.	Designing Women	CBS	11.6
22.	Hooperman	ABC	11.2
23.	Blue Skies	CBS	11.1
24.	J.J. Starbuck	NBC	11.1
25.	"Crash Course"	NBC	11.0
26.	Miami Vice	NBC	10.9
27.	20/20	ABC	10.8
28.	227	NBC	10.7
29.	48 Hours	CBS	10.7
30.	The Equalizer	CBS	10.7
31.	Wiseguy	CBS	10.6
37.	Facts of Life	NBC	9
38.	"Passion Flower"	CBS	9
39.	Full House	ABC	9
40.	Jake and the Fatman	CBS	9
41.	I Married Dora	ABC	9
42.	Spenser: For Hire	ABC	9
43.	Perfect Strangers (Fri.)	ABC	9
44.	Simon & Simon	CBS	9
45.	Sonny Spoon	NBC	8
46.	Monday Night Baseball	ABC	8
47.	"Slap" Maxwell Story	ABC	8
48.	Beauty and the Beast	CBS	8
49.	Bronx Zoo	NBC	8
50.	Cagney & Lacey	CBS	8
51.	Highway to Heaven	NBC	7
52.	Days and Nights of Molly Dodd	NBC	7
53.	My Two Dads	NBC	7
54.	TV Bloopers & Practical Jokes	NBC	7
55.	Family Ties	NBC	7
56.	"Camille"	CBS	7
57.	Mama's Boy	NBC	7
58.	West 57th	CBS	6
59.	Tour of Duty	CBS	6
60.	High Mountain Rangers	CBS	6
61.	"Star-Spangled Celebration"	ABC	6
62.	Hothouse	ABC	6
63.	Sledge Hammer!	ABC	6
64.	Summer Playhouse	CBS	5
65.	The Charmings	ABC	5
66.	Hotel	ABC	5
67.	America's Most Wanted	Fox	5
68.	Disney Sunday Movie	ABC	4
69.	MacGyver	ABC	4
70.	Rags to Riches	NBC	4
71.	Supercarrier	ABC	4
72.	Married . . . With Children	Fox	4
73.	21 Jump Street	Fox	4
74.	"Home Again"	ABC	3
75.	It's Garry Shandling's Show	Fox	3
76.	Duet	Fox	2
77.	Tracey Ullman Show	Fox	2
78.	Family Double Dare	Fox	2
79.	Boys Will Be Boys	Fox	1
80.	Dirty Dozen	Fox	

Nightingales, 1989. NBC tries to bury the pilot, but viewers are curious.

A Women-in-TV Clout Chart: Who's Got It and Why

Grandes Dames
Meta Rosenberg
Ethel Winant (NBC)

Calling Their Own Shots
Lillian Gallo
● Fay Kanin
◗ Joanna Lee
Lin Bolen
◗ Lila Garrett
◗ Susan Harris
● Gail Parent

Writers Whose Pens Are (Unfortunately) Mightier Than Their Swords
● Ann Marcus
● Caryl Ledner
● Margaret Armen

Pushy, Pushy, Pushy
● Susan Silver

Most Enviable Position at a Studio
Andrea Baynes (Columbia)

Cleaning Up Her Act
Karyl Miller

Taking Care of Business
Sybil Adelman
◗ Pam Chais
Pat Nardo

Taking Care of the Quota
Christine O'Connell Grierson (Warner's)
Mae Helms (CBS)

In a Holding Pattern
Roberta Haynes (20th Century-Fox)
Nancy Malone

War-Horses
Maggie Duffy (ABC)
Barbara Schultz (KCET)
◗ Jean Holloway
Renee Valenti
Madelyn David
Joanne Brough (CBS)

If They're Part (but Not All) of a Package It's a "Go"
Jacqueline Babbin
Charlotte Brown
Juanita Bartlett
● Rita Lakin
● Blanche Hanalis
● Dalene Young
● Barbara Turner
● Eleanor Perry

Even with Talent, It's Nice to Have a Little Help from a Friend
Jane Wagner

If You Don't Like What You're Seeing, Blame Them
Deanne Barkley (NBC)
Esther Shapiro (ABC)
Marcie Carsey (ABC)

If You Don't Like Who You're Seeing, etc.
Ethel Winant (NBC)
Jane Murray (TAT)
Pam Dixon (ABC)

Causes, Causes
Marlo Thomas
Virginia Carter

Well, It Sure Beats the Convent
Christine Foster (Columbia)

Least Publicized Talents
Mimi Roth
Maxine Ellis
Emily Levine

Power Failures
Joan Rivers
Louise Lasser

It's Nice to Have a Network Behind You When You've Written a Novel
Deanne Barkley (NBC)
Joyce Burditt (NBC)

Rising Stars & Dark Horses
Nell Cox
● Linda Bloodworth
Diana Dreiman
Iris Rainer
● Lynn Roth (20th Century-Fox)
Marilyn Freeman
Sue Milburn
● Nancy Schwartz
Gail Honigberg
Deena Kramer (NBC)
Deborah Leschin
Stephanie Kowal (Universal)
Beth Uffner (Warner's)
Mariko Kriss (Paramount)
Nancy Sackett
Rosie Shuster
Judy Coppage
(Hanna-Barbera)

Been Down This Year, Looks Like Up for Next
Joan Darling
Viva Knight

Don't Call Us Sexist, Just Call Them Sexy
● Lynn Roth (20th Century-Fox)
Lara Lindsay (MGM)

Writer's Writers
● Carol Sobieski
◗ Treva Silverman

Eccentric's Eccentrics
Monica MacGowan Johnson
Marilyn Miller

Sour Power
Joyce Selznick

Thank God for Skirttails
● Erma Kalish
● Carol McKeand
Lynn Farr
● Elizabeth Hailey
Tina Pine
● Elinor Karpf
Adele Styler

Thank God for Coattails
Nancy Greenwald
Dawn Aldrich

Dowager Queens
Lucille Ball
Carol Burnett
Mary Tyler Moore

Trappings of Power
A Betamax (at home)

Any wine-colored car, preferably a Volvo or BMW—or a Champagne Delight VW

Self-correcting IBM typewriter

The Joan Didion/Fay Kanin writing caftan

Cartier pigskin-strapped, ivory-faced tank watch worn on the same wrist with a thin gold bracelet, or: gold Rolex watch; no other jewelry

An extremely fast, clipped telephone voice and equally fast push-button fingers

Charge accounts at Country Club Fashions, Dorso and/or Dinallo

A happy female secretary

Large wineglasses of Perrier served in the office

Specially written material for your answer phone, the funnier the better

Hermès Agenda lizard datebook

Slouchy, expensive tweed blazer worn with (very) open silk shirt and unknotted, rectangular cashmere scarf with slight fringe

Two phones at home: one listed, one unlisted

Long brown More cigarettes

A fur coat (not from an endangered species)

A high energy level

Stroke Spots
Ma Maison
Moustache Café
La Serre for lunch
The Palm
The front room at La Scala
L'Ermitage
La Bella Fontana in the Beverly Wilshire (never the El Padrino) for private luncheons
Imperial Gardens on Sunset

Places Where You Can Actually Do Business
Du-Par's, Studio City
Sports Deli, Century City
Cantor's
Chadneys, Burbank
NBC commissary

Women in power at last, 1989. ●Women writers; others are executives.
For a laugh, don't miss "Trappings of Power."

A SHOW NOT WORTH WATCHING

We Watch Anyway

TV LOG LINE: March 7, 1972
Movie of the Week, ABC
The Rookies
Young men and women train to become police officers.
Producer: Aaron Spelling. Director: Judd Taylor.
Script: William Blinn, based on a story by Rita Lakin.
Cast: Darren McGavin, Georg Stanford Brown.

(Kids are 12, 16, and 20)

The kids were excited, getting ready to watch my show. I had not planned to see the damned thing, but the children took it for granted we would. We always watched Mom's shows. I didn't confess why to my children—what was the point? Why spoil their evening?

Naturally, the menu was the usual, popcorn and sodas. Junk food for a junk show, I thought sarcastically.

Joan had at the ready her little Brownie camera to capture forever the fast moment my name flashed on the screen.

Bob said he'd be working late at the studio, editing. But I knew he didn't want to see this show, even though I had hoped he'd sit through it with me. I wanted his support.

Joan asked, "How much time is there after the 'Created by' credit goes on? When does the 'Written by' credit go on? I want to snap both." Everyone in my household knew Hollywood jargon.

"Only a minute or so, but this time it's only 'Story by.'"

"Really? How come? You always get 'Written by.'"

I tried to bank my sarcasm. "Speaking of stories, this one's too long to explain. Some other time, okay?"

"Sure." And then she was off to the kitchen to make coffee.

Finally we made ourselves comfortable, curled up on couch and floor. Joan snapped photos of my credits as they rolled by, and all three cheered for me.

I thought of earlier days when my sister, Judy, and I would make it a fun evening. But Judy was long gone. She and her husband, Paul, were living in their motor home, still traveling the country, having a great time.

The movie was on. I watched, inwardly groaning. Bill Blinn was a good writer, and this was not good. I smelled a lot of network interference.

As for all my research to get the police training right, not a snippet of reality crept in. Not a word of mine, not a character, not an idea. Cardboard cops in cardboard situations creakingly done yet again.

The only high spot of the evening was Gavin's baseball scene. "Look at it this way, Mom: I got my second role in a TV show. And I got up to bat."

Sue chimed in: "Some batter you were. You almost drilled the cameraman with a line drive up the middle."

With that, they jumped up and down, high-fiving each other.

But little by little, boredom set in. Joan yawned and shrugged and left the room, a book in her hand. Followed by my kids, with excuses to stop watching.

"You need to do homework? That's your excuse to leave? That bad, huh?"

As Gavin walked out he tossed back at me, "Not one of your best, Mom."

You could say that again.

Finally I was alone and could turn it off.

When Bob got home at last, he wasn't interested in discussing it. "I'm beat. That one scene took forever." He didn't look too happy.

"A problem?"

He was angry. "Gershuny is driving me crazy. He accused me of taking too long with too many shots. I said to him, This is a movie, for God's sake; we need to use as much time as it needs. And do you know what he had the nerve to tell me? He hired me because I was a TV director. I was supposed to know how to shoot fast and cheap!"

With that, he lumbered up the stairs, shaking his head.

REVIEWS: Kevin Thomas of the *L.A. Times*, still being kind to me, said he liked it. Called *The Rookies* "a winner," said it would make a great series. Cleveland Amory of *TV Guide*, however, called the characters "so one-dimensional, they are almost ludicrous."

Once again, in my battles with Aaron for Class vs. Crass, I lost.

A FUNNY THING HAPPENED on the way . . .

A month or so after *The Rookies* went on the air, I was driving on the Hollywood Freeway to a dentist appointment, singing at the top of my lungs to one of my favorite tapes, *Jesus Christ Superstar*, when—oops!—I got pulled over by a cop.

What had I done? I knew I hadn't been speeding.

"Driving too *slow* in the fast lane," he informed me.

I was going to get a ticket for not speeding but singing and having a good time?

"Oh, for goodness sakes, gimme a break." I didn't even realize I'd slid out of the slow lane. I tried to talk peacefully to the peace officer about not getting a ticket.

"Show me your license."

"I have a toothache and I'm in pain; I wasn't thinking straight." That didn't work.

"Registration."

I dug it out of my glove box, causing its contents to spill out onto the passenger seat and floor. Hmm. A leftover sandwich from who knows when. The second glove of a pair I'd been searching for. Some stale mints. A half dozen gasoline receipts that had been tossed in. Other little treasures to examine later.

I pleaded. It would be embarrassing to tell my friends I'd been ticketed for going too slow. "Have mercy."

He ignored me.

I tried name-dropping. "Do you happen to know some North Hollywood cops named Darla and Jim?"

He didn't answer, so I guess he didn't know them.

"Nice couple. Partners. Like to eat at Ben Frank's." I added.

He kept writing. I hated when they wore those large mirrored sunglasses so you couldn't see their eyes, couldn't tell what they were thinking.

This was my last attempt. I tried to look important. Head up, puffed-out chest. "I'm a writer. I created that famous TV police series *The Rookies*."

He finally looked at me. "Hey, lady, quit while you're ahead. I hated that phony show." He shoved the ticket at me.

As I drove off I mumbled back at him, "You shoulda read my pilot."

But at least I felt vindicated. I knew I had been right about *The Rookies*.

THE SERIES was ordinary and dragged out for a lifeless four seasons. Would it have been different if I'd had my way? I'd like to think so.

WEDDING BELLS

Bob and I Get Married, and I'm Told an Omen

April 1972

ob's divorce was final, and *Lapin* had completed shooting and the film was almost finished being edited. He was excited about the upcoming private test screening with a live audience. He knew he had a winner.

So one morning, as I was enjoying my first cup of coffee, he cheerfully greeted me with "Let's get married." I was stunned. Sometimes he reminded me of a yo-yo, with all these highs and lows.

Up until now, I'd found excuses not to marry, and finally, a man had come along who managed to crack my defenses. None of the men I'd met had eased me into marriage, *eased* being the operative word. The secret I never admitted, even to myself, was that I was afraid to commit again, afraid I could never love again, and afraid that another husband could *die* living with me.

"Stay single, stay safe" was my motto. Unless . . . unless someone talked me into another plunge into matrimony. And someone was doing just that.

What was I getting myself into? I suddenly had pre-wedding jitters.

I must have been at the point when I felt I had to stop saying no to every man I met. This man didn't ask; he told me we'd marry. He was the only one who talked me into it. And yet . . . I still didn't sense I knew him well enough. Would I feel safe with this man, as I had with Hank?

Apparently my new captain was steering the ship. I wasn't ready to rush into anything yet. I assumed planning for a wedding would go on for a while, and I'd have time to adjust. But Bob said, "Let's just do it. We can squeeze it in before the screening."

Squeeze it in? He was pulling me along with the sheer force of his personality

IT WAS WHIZ, bang, and before I knew it, Bob and I were married out on our huge brick patio with its lovely adjoining garden. (A garden, which by the way needed a knowledgeable, costly gardener, the beginning of a long line of new, unexpected expenses.)

It was all happening too quickly. How did my kids feel about our big event? I don't recall asking, so I had no idea what they were thinking as they watched us marry. The same for Bob's son, who was there—how did he feel? I hadn't thought to invite Howard to come home from college for the event. He was more puzzled than hurt; he chastised me later: How could I forget to invite my son?

I called up my folks and told them after the fact. Although Bob's parents lived in town, they weren't invited either. Nor did I invite my close friends. Not even my sister, Judy.

How odd of me, and why didn't I question this behavior, which was so unlike me? Mom pretended not to be upset, but she was. "I was just there," she commented, "but I could have come back."

Bob convinced me that we shouldn't make a big deal of it. Hadn't we gone through the overdone big weddings the first time around? "We could have a party later," he reassured me, (a party that never happened). I even went into my closet and took out an ordinary dress in which to get married. Why didn't I think to buy a new outfit?

I chalked it all up to Bob's rushing me, not giving me enough time to think. He just took charge and I followed blindly.

Bob's brother, Arthur, also a scriptwriter, and his wife, Ursula, a self-proclaimed astrologist, were the only guests at our no-frills affair. Arthur was entirely different from his brother. Where Bob was thin, lanky, edgy, and acerbic, Arthur was chubby, slow-moving, and sweet. Ursula was German-born and Gypsy-like. Her idea of interesting wedding conversation was to inform me she'd been forced into the Nazi Hitler Youth movement as a child, which horrified me. Though she did say she hated it. And here she was, married to a Jewish man in California. I wondered how that had come about.

When the short ceremony was over, as the rabbi (whose daughter was also a screenwriter—isn't that *so* Hollywood) and my new in-law witnesses were leaving for home, Ursula bent over and whispered to me in her thick accent. "You shouldn't have married him. You'll be sorry."

Huh? I thought, what nerve!

With that, swirling her voluminous multicolored skirt, which was much dressier than what I had worn, she hurried off to Arthur, who was holding their car door open for her.

Would that I had listened.

I looked around my fancy garden. All that was left of my wedding were a scattering of paper cups, a few empty champagne bottles, and a puzzled bride.

WAS IT THE RING on my finger? The marriage license in my hand, which finally gave me permission to love again? To stop holding back, to completely surrender myself to love, to let the overwhelming feelings enter? To offer every fiber of my being? There had been so much I wanted to give, and I hadn't known I had been waiting.

I lamented what I had missed all these years by remaining faithful to a memory. My flowering self had reopened.

But was that very ring on my finger to become the noose around my new husband's neck? We've all heard the expression "a marriage made in heaven." In retrospect, looking back, I can only sum up my experience as "a marriage made in irony." And "Killing Me Softly" was indeed our theme.

When the honeymoon was over, the honeymoon was over.

And the deconstruction of Rita began.

SUCCESS:
A TWO-EDGED SWORD

How Could I Explain What Went Wrong?

Was it the disaster of his movie *Lapin 360*? Maybe. Maybe not just that. The test screening turned into a nightmare. Things had been going so well. The invited audience was totally involved; people were riveted to their seats, seemingly holding their breaths. We were standing in the back, holding hands and grinning.

Then it all changed. The movie came to its dramatic close. The mother and child, trying to escape, were brutally gunned down by the bad guys. A gasp echoed throughout the theater. A pause, and then, to our horror, the viewers were booing, even shouting. People got up out of their seats and stormed out, muttering angrily. It was as if Bob had done too good a job making the audience care, then killed off their heroine and her baby. People were first shocked and then infuriated. They had been led to expect a happy ending.

We stood there, watching them leave, the theater emptying as they poured out into the lobby, where they were meant to fill out response cards. I peeked out at them. Surely they were writing angry comments. Many ripped up the cards in protest. How ironic, I thought. The movie must have been effective to have caused such an outbreak of emotion.

The only ones left in the theater were members of the cast and crew and the executive producer-owner.

"Well, that's that," Bernard Gershuny said, in a blame-filled tone of voice. "My money down a toilet."

Bob rushed over to him, still reeling from the unexpected audience reactions. "What are you talking about?"

He shrugged. "My wife warned me. Stick to selling novelty hats. That's a business, you know."

"We have to fix it."

"Fix what? It's broken."

Bob was waving his arms wildly. He was turning purple. "Why do you think we have these paid viewings? To get audience response. Well, we got it, and they told us loud and clear they loved the movie but didn't want the characters they love to die."

Watching my husband in pain, I remembered sadly all the heated discussions they'd had about how to end their film. Happy ending? They'd gone for tragedy. They'd made the wrong choice.

The cast and crew silently tiptoed out. They wanted no part of the fireworks to come. They stopped on their way out to speak to Bob and said how sorry they were, that it was really a good piece of work. Especially remorseful was his good friend Les Green, who had done the editing. But Bob didn't hear them. He was fixated on Bernard.

"Too late," Gershuny said, picking his coat up from his seat and starting for the door.

Bob wouldn't let him leave. "We go back and reshoot the ending and reedit and we've got a great picture!"

Gershuny pulled his arm away. "Mr. Hot-Shot Director. With what? What is this 'we'? 'We' are out of do-re-mi. This is it. Goodbye."

And that was that. Bob was devastated and I felt terrible for him.

THE LAST BRIDE OF SALEM

RL Square Is Born

I t was gloom and doom in our beautiful $100,000 Beverly Hills Canyon dream house. The failure of *Lapin* hit Bob hard. "It wasn't your fault," I kept telling him. "Your movie was terrific." But he was inconsolable.

I talked about my own career failures. "Remember the fiasco of 'Shattered Glass'?"

A slight nod at that.

"And didn't *Rookies* just fall through? One has to pick up the pieces and go on." It got no response.

"Hey, we're a team," I reminded him, "Remember when we came up with RL Square? Well, now is the time to make it happen. We'll come up with good projects for us to do together."

Bob seemed to perk up.

WE GOT LUCKY pretty fast. ABC was willing to let us do a project for them.

"But daytime?" Bob was not too thrilled about that. I could imagine him thinking, From a feature film to daytime, what a comedown.

"It lets us work together. It's not as if we're doing a soap—they're still movies." They were calling this new series *The ABC Afternoon Playbreak*.

We came up with an idea for a gothic horror flick and the network liked it.

So I wrote "The Last Bride of Salem." Lois Nettleton, still going strong after *Women in Chains*, played a young mother who realizes her husband, played by Brad Dillman, and her child are being possessed by descendants of the Salem witches.

Bob was executive producer. He didn't direct, because daytime shows were not filmed, they were taped, so we hired Tim Donovan, well-known in that field.

This was a win-win situation for us.

We were given a big write-up in the *L.A. Times* with a flattering photo of the two of us at our desk in our beautiful den. The reporter congratulated us on our talent and called us "adventurous."

MONTHS LATER, a congratulatory telegram arrived for Bob from the National Academy of TV Arts & Sciences. They were announcing nominees for the Daytime Emmy Awards.

Bob had been nominated for Best Executive Producer of "Last Bride." And I was delighted to see that Lois was nominated for Best Actress.

What good news. I happily congratulated Bob. But I was surprised my name didn't come up also. It would have been fun being recognized with an award as a husband-and-wife team.

"What thoughtful person recommended you?" I asked, smiling.

"I did," was his answer. "I nominated myself. That's how it works."

What! In a shocked moment of disbelief, I realized that when he had nominated himself, he hadn't thought to tell me to do the same. How come he didn't think of me? If it had been reversed, of course I would have thought of him.

He didn't win the Emmy.

RL SQUARE WASN'T GETTING any other projects as a company, so Bob and I went back to nighttime TV as solo acts.

I didn't know it then, but it was never going to be about me. It was always going to be about Bob.

This was a clue, a portent of the future. The handwriting was on the wall.

TROUBLE

The Last Bad Days

I wanted to understand what catapulted us into a tailspin.

Bob began to seriously drink at night. One martini escalated to three. He was changing before my eyes. The cocoon disappeared and the real world had seeped back in, and so did the real Bob Lewis.

His was an underbelly of need. I didn't recognize the scope of that need. He desperately wanted success. I thought of it as a typical male thing, men still believing that they had to come first because they were better than women. And I was continuing to move faster along the career track than he was.

I wanted him to earn more than I did.

He needed to fill the empty holes in himself. The Beverly Hills house had been the first step in living up to his desired image of himself. It wasn't enough. *Lapin* had been the next step, and that had failed. Out of his insecurity and feelings of inadequacy, he became angry. He felt entitled and couldn't understand why he wasn't appreciated.

He ranted about the ungrateful people he worked with. Everyone was to blame, never himself. Since it wasn't safe to let the world see his rage, I was forced into becoming his safety valve.

Dr. Jekyll, with the aid of martinis, transformed into Mr. Hyde. The nights turned into horror movies. He couldn't sleep, so he kept me up, leaning over me, belittling me, battering me emotionally.

One night he berated me for hours for my lack of cooking skills. He moaned, "Why, oh why, did I marry two women who didn't know how to cook! Any fool could be a better cook than the both of you." To spite me, he bought and studied cookbooks and then took over cooking our meals. I was relegated to cleanup.

He demeaned me as a woman. How I dressed. Whatever my opinion, he argued against. So I stopped having any. He continued to undermine me.

Night after night, wearing me down, wearing me out. I moved foggily and exhaustedly throughout my days. Why didn't I stop him? He didn't seem to be able to stop himself. For a while I must have been seen as a totally accepting mother. Now was he turning me into the real one, the critical one? Was he repaying his mother's fury, doing to me what she did to him? He was killing me. Less softly.

The only area in which I was secure with him was my writing. He nurtured that. I was still his meal ticket.

I was changing as a result. I fell back into that 1950s trap of being "the little woman" again. How naturally I fell into that role. Somehow, the accomplished person I had become melted away. I became the simpering "yes, dear, anything you say dear" wife. And I willingly let him take charge of my life. I turned over the business details, and the household bills and all money and banking to him. His name was added to the house and both cars. I was relieved to be rid of all that responsibility, unconsciously still believing I needed a man to make my decisions.

Maybe I wanted to repeat and recapture and complete the experience of being a wife and partner that I'd lost when Hank died. I believed Bob would love me and take care of me, as Hank had. It was as if I'd been emotionally holding my breath all those alone years, which were finally at an end. I'd be rid of all my cares and be able to live the way I wanted again. I could concentrate on what really mattered to me as a woman—my marriage, my kids, and my writing.

He was no longer the caring husband I'd thought I married. I was no longer the capable wife *he'd* married.

I used to think being an abused wife meant getting smacked around. For me, I understood later, it could be also mean being battered with words. What irony: My writing was all about words, and in these fights I was mute.

I was desperately trying to balance the marriage and my job. By compartmentalizing myself, I managed to keep working. It was a miracle that I did as well as I did, on all those projects that came during those awful years. None of my friends or the people I worked with knew the stress under which I worked. I would have been too embarrassed to let them see what a fool I'd been. What's that line—laughing with tears in my eyes? Truth is, I was happy only when I was at work.

I was caught in my new husband's thrall, and he overpowered me and controlled me. I lost any will of my own.

And he stayed on course. As always, it was all about Bob.

SUNSHINE

Meeting the Head of Universal Studios and Being Stupid

1973
Universal Studios

A highly touted, important project came along called *Sunshine*. It was based on an *L.A. Times* magazine article true story about a woman who kept a tape-recorded journal while she was dying. She made the tape for her daughter to listen to when she had grown up. It was top priority, and writers were lining up and would kill for it.

It was so huge that Sid Sheinberg—at this time the head of Universal Studios—was in charge of making it happen. There was already a lot of press about it, and viewers were anxiously waiting to see it.

And who did he call? Me. He called *me*? I guess I was still on the A-list. I was astonished, tense, and excited just thinking about it.

The day before I was to attend this meeting, Bob informed me he was going to tag along with me. I didn't think he should do that, but my husband insisted, he was going along to protect my interests. He was adamant that this project was too important and had to be handled carefully. Big money and a major career jump were involved. I assumed he meant mine.

Sheinberg was surprised to see him arrive at the meeting but showed good manners, and he was friendly. He directed his conversation toward me and informed me how much the studio was involved in this production, and I listened avidly.

To my astonishment, President Sid offered me this prize. What I realized instantly, as I sat there on cloud nine in his magnificent office high up in the Black Tower, was that this assignment would definitely raise me into the glorified strata of writing motion pictures.

Bob, sensing that Sid was ignoring him, leaned back in his chair, took out a cigar, and made a big deal out of lighting and puffing it. He glanced around like a man taking over the room. "Sid," he said, with grandiosity, "did you know I just finished directing Henry Fonda in *The Alpha Caper*? Harve Bennett producing. We shot it on your lot?"

I couldn't believe what I was seeing and hearing. My husband was showing off, preening and behaving insufferably. Waiting for some acknowledgment or admiration.

I was so embarrassed. Sid merely nodded, but I shuddered at the look of disdain on his face.

My head was so clouded with this image, I hardly heard anything more of the script discussion. Finally, to my relief, the meeting was over.

Sid Sheinberg sent me home with all the research and said he'd wait to hear from me once I had time to think about how I would write it.

Bob effusively said goodbye and stated that he was looking forward to seeing Sid again soon.

≈

Later
At home

No surprise, hubby Bob was panting at the thought of directing *Sunshine*. Totally unaware of having spoiled my meeting. All he could focus on was this was his next big opportunity to jump into the really, really big time. Since Sid had already met him, Bob was sure he was a shoo-in. "Did you see how his eyes lit up when I mentioned directing Fonda?"

"No, I must have missed that," I said, trying to be sarcastic. Bob didn't notice. Besides, I was still upset. How could he have inappropriately pushed his own agenda? And to have brought up Harve Bennett's name when he knew how much that man hurt me? I would never have behaved like that, nor would I ever have worked with a producer who hurt *him*.

Bob gave me an order. "Just you remember. You reject the project if we aren't *both* connected to it!"

I couldn't believe he was telling me to go to a major studio head and demand that my husband direct. "Bob, you can't mean that?"

"We're a team. We should do it together."

"We're a team only if the projects are ones we come up with. He's doing the hiring. You can't expect me to give this man orders."

He did expect exactly that. So it was *his* career jump he was thinking about.

After hours of badgering me all night long in bed, keeping me up, with me begging him not to make me do this, finally, exhausted from no sleep, I gave in.

The next day I asked for a private conference with Sid. The meeting was short and unbearably painful, but I crawled my way through, feeling sick to my stomach.

Sid Sheinberg's response was to decline the both of us.

≈

When he took the project away from me, I cried all day. Why had I done what in my heart I'd known was wrong? All wrong. Now the head of Universal Studios would never hire me again. A vitally important door was closed to me. Why the hell had Bob made me do that? So much for his protecting *my* interests.

Sid Sheinberg hired Joseph Sargent to direct it. Sargent was an A-list director with thirteen years of solid good movie credits. He did a wonderful directing job. After winning four Emmys, he went into directing feature films.

Sid gave the writing assignment to my old friend Carol Sobieski. It couldn't have gone to a better person. She wrote a brilliant script and she too won many awards for it, and it catapulted her into writing for feature films.

Carol, a beautiful woman inside and outside, died much too young at fifty-one after a full career as a successful feature film writer. She'd evolved, as I'd expected, into a celebrated writer, deserving of her many awards. She was a woman of grace and beauty, and hundreds turned up at her funeral to mourn such a loss and to celebrate her life.

A little piece of me died when I watched Carol's *Sunshine*.

I thought, ironically, that a big piece of sunshine had gone out of my marriage.

A SUMMER WITHOUT BOYS

An Embarrassment of Riches: A Tale of Two Movies

TV LOG LINE: December 6, 1973
Special Saturday Movie, CBS
A Summer Without Boys
Set in the World War II years. A coming-of-age story.
A teenager finds love and disappointment on a summer vacation.
Executive producer: Hugh Hefner. Producer: Ron Roth. Director: Jeannot Szwarc.
Teleplay: Rita Lakin. Cast: Kay Lenz, Barbara Bain, Michael Moriarty.

Thankfully, finally, I had two fine job offers at the same time. CBS and ABC each hired me to write a movie. I wrote them back-to-back, and they were produced at the same time. Both were favorites at the time because at last I was dealing with the kinds of shows I knew were right for me. I'd finally been given the chance to do stories about women, character-driven plots with emotional underpinnings.

My first story meeting was a surprise. And who should be the first to give me the chance to write something meaningful about women? The company called Playboy Productions. Yes, Playboy, as in Hugh Hefner of *Playboy* magazine fame. The one who invented Playboy Bunnies. Irony abounds.

However, I never visited the Playboy Mansion or Playboy Club or met Hugh Hefner. And I certainly never wanted to see or be a Bunny. An offshoot of his many business ventures was Playboy Productions, a respectable mainstream company producing feature films and television.

At my meeting with Ron Roth, this highly intelligent producer asked me what I'd like to write about.

That was a first, being asked what I'd *like* to write. I was in awe.

It had always been about what was commercial or what was timely. I turned over possibly salable ideas in my mind. I couldn't ignore this challenge. What I *wanted* to write! Whatever possessed me to try to sell this idea in this male-dominated company? I meekly said, "I would like to write a movie exclusively about women."

He repeated, "Write what you want."

Okay. I pitched him the idea that came to my mind. I had a desire to write a movie that was actually autobiographical, and that was fine with him. Again, a first. What a treat, not having to try to guess what would interest a buyer. Another first, this one the most amazing of all: There wasn't one change. Every word remained mine. Unheard of.

A Summer Without Boys was loosely based on a true experience I'd had as a teenager. After ten years of writing for TV, I had a chance to revisit the girl I once was.

The story took place in 1944, played against the fact we were at war; this was my own coming-of-age story about a teenager's lonely summer spent in the Catskill Mountains in New York State.

It was traditional during New York City's unbearably hot summers that wives would take the children and travel to a resort where it was cooler while the husbands would stay in the city and work. (Remember, there was no air-conditioning at that time.) Between that and the fact that many husbands were at war, the only guests at the resort were women, children, or older people.

Not only was I writing about women, I was also adding a subtext of a cultural and religious phenomenon. The Catskill Mountains were filled with Jewish-owned hotels ranging from the expensive and well-known, such as Grossingers and the Concord, way down to the small, inexpensive hotels that were more like communes (mutually supportive communities). These were known as *cuch-a-lains*, translated from the Yiddish phrase meaning "cook alone," which meant instead of being waited on, all the women did their own cooking and serving for their own families.

In my teleplay, as in my real experience, my mother did take me up to these mountains for the summer, and there was only one young man helping out at that inexpensive resort—a man who was classified 4F, unfit to fight in the war.

I took a writer's liberties; my mother did *not* have an affair with this man. But since a drama needed "drama," I played her as an unhappy, lonely wife, looking for love. My real mother, Gladdy, didn't mind that I gave her this forbidden romantic interlude; it amused her. "Who knew I could be such a brazen hussy?" she commented happily. "But don't ever let your father see it."

Barbara Bain played the mother and Michael Moriarty played the only available male. They were wonderful. Barbara had already done a lot of TV, winning an Emmy for her role on *Mission Impossible*. Michael had won awards for two of his TV movies, *Bang the Drum Softly* and *The Glass Menagerie*, with Katharine Hepburn.

My character, Ruth, played sensitively by newcomer Kay Lenz, demonstrated teenage angst beautifully. There was only one other girl on the premises my age, who I named Lenore, played incisively by Debralee Scott. As in real life, this girl I befriended was definitely a bad influence, leading me to do things I never would have dared on my own. (I cringed when I watched the scene where I stole a lipstick from Woolworth's at her insistence.) Of course, in real life, I never saw "Lenore" again once the summer was over.

Writing this script brought back a lot of memories. Part halcyon days—picking huckleberries, swimming in the lake, and reading books. Lots of books. Part worrying what to do with my life. Would I ever fall in love; teenage stuff like that.

I wondered whatever happened to Lenore, and I often fantasized about her seeing this movie and recognizing herself in it.

However, Playboy only went for the drama of wartime and romance. The movie ignored the Jewish background I presented. Playboy Productions wasn't interested in the political ramifications of that time. "American" hotels were restricted from having Jewish clients. Jewish hotels were built in response to that segregation. However, the vacation place as shot in my TV movie could have been in Anywhere, USA.

I had already been able to deal with that sensitive subject matter, on, of all shows, *Mod Squad!* An ordinary cop show let me deal with anti-Semitism.

Funny, though, that a company that denigrated women let me write a sensitive story about women.

Reviews were good. Dave Kaufman in *Variety* wrote, "Rita Lakin turns back the pages of time for this nostalgic glimpse of the days of WWII . . . an arresting picture of another era, another time, another world . . . An offbeat tale and a rewarding one." He raved on and on about its merits, making me blush with pleasure.

But I had to admit, in the midst of all this glory, I made the next foolish error that would haunt me through the rest of my career. Right after I'd finished the script, Bob started nagging me. Once again, he brought up the director job.

"Sheinberg made a mistake not giving me *Sunshine*. You have to get me this one."

"How can you even ask that of me? It didn't work last time. It won't now."

His eyes narrowed. "Because you want me to succeed, don't you?"

I was feeling panicked. "Ron Roth already has a director in mind, someone with a lot of credits." A French director, Jeannot Szwarc, who already had a fine reputation.

"He wants you, he has to take me."

I saw myself being dumped off this project as well.

Bob kept demanding. I felt trapped. I knew it was wrong, but once again I gave in and did as he asked.

Out of the desperate need to please my husband, I stupidly insisted to the producer, Ron Roth, that I get my way.

To his credit and my relief, Roth didn't fire me, but of course he turned Bob down.

Ron Roth never spoke to me again. And even though he praised my writing, I'd never have a chance to work on any of his other projects after that. Another important door was shut to me.

≈

THE ABC TV PRODUCER was okay with Bob as part of the deal, so he finally got to direct on this second project. My husband never apologized for making me lose *Sunshine*. Or, even worse, for making me lose the respect of two important men.

MESSAGE TO MY DAUGHTER

TV Movie Number Two

TV LOG LINE: December 12, 1973
Special Saturday Movie, ABC
Message to My Daughter
Flashbacks carry this poignant story about a confused teenager
looking for emotional strength from her dead mother's tapes.
Producer: Charles Fries. Director: Robert Lewis. Script: Rita Lakin.
Cast: Martin Sheen, Bonnie Bedelia.

was so lucky to have Martin Sheen, in a double role, playing the father and, in flashbacks, husband to Bonnie Bedelia, the wife/mother who died young. Sheen and Bedelia were wonderful. Two genuine, believable performers, who've had long, steady, successful careers.

WITH BOTH of my movies being shot at the same time, I was torn between the two projects, wanting to be on both sets. Bob expected me to be on his set constantly. It was making me nervous. He was shooting some of the more emotional scenes in a way I felt was shallow. Naturally, I didn't comment.

One morning, I said, "They're shooting my *Summer* movie on location at Lake Arrowhead, and I'd love to go up there." It was something I really wanted to do. And frankly, I needed a break from a movie that wasn't turning out they way I'd felt it should.

"No," he said. "I need you here." He didn't even bother to look at me; he was looking over the script in his hand. I had a sudden memory of Harve Bennett keeping me away from my *Mod Squad* show. He had kept me "busy" doing useless work, and Bob kept me "busy" doing nothing but standing around watching the "great man" work. No wonder the two of them liked working together. They were so alike.

No matter how much I begged, my darling husband refused to let me go.

An Aside

Things were changing for women, though it was still rare to encounter other women in my industry.

One of the major moments of that year was tennis star Billie Jean King easily beating star player Bobby Riggs, who had proclaimed men were superior to women. Especially in tennis. It turned out to be the most watched tennis match in all history.

And very big news. In *Roe v. Wade*, the Supreme Court voted 7-2 that laws prohibiting abortion were unconstitutional.

I dealt with the subject of abortion in my movie, when the daughter, Miranda, played by Kitty Winn, tries to abort her baby. I wrote the kind of scene that was still happening and spoken about in whispers. The law said they couldn't be prohibited, yet abortions were still hush-hush, considered a sin and performed in unsanitary, dangerous places.

In real life, living in Los Angeles, I was aware of the many women traveling south to Mexico for cheap abortions, and some never lived to come home.

THE MOVIE FINALLY AIRED, and it received the only kind words from columnist Bill Mayhan, who did a series about the filming of *Message*, in a magazine called *The Evening Outlook TV Week*. He wrote, "Rita Lakin, one of the better writers in this town, came up with an especially appealing story. . . . That, in essence, is the major reason this film will be a superior Movie of the Week." Bill also commented that Martin Sheen, Bonnie Bedelia, and Kitty Winn made a sensational trio. He was right about them, but not about the movie.

Alas, this movie did not get good reviews. The story didn't hold together well, and *Variety* commented, "The film was not helped by Robert Michael Lewis' lethargic direction." Bob threw a fit.

So much for my wifely good intentions. I was feeling more and more like a doormat. Or was that a dishrag? When would I realize what this was doing to me?

Unfortunately, not until much later.

BOB FINALLY did get to direct better projects, but the damage to our relationship was done. I no longer trusted him to care for me. I no longer felt any closeness. I might have still been living in the same house, but I felt alone.

I still felt I had to try.

An Aside: "Wolves"—A CBS Movie That Never Happened

January 1974

Sometimes—actually, frequently—in Hollywood, a full script gets written and approved by a network but never gets produced.

Even A-list writers are not immune, and in 1974 it was my opportunity to write a thriller. I'd never had the chance to tackle a suspense story, and it was fun to write a kind of *Ten Little Indians* plot. It included a great villain—a successful, cruel movie star I named Lila Carmichael, who invited ten people away for a weekend at her mansion on one of the San Juan Islands. These people had known one another in their past. All were in terrible financial and career straits, hopeful that Lila would help them. No one realized that Lila had made them the failures they were today. What she planned was her long-awaited revenge for what they had done to her in school when they were all young.

Sue Cameron, a columnist for the *Hollywood Reporter*, wrote, "Writer Rita Lakin really did a super job on her suspense story, 'Wolves,' aimed as a movie for CBS, but it is so scary that CBS might not put it on. We know they're nervous about violence, but suspense, too?"

The sad truth was, fear of suspense had not stopped its production, but the illness of producer/director Leonard Freeman, who had a dangerous heart condition, had. Just before filming was to start, the much-admired man went into surgery and died of complications on the table. The date was January 20, 1974.

With so many people grieving, no one wanted to continue with the project.

A WEDDING AND A VACATION

Adventures in England

August 1975
Holbeach, Lincolnshire, and London, England
(Kids are 15, 18, and 22)

My son Howard met his lovely English wife, Jennifer Taylor, while he was still at Antioch College. She was traveling on vacation and stopped over in Ohio to visit a friend. She met Howard, and two continents were joined.

Bob and I attended their wedding in the county of Lincolnshire on the east coast of England. We met her folks, Effie and Percy, and a large number of charming relatives. The family business was growing tulips, which surprised me until I looked at a map and saw that this part of England was directly parallel to Holland across the North Sea.

Our pleasant trip was marred only by extremely high temperatures. The hosts of our quaint bed-and-breakfast, unused to such weather, continued to make the beds with heavy, scratchy woolen blankets, which we kicked off nightly.

It was a lovely wedding, and we were welcomed into a new branch of the family. Howard and Jenny left immediately after for their honeymoon.

It had been Bob's and my plan to do a little traveling while overseas. I thought of the trip as the honeymoon I never had, and hoped it might help bring us back to where we had been only three short years ago.

However, I didn't see much of him. Bob couldn't bear being this far away from the Hollywood scene. He spent most of his time finding phone boxes from which to call his agent or his answering service, hoping to hear about potential jobs. He finally went back to the States, his anxiety level too high for him to relax.

I decided I needed a vacation from my husband.

Frances was a gal I knew from L.A. She was not a close friend, more like an acquaintance. She lived in our neighborhood. We often had morning coffee together and talked about places we dreamed about visiting, especially Europe. What a coincidence, she'd be in London when I was in Lincolnshire.

So I called her at her hotel, lucky to find her in, and asked if she wanted a roommate. Her response? "Get on the train and come on down." The room already had twin beds.

I WAS ALREADY learning that when you think you know someone, you never really do until you've lived with them. I was soon to learn it was also true about traveling companions.

With tour guidebook in hand, I was determined to see many of the famous London landmarks that I'd read about for years. I loved English literature, and now was my chance to breathe the air of my women writer favorites. The Brontë sisters. Jane Austen, Elizabeth Barrett Browning, Mary Shelley. I could hardly wait.

Frances had a different itinerary, which I soon gleaned. The subject hadn't come up over coffee: Travel for her meant freedom from inquiring eyes, the chance to be anonymous, to pick up any man who appealed to her. She also informed me she was a night owl: She had come to London to have nonstop *fun!*

Oh boy . . .

My first evening, I was revved up after dinner and decided to take a walk. Frances was not interested, so I left the hotel, chose an arbitrary direction, and off I went, map clutched in hand.

I learned later that night Fran had gone off with an Irishman she picked up in the hotel bar.

The *veddy* proper hotel we stayed in gave us only one key, which caused a problem. It was finally solved by me keeping the key and Frances having the bellman let her in with his passkey, almost always at around 3 a.m., and, of course, waking me. With my eyes barely propped open, my disheveled roommate would insist on catching me up with the candid details of her "fun" nights. As we say these days, TMI. Way too much information.

MY MAP that first evening took me to an area called Soho, and I happily strolled. By nearly 10 p.m. I thought I ought to head back, when suddenly a man appeared at my side and said, "Hello, luv. Nice night, *innet?*"

He was polite, so I nodded, being equally polite. He was well dressed. Tall, not bad-looking, a tad on the paunchy side. Lovely English accent. But hadn't they all? He walked alongside me and asked some rather peculiar questions. Like where should we go? Did I have a bedsit of my own? (I quickly translated it from all my reading as a living room with a bed.) Then he took my arm in his. I thought it rather forward of him.

I stopped walking. "Who are you?" I asked. "I assumed Englishmen had good manners."

He looked at me, startled. "Your accent . . . You're an American. . . ."

"Yes." And being prickly I added, "And you are an Englishman. *Your* accent . . ."

He stepped backward. "Oh dear, I believe I've committed a faux pas. Do you know where you are?"

Still being testy, I answered, "When last I looked, I was in London."

He actually gasped. "Oh my God, you're a tourist." Even though it was dark, under the lamplight, I could see him go red in the face.

He practically stuttered. "Please, may I buy you a coffee? And let me explain?"

I was the one turning colors a few minutes later in a coffee bar, after he enlightened me that I had wandered into a section of Soho where men commonly went seeking assignations with ladies of the night. He'd been watching me, and he "rather fancied me."

He thought I was a hooker! Even though I was dressed ever so properly. He thought my schoolteacher-like skirt and sweater were my "costume attire."

By the time we finished chatting, we were both laughing.

Wilfred, who was a barrister, became my tour guide and friend. He introduced me to a London I would never have found on my own.

ANOTHER ADVENTURE in my London chronicles: The hotel served high tea in the hotel lobby at four o'clock. Most afternoons, I managed to return, tired and happy, from my sojourns in different sections of London, especially my favorites, the Victoria and Albert Museum and the Tate Gallery. I had no idea where Frances was.

The lobby was filled with guests from all over the world. High tea was perfect—the scones and orange marmalade, the clotted cream, the crustless cucumber sandwiches the dry sherry, the petits fours for dessert. And the tea, the wonderful tea. So elegant.

I basked in the absolute pleasure of this hour daily.

And every day, seated nearby at a large, round table was a group of obvious Middle Easterners. The only male was probably a sheik, a shah, an emir, or something like that. Around fifty, he was heavy and wore a voluminous white robe I later learned was a keffiyeh, and a turban with a rope circlet, an agal. Also at the table with him was a group of five extremely young girls who looked somewhat alike.

I speculated about the girls. Were they about fifteen years old? Surely they couldn't all be his daughters? Did he have them with five different wives? Were they relatives? His daughter and schoolmates on vacation? Surely they couldn't be a harem? Or could they?

And while I kept staring at them, the only male was staring at me.

That particular day, after tea, I entered the elevator—the "lift," as it's known over there—heading for my room. The door closed slowly, leaving time enough for another passenger to get in. To my surprise it was the "sheik."

My room was on the tenth floor. The man didn't press any buttons, nor did he get off on any of the lower floors.

He was staring at me with an expression I couldn't read. I worried. Had I offended him by glancing over at his table? Was my curiosity going to get me a dressing-down for rudeness? I wouldn't meet his eyes.

But his voice carried me back. A strong, guttural sound. "Tomorrow I leave on trip on private plane. You will come with me."

Huh! He couldn't be talking to me, but there was nobody else in this car.

I managed a brilliant riposte. "What?"

"First we stop Dubai."

My hands went up as if to prevent his words. "Listen, I think there's some mistake here."

"First, you like to shop? Dubai is good."

First? I didn't like to think about second.

In a panic, I hit all the elevator buttons going up. But they didn't open. Was this an express car?

"You do not pack. I buy you wardrobe."

Oh boy. "Sir," I said. I didn't know how to address him. Your Royal Highness? Or was that the queen? Your Shahness? Sir Emir? "I don't know what you're talking about. I have no intention of going to Dubai, wherever that is."

He moved a few inches closer. "You will go."

I was backed against the door. Why wasn't anyone getting on? How come they didn't have elevator operators? This was a fancy hotel. Should I sue?

Stubborn me. "I won't go."

Stubborn him. "You will." I could feel his breath on my face and the elevator rail digging into my back. He must have had the escargot for lunch. Ugh, he had to eat snails? The garlic was overwhelming.

Impasse.

"Why are you bothering me? I'm forty-four years old. I'm not your choice of age group." Cheap shot. Thinking of those fifteen-year-old girls. Decided now that they were a harem.

My back was pressed hard against the door. His arms were braced, surrounding me; he leaned his hands on each side of the elevator.

I was sweating. What was I going to do? More important, what was *he* going to do? Even more and more important, when was the damn door going to open? I was trapped. Too late. I couldn't turn and reach the emergency button.

I babbled. I had no idea what would come out of my mouth. I wished I had eaten garlic as well. Why should I suffer his bad breath alone? "I won't go. You can't make me. Besides, you can't show me off to your friends. They'd laugh at you. I'm Jewish."

Eyebrows raised. For a long moment nothing happened. I kept hyperventilating. Finally he pressed a button and the next door opened. I almost fell out. The door closed on him glaring at me.

I didn't go to tea the next day, but then I thought, I'm not going to let him spoil my favorite time. The day after, I arrived promptly at four and looked around.

There were Japanese tourists at his round table.

The shah and his juvenile group were gone.

I kept thinking of those young girls and worrying about what their lives were like.

AT HER INSISTENCE, I agreed to go to dinner with Frances and some new friends of hers. They were American men, from Texas, and they were a lot of laughs, was her report. And very rich. There were four of them, and she wanted to share the wealth, so to speak. Since we hadn't spent any time together on this trip at all, I reluctantly gave in. But I warned her, no hanky-panky. "No bringing Texans up to our room. Got it?"

She said, "Sure. Hey we need to eat, right?"

The restaurant was Mirabelle, an upscale restaurant in Mayfair. At last, some-place to wear the only dressy outfit I'd packed, the one I'd worn to my son's wed-ding. I thought about the honeymoon couple, which unfortunately reminded me of my husband back home, so I stopped thinking and concentrated on my misgiv-ings about an evening out with Frances.

I was introduced to PJ, SL, CBK, and BC. Fine with me. If that was the way they wanted it. We'd already had LBJ in the White House. It would be four years before *Dallas* came on and the world would know JR and all the rest of his ini-tialed friends.

Naturally, the Texans were over six feet tall, and of course they wore their cowboy hats, which they didn't remove. Strike one. Just from their boisterous entrance, I could see the maître d' was already alarmed.

Strike two. They drank a lot! As did Frances. And got noisier with each bourbon bottle they emptied. And what the heck was branch water?

Their behavior was enough to brand them "Ugly Americans." If only I could have reassured the traumatized waiter that not all Texans were like this, only friends of Fran's.

And then it got worse. PJ decided to notice the ashtrays that held their cigar butts. Holding one up, he announced, "Well, ain't this a purdy doodad. What say we take them home as souvenirs?"

"I think they're pewter, kind of expensive," I whispered.

I saw the waiter blanch and hurry away.

Oh lord, what next? Were they going to call the bobbies?

Within moments, the waiter arrived with help. With a straight face, he said, "Compliments of the house," as he gave out six cheap glass ashtrays with the name of the restaurant painted on them. As at the same time, his helper cleared all the valuable pewter off the table.

"Well, thank ya kindly," said CBK, reaching for the "souvenir."

Apparently the management, used to shoplifting types, was prepared.

I thought dinner would never end, but finally, it did. I couldn't look the maître d' in the eye as we left. I was mortified.

I still own that little glass ashtray, and it always brings back memories of that evening. Now I laugh. Then, I'd expected an "international incident."

When Frances and I finally got home to L.A., somehow we didn't see much of each other anymore. I guess I was too tame for her, and she was more excitement than I needed in my life.

Wilfred, the man who'd thought I was a hooker, and I stayed pen pals for a while, but then, as happens, we just stopped writing. Was I attracted to him? You bet. But I still believed in my marriage vows. My rule number one: No cheating allowed.

And I went back to the man I was still sort of married to.

WHEN I ARRIVED HOME, my children called a private meeting. I'd hardly carried my suitcase upstairs before I was immediately summoned. It was held in Gavin's bedroom, with the door shut.

"Why so secretive?" I asked playfully. "Which one of you is in trouble? And which one is protecting the culprit?"

Gavin started with, "Howard agrees with us. He says it's unanimous."

This was a surprise. "You spoke to your brother? Are they home from their honeymoon already?" I'd lost track of the time while I was away.

Sue added, "They just got back. He said he got the same letter that we did. It was waiting for him."

Curiouser and curiouser. I sat down on Gavin's bed. Jet lag was setting in. If I leaned back, I might fall asleep, so I stayed upright. "Is this something bad?"

Gavin straightened his shoulders, looking serious. "We think so."

"All right, cut to the chase. I can't take much more of this suspense."

Gavin's voice took on a somber tone. "Bob says he wants to adopt us. We took a vote and we voted unanimously, no. No way, nohow."

Sue crossed her arms, indicating the strength of her opinion. "We already have a daddy, even though he's gone."

Gavin nodded vigorously. "We are not going to change our names."

To say I was surprised was an understatement. Why had Bob asked for that?

It made no sense. Did he think I wanted him to adopt my children? I didn't. Though I thought perhaps he meant well, it was too late now for him to want to be in my family.

This bizarre conversation made me realize how negatively my children felt about the man I had married.

What had I done? To them and to me?

SEX AND THE LAW

A Great Morning After, and I Get an Odd Phone Call

TV LOG LINE: September 8 and 15, 1975
Medical Center, CBS
"The Fourth Sex"
Dr. Joe Gann finds himself helping a doctor friend decide a major medical change in his life.
Executive producers: Frank Glicksman, Al C. Ward. Producer: Don Brinkley.
Teleplay: Rita Lakin. Director: Vince Sherman.
Cast: Chad Everett, Robert Reed.

I was asked by Frank Glicksman to write a script about a man who wanted a sex-change operation. Once I got over my surprise, I was honored. He'd already produced 147 episodes of *Medical Center* and had written some of them as well. (His final production tally: 171 shows!) While most series made for TV were still escapist dramas, Frank's were well respected, known for dealing intelligently with important topics of the day in medicine. The subject of sexual-reassignment surgery was so new and so compelling that it was decided it would take two hour-long episodes to tell the complete story.

I liked Frank, I liked the assignment, and I welcomed the challenge of reading up on this new medical event—not only about the medicine, but about the psychological problems that came with this kind of procedure. Actor Robert Reed was set to play the doctor, friend of lead character Dr. Joe Gannon, played by Chad Everett. I was in awe of Reed's powerful performance of this complex character, and in fact, he was nominated for an Emmy for this work. It felt good to see that the show did well in the ratings and had fine reviews. The subject got a lot of attention. A most satisfying writing experience.

By NOW, Bob was finally getting enough assignments of his own, and was given his own office at each studio, so we were both kept busy and hardly saw each other. His great claim to fame so far was a TV movie called *Guilty or Innocent: The Sam Sheppard Murder Case* with actor George Peppard. Another "hit" by producer Harve Bennett, Bob's new best friend.

It was the morning after the second of the two-part *Medical Center* had aired. Picture this: I was home, at my desk, glancing out the window at my busy bird feeder in the backyard, where the birds were fighting for purchase as I doodled, concentrating on my Sunday crossword puzzle.

I'd given myself a day off. No writing today, just beaming from the positive words being tossed at me for a job well done. The phone rang constantly.

Then a different kind of phone call. I picked up thinking it was another con- gratulatory call, and I was all smiles.

It was a man who introduced himself as a lawyer, calling from New York City, wanting to speak to me about the show I'd written. I was only half-listening.

He was representing his client, who happened to be a doctor who had lived this entire situation of sexual-reassignment surgery and wanted to know if I had been writing his true story.

"Oh," said I, still stuck on a five-letter word meaning *orange* or *Indian*. Did any warning bells ring? Did I suddenly go into terror mode? Could this mean a potential lawsuit? Did I immediately say, "Let me give you the production office number? They'll connect you with the legal department." Actually, no. You have to remember we were still in the seventies, which was more or less still a naïve time. Paranoia was not rampant yet.

I kept concentrating on my puzzle. The answer was *Osage*.

"You *are* Rita Lakin?" he asked.

I said, breezily, still in a my good mood, "That's me."

"Mind if I ask you some questions?"

"Sure, why not?" Still no red flags.

"Do you know Dr. (Name would be left out here for obvious reasons. But I don't remember it, anyway) or have you heard of him?

"Nope, can't say that I did."

"How did you come to writing this particular story?"

"My producer is well known for doing current medical stories and there had been a number of articles on the subject. So he asked if it interested me and it did."

By now one would think, *Stupid, hang up the phone,* but I was still concen- trating on my puzzle, birds flitting about the yard, and the new distraction of my kids laughing at and egging on our dog, Linus, who was running around in circles trying to catch his tail. Dummy.

"Why did you make the man a doctor?" I could hear the scratch of a match. He was smoking.

"Because it's a medical show. And it's easy to connect stories that way. I wrote him as a friend of the main character."

"How did you decide to send him to that specific part of Africa for treatment?"

"Research told me that was the place people went for such procedures that were part of a lengthy treatment plan."

I now glanced through my mail. Bills mostly. Outside, Linus was barking hys- terically.

The lawyer continued his interrogation. "Why did you give him one son, as opposed to a larger family, or even a daughter?"

"Simple. If they had a big family I'd have to write about all of them. It would slow the story down. A son made more sense than a daughter. A son might feel more threatened by his father's choice. My choice came out of laziness. One son was enough to make my point."

"And that scene with the wife. Where did you get that dialogue?"

I was getting bored. How much longer . . . ? "Out of my head. What else might a wife say to a husband who no longer wanted to be a man and wanted to leave the marriage to become a woman?" A bit sarcastic now.

There was a silence. Then the lawyer said, "Thank you for your candor. We won't be bothering you again." He hung up.

I finally reacted to what had just transpired. It dawned on me that I had just dodged a bullet! That the doctor he was representing thought I told his true story without permission. And a major lawsuit would have been the next step.

Dummy. Me.

In 2009, I was honored by a gay-lesbian group of members of the WGA for being a pioneer in their movement. I had no idea that I was doing something unusual when I wrote "The Fourth Sex." At the time I wrote it, in 1975, *gay* was a word one hardly heard. Gay issues and gay rights were rarely discussed. And transgender was off the radar altogether. To me, the topic was a worthwhile assignment. An important story to tell.

Shadowing up behind these people was the illness that had no name yet, that was beginning to kill. It wasn't until the early 1980s that the world first became aware of men dying of a new and rare disease called AIDS.

A year later, I did another *Medical Center* movie for Frank Glicksman, titled "Us Against the World." It was about the difficulties women endured in order to become surgeons and how treacherous that road was for them to travel. Dealing with the chauvinistic male surgeons who didn't want to let women into their private club, they were demeaned because of their gender. It starred Meredith Baxter-Birney, Donna Mills, and Theodore Bikel, all well-known respected actors.

Once again, we were ahead of our time.

Recently, when I had to go into the hospital for a medical procedure, my doctor was black. And a woman. And a surgeon. And I felt so good about it. I wondered if anything I wrote helped to make these changes happen. So by the end of the seventies I was accidentally turning into an activist, when I didn't even know that word.

HEY, I'M ALIVE

An Intriguing Producer and an Actress Who Can't Do a Bronx Accent

TV LOG LINE: November 7, 1975
Hey, I'm Alive, ABC
A pilot in Alaska gives a college student a lift to San Francisco with dire results.
Executive producer: Charles Fries. Producer/director: Lawrence Schiller.
Teleplay: Rita Lakin, from a book by Helen Klaben and Beth Day.
Cast: Edward Asner, Sally Struthers.

This ABC MOW marked the first time in all the biopics I wrote that I actually met the real people who lived the story. And I worked with a most unusual and peripatetic producer/director, Larry Schiller. A good experience all around.

The story. Helen Klaben was a young woman of twenty-two, from New York City, traveling alone around the country. She ended up in Alaska and, looking for a ride to San Francisco, she met Latino Ralph Flores, and paid to ride with him as a passenger in his private plane. The plane crashed. And they survived the impossible—forty-nine days without food or water.

What made the story fascinating was that they didn't get along. They fought most of the time. Furious at him for not keeping his plane in safe condition, Helen blamed Flores. There were no medical supplies, no food, no working radio.

Ralph Flores was a religious man who blamed Helen for the crash by accusing her of rejecting Jesus Christ. He told her they would never be rescued unless she read his Bible cover to cover. And he insisted they refer to each other as "father" and "daughter" to prevent improprieties in their behavior. So here I was, writing an adventure movie that dealt with religion as a subtext.

Helen had no intention of reading his Bible. Finally, weak and exhausted, thinking they were doomed, she gave in. Remarkably, the day she finished reading the last page of the Bible, they were rescued.

A unique two-character piece.

When I met Ralph and Helen at a party at Larry Schiller's house, they still were unfriendly to each other! It was fun watching them react to meeting Ed Asner, who played Ralph, and Sally Struthers as Helen Klaben. The actors were comfortable but not the real people, who seemed awed by the well-known show business folk.

Larry's background was fascinating. A former *Life* magazine photojournalist, when told of the rescue of these two people, he immediately chartered a plane to get to them first before any other journalists. He talked the survivors into signing a contract to allow him to make a film about their experience. He'd first do the story for *Life* magazine, then follow up with a television film.

Larry had a remarkable career doing just this kind of thing. He wrote about famous people like Marilyn Monroe, Gary Gilmore, Lee Harvey Oswald, the Charlie Manson girls, and O. J. Simpson.

Our movie garnered a lot of affirmative reviews. My favorite line was by columnist Morna Murphy, who wrote, "The question this excellent film raises about survival and meaning of faith are intriguing and strangely humbling."

The fun part for me was trampling with the crew around in the snow during the day and spending evenings in Vancouver listening to Larry tell stories of his most amazing life.

I attempted to teach Sally Struthers, of *All in the Family* fame, how to talk with a New York accent so she might sound like Helen Klaben.

"Arrenge," I'd say to her, dragging out the *aaarrr* sound as I pointed to a glass of orange juice.

"Orange," she'd answer back.

"No," I corrected her. "Too Californian. Say *arrrrr*, like that."

"Errr," she tried. She giggled and never got it right.

"Fuggeddiboudit," I told her in Bronxese, now giggling also.

"Huh?" Sally played it her way.

AN UNUSUAL JOB FOR A WOMAN

Executive Producer, *Executive Suite,* Executive Problems

TV LOG LINE: September 1976
Executive Suite, CBS
Big business in the boardroom and bedroom.
Executive producer: Rita Lakin. Producer: Buck Houghton.
Cast: Mitch Ryan, Stephen Elliott.

I was offered a job, out of left field, at MGM studios, for a CBS series that was already on the air on Monday nights. I was hired to be an executive producer of this show called Executive Suite. I repeat. Executive producer. Not a writing job. This was something I never could have imagined.

By definition, an executive producer was THE BOSS. He answered to no one. He made all decisions. His word was law. I keep saying "he." They were always men, high-powered men. They were not writers, these men. They were businessmen, moneymen who were responsible for the full production of a show; they were politicians when necessary.

The shows I'd worked on had such powerful executive producers. David Victor. Dick Berg. Orin Tovrov. George Eckstein. Aaron Spelling.

The hierarchy worked like this: The executive producer hired producers to work under him. They were line producers and did all the nuts-and-bolts work for the production, and creative producers, like Harve Bennett, who dealt with the scripts on a creative level.

So here was *Executive Suite.* Originally a novel by Cameron Hawley about big business, in 1954 it became a movie starring William Holden and Barbara Stanwyck. Twenty-two years later, CBS bought the TV series based on the book, about people who ran a big company, their employees and families. They considered it the first nighttime soap since *Peyton Place,* and many well-known executive producers, such as Don Brinkley, Norman Felton, and Stanley Rubin, took unsuccessful turns trying to make it work.

So here's how it went down. CBS was upset because of the show's poor ratings. But they were opposite, and couldn't beat, *Monday Night Football.* So what did CBS do? They unfairly fired the entire crew of talented people. Naturally, all were tremendously upset. And so was MGM.

CBS decided they needed another person to run the show, someone who understood nighttime soaps, which is the way they saw the show. And suddenly this job was offered to me, because of *Peyton Place*. I'm sure they tried to get the men—Gleason, Wilder, or Siegel—but I bet they were all busy or turned it down. The lady writer won by default.

What to call me? There was no name for a writer who was a producer. There was no title that identified me, so they negotiated a deal under the title of executive producer. In another five years, writers occupying this position would be given a new name, an important new job description. These writers (who now also produced) would be called supervising producers/showrunners. (See "An Aside: Steven Bochco.")

So what was I supposed to be when I suddenly was crowned with this fancy title? I think the right answer to that was "hoped-for miracle worker."

I had no time to think about all the above. It was another situation like *The Doctors*, where I was thrust into a losing proposition. However, CBS promised to do *anything* to help me turn the show around.

My title meant zilch to me. I just jumped in and worked incredibly hard doing whatever I thought would fix the show. Buck Houghton, a line producer, was on board to help me. I hired an amazing, charismatic young talent, an actor named David Dukes, to be the new star. I commissioned new scripts to be written using my ideas for the forward direction. A slogan was born and bandied about: I took the show "out of the boardroom and into the bedroom."

The entire cast and crew were incredible. Everyone pitched in to make things exciting and refreshing and innovative. And we all believed we'd made the miracle happen. But did we ever get the chance to put the new shows on? No.

What was it that CBS did to "help?" They changed the night that the already crippled show was on, to Friday (my personal name for Friday night programming was "Death Valley,") and once again forced it against an impossible mountain, this time the wildly successful *Rockford Files*. Splat!

Someone must have pushed a panic button. All our heartfelt hard work for nothing. All our new scripts were dumped.

When CBS called me in the middle of the night to tell me to pull the plug the very next day, I had an experience I would never have dreamed I'd have. I walked onto the set and when I made the announcement to nearly a hundred people, many began to cry. In January 1977, the show was dead after a total of eighteen episodes, none of them mine.

And I cried too.

The next day, over breakfast, Bob was surprised I was still at home. I told him my bleak news. By now, our relationship was such that that all he could say was, "They should have hired me as the exec producer, instead. A man would have succeeded."

I didn't bother to argue with him. It was too exhausting.

Maybe CBS felt they owed me, for not backing me as promised, for the debacle of *Executive Suite*. On an amusing yet ironic note, and certainly a costly one, I was offered the opportunity to create a new series for CBS. Ordinarily, I didn't turn down jobs, especially the chance to create a new series, but this one sounded so dull and cliché-ridden. I could just imagine my good-old-boy heroes riding around in their pickup trucks with a dead buck deer with huge antlers tied on their hoods. Drinking hard liquor, talking about oil as they brought their trophies home to their trophy wives. Not my cup of tea. Who would watch? Who would care? Certainly not me. I remembered the rich, obnoxious Texans oilmen I'd had dinner with in London. No thanks.

So in 1978, I turned down *Dallas*.

And the birth of JR Ewing.

I hadn't even bothered to tell Bob about the offer. He would have screamed at me if he knew I'd turned it down.

Dallas ran an astonishing record-breaking fourteen years, 357 episodes. I can't even begin to calculate the amount of money the creator of that show made, including years of summers and international reruns. An astronomical figure.

(An amusing sidebar: My brother-in-law, Arthur Lewis, wrote and produced that show for years, and so did my son, Howard! More on that later.)

I had forgotten the lessons of Aaron Spelling. The clichés won once again. Need I say more? But I wasn't sorry. Money isn't everything, I told myself.

Woulda, coulda, shoulda.

DORIS

My Best Friend Surprises Me by Asking a Most Unexpected Favor

1978
MGM commissary

led my friend Doris through the front section of the MGM studio commissary heading toward the VIP back area. "Get this," I whispered. "The VIP dining room is called the Lion's Den."

I didn't even have to tell the attendant at the door who I was.

"Good afternoon, Ms. Lakin." He picked up two menus and walked us to my regular table.

"Impressed yet?" I asked her, smiling self-deprecatingly, as if to say, *Can you believe it? Your old pal the Valley housewife getting the VIP treatment.*

The well-appointed room was huge and the tables were filled. I recognized some of the actors who were shooting on this date. Seated at the *Dallas* table were stars Barbara Bel Geddes and Patrick Duffy.

Doris, being Doris, wasn't impressed. She was too busy being tense.

I ignored that for the moment and jabbered on. "Even though they've canceled my show, I still have cachet in the MGM commissary. In this business, one never knows whether an executive producer might get another gig. So people stay nice to you until they can nail down your status for sure."

This attempted funny line was also ignored. Other friends had been making jokes about my hot-shot executive-producer rank. I always countered with something like, "It didn't last long, did it?"

Usually Doris and I lunched in restaurants around the city, since my being in showbiz was continuously ignored by her. I was surprised when she suggested we have a meal in a movie studio.

The minute her bottom hit the seat, Doris immediately scrounged around in her purse for her cigarettes. She found her crumpled pack of Salems, straightened out one of its limp cigarettes, and dangled it out of the corner of her mouth. She then began the usual search for her lighter. Since her purse was large enough to accommodate her VW Bug (ha! only a slight exaggeration), this took time.

Our waiter was alert. He hurried over and snapped open a lighter for her. Once she lit up and inhaled deeply, she almost relaxed.

Before our waiter could back off, she grabbed his arm and asked for a double espresso.

"So, I hear you're all going to Alaska for a vacation. Kids, grandkids. All eight of you? When are you going?"

Doris shrugged, voice flat. "Larry's in charge of it. Ask him."

I wasn't used to seeing Doris depressed. I decided to try to cheer her up.

"So I'm going to do another TV movie. Wait till you hear my CBS gossip." I sat up straighter in the elegant dining room chair, the better to emote. "We need to get the network to approve before I can even start writing. I go to a pitch meeting with the producers, Tom Kuhn and Alan Landsburg, and there's this twelve-year-old teenybopper sitting in the office all by herself. She's in charge."

Doris arched an eyebrow in disbelief at my comment about her age.

"Well, she looked that young."

The waiter came by and informed us of the specials. Doris handed him her menu and nodded at me. "You pick something."

"Make it the house special, the chopped Greek steak." He nodded, left a pack of matches, and off he went.

I buttered one of the fresh warm rolls while waiting. "I heard that Louis B. Mayer, who started this studio, used to have a craps table in the commissary so he could play at lunchtime. I read he and his friends threw the dice to see who would pay for lunch. I love showbiz historical stuff like that. Where was I?"

Doris chain-smoked another cigarette, this time using the book of matches the waiter had left on the table. "Something about the woman at your meeting."

"Right. Anyway, the network had already approved the idea of taking the popular song 'Torn Between Two Lovers' as the theme of the movie. I was at this meeting to fill the network execs in on our agreed storyline. Tom and Alan let me do the spiel we'd all agreed on. Wife, happy in her marriage, meets a sexy man and to her own surprise, she is attracted to him. So I'm relating the plot points to Miss Underager and I'm building up to this emotional act end. I say pointedly, 'The wife sleeps with this new guy one afternoon, and that evening her husband arrives home unexpectedly from his business trip and he immediately wants to have sex with his wife.' Wow!"

"Sounds intriguing. What happens next?"

"You're not going to believe this. I'd paused for effect, waiting to hear the network babe's shocked comment. And what does this girl-child say? She says, 'So?'"

"I replied, astonished, 'So? What do you mean, *so*?' Alan and Tom were staring at the woman, equally surprised.

"Little Miss Muffet looked at the three of us, wide-eyed. 'What's the big deal? So she sleeps with two guys. Where's your conflict?'"

This finally got a rise out of Doris. She laughed.

"The rest of the meeting was a shambles. But in spite of her, this deal was going ahead. My producers had clout."

Our lunch arrived. I ate my studio's signature salad. Doris picked at hers. "Okay. What's going on with you? Something's obviously wrong."

She pushed her plate away. Her voice was low. "You remember my story in the *Post*? 'The Mexican Maid'?"

"Of course I do. How many times did I read it and we critiqued it till you finally got it perfect? I loved that story. But that was a few years ago. What about it?"

"I got a call from someone who read it and hadn't forgotten it."

"And why not? It's a beautiful story."

"Yes. Anyway, she was a book publisher and said she wanted me to expand it and turn it into a novel."

I almost jumped out of my chair with excitement. "What fabulous news! Your dream has finally come true. To be writing novels! We should celebrate!"

She ground out her cigarette in the ashtray angrily. "That happened a year ago."

My fork was headed for my mouth, but I stopped short. "You're kidding! And this is the first time you tell me about it?"

"For a whole year, I've been trying to write this novel and I couldn't do it. I just couldn't do it."

"What are you talking about? Of course you could write it."

She leaned across the table, her eyes wild and scary, like turning, spinning windmills. "I tell you, I couldn't. I tried to expand it. I tried every which way. I added characters and situations. Nothing worked. That's all I'm good for, to write short stories. And that's not enough anymore."

"Why didn't you tell me? Surely I could have helped you work the plot out."

"Because this book editor was personally working *with* me. And she finally got tired of me saying, 'I don't see what you mean. . . . I don't know what you're telling me. . . . I don't know how to do it.' She gave up on me."

"It's not too late. I'll sit down with you and we'll solve it."

"No!" Her fingers clutched her napkin, crushing it. "I never want to look at that damn story again."

I nibbled at my food, not knowing what to say.

"It's no longer enough to stare at the walls and come up with stories that occasionally sell. I feel like I'm going crazy."

I THOUGHT BACK to the time a few years ago when Doris and her husband, Larry, decided to do reconstruction work on their exquisite Mexican hacienda–style house. I remembered going over while they were in the planning stages, and the two of them walked me through the house, explaining the changes. A bigger den for their expanded video and library. Enlarged bedrooms for Gail and Nancy, their daughters. The restructure of the extra bedroom for a bigger workroom for Larry's many hobbies.

After the tour was done and we were sipping cappuccino, made from their new espresso machine, I glanced around. "Something's missing," I said.

"Like what?" Doris asked.

"When do you stop writing on the dining room table? Where's *your* room? An office to write in? Don't you count?"

Larry and Doris stared at each other. It had never entered their minds.

"Doris?" Larry asked his wife. "Would you want this?"

She thought for a moment. "Yes. Yes, I do." She hesitated. "But there's no more space."

He got up and headed for the phone. "I'll call the builders and we'll think of something."

And they did. They extended out a wall of the house and Doris finally had an office of her own. She was nearly forty years old at that time.

I EXAMINED DORIS closely. She seemed like someone in a lot of pain. I asked quietly, "What *would* be enough?"

"I want to be involved twenty-four/seven. I want every minute of every day filled! I *need* every minute filled."

I waited, thinking she'd tell me why, but maybe she didn't have to. I was reminded once again of Betty Friedan's famous quote hanging on my office wall. I knew it by heart. "The only way for a woman to find herself, to know herself as a person, is by creative work of her own. There is no other way."

I asked carefully. Doris seemed so fragile to me right now. "And how do you think you could do that? Fill every minute?"

She took a deep breath. "I want what you have. I want to write scripts and get into the television-writing business full-time. I want you to get me in."

Whoa! I'd never expected to hear that. I had to feel my way carefully; she was like a skein of wool unraveling before my eyes. I didn't get it. "I thought you hated TV."

"I don't anymore. Can you get me in?"

I stared at my friend, who was in tears now.

It had taken me sixteen years to get where I was. She was asking the impossible.

TORN BETWEEN TWO LOVERS

I Do the Impossible

TV LOG LINE: May 2, 1979
Torn Between Two Lovers, CBS
A wife finds herself in love with two men: her husband and a stranger.
Based on the song by Peter Yarrow and Phillip Jarrell.
Executive producer: Tom Kuhn. Producers: Alan Landsburg, Joan Barnett, Linda Otto.
Screen story: Rita Lakin. Teleplay: Doris Silverton. Director: Delbert Mann.
Cast: Lee Remick, Joseph Bologna, George Peppard.

I asked Tom Kuhn and Alan Landsburg to meet with me. Once we were seated, I said it straight out—I didn't know any other way.

"I know a writer who is very, very good and wants to write for TV." I told them Doris' short-story credits and they were impressed. "The Mexican Maid" had made it into an anthology of the best stories of 1971. I handed them copies of all her stories.

To my surprise, they sat there for a few minutes, engrossed in reading. I'd assumed they would take the stories with them and get back to me another time.

"Impressive," said Tom. "She writes beautifully."

Alan took a few more minutes, looked up, and agreed.

Alan said, "Well, we'll be glad to think about her for some future project." He shrugged. "Who knows when that might be."

"I have an idea," I said. "What about our movie, *Torn Between . . .*?

They looked puzzled, and rightly so.

"What, replace you? We're happy with our choice," Alan said, amused.

"I have a plan. I'll write the story and I'll have it completely outlined. And we let Doris Silverton write the script. As you can see, she's fabulous with dialogue. I'll be monitoring every page. . . ."

Tom said, "I've never heard of anyone doing this before."

Alan added, "This is a class project. Why would you give it up?"

"Always a first," I said cheerfully. "And if you aren't one hundred percent happy, I'll rewrite the entire script, free. Now that's an offer you cannot refuse."

≈

I did a very complete story outline to let Doris know exactly what was expected. She did the script. The script was wonderful. Everyone was satisfied. We were lucky to have the elegant Delbert Mann directing and fabulous actress Lee Remick as our lead.

And the very next movie that came up for them, they gave to Doris to write the whole script. She wrote the Jayne Mansfield biography (starring Arnold Schwarzenegger!) to highly impressive reviews.

By then I was working on a new pilot, so we were both very happy.

It amused me to note that though my friend claimed to hate showbiz, once she got in, she was like a whirling dervish unleashed. She never stopped working. She did a number of movies for TV and, to my amazement, eventually took a job on the number one daytime soap, *General Hospital*, working with a producer who was a workaholic and drove her writers. When I asked her why a soap, considering her nighttime credits, she said she was fine with it, because she got her wish: she was finally busy twenty-four/seven!

1977
A series of phone calls

Gavin at Age 17

"Hey, Mom, hello. Happy seventeenth birthday to me."

It delighted me that Gavin always made this cheerful phone call to me on every birthday, always before I had a chance to call him.

"And thank you yet again for being the wonderful, loving mother you are and thank you again for having me."

"You're welcome."

This semiformal, amusing ritual had started in his early teens, and now he was away from home.

My expected line followed: "And thank you for being a great son."

We both laughed. I asked, "How many more years are you going to keep being the one who phones *me* on *your* birthday? Though I love it."

"Forever."

Ritual over. "So how's life as a new college boy?"

"Sometimes I hate it and sometimes I love it. I'm already thinking of switching majors. Gotta go, see ya on spring break." He hung up.

His birthday always made my day.

Howard at Age 25

"Mom, hi there, it's your firstborn and your masterpiece calling." Howard and I had this inside joke. The punch line came from a *New Yorker* cartoon, of a matronly mother introducing her son to her guests.

"How's Jenny?"

"She's fine, still working at the bank and liking it."

"What's up?"

"Remember me telling you about that scriptwriting course I was taking at UCLA? From Paul Schrader, you know—the guy who wrote *Taxi Driver*?"

"How could a mother forget?" I teased. My son was now finishing up his UCLA graduate school program after getting his bachelor's degree from Antioch College. Up until now, he'd had no idea what career to pursue.

"Well, I just got my grade on the script I wrote for my term class project. Want the good news or the bad news first?"

"Uh . . . maybe the good first . . . ?"

"Schrader gave me an A, and you know what he told me? That I was wasting my time taking his course, because I was already a pro. I should get the hell out of school and go to work as a writer. Must be in the genes. Who knew?"

I was puzzled. "So what's the bad news?"

"Your devious plot to make all your kids hate showbiz didn't work on me. I'm going for it. I want to be a writer like you. Maybe we might even work together on something. Well, now all I need is to get an agent and kick some ass. I am so buzzed. Isn't it great?"

Oh my . . .

Susan at Age 21

"Mom?"

"Hi, Sue. So how's the weather up in Eureka?

"Raining as usual."

"I hope you're keeping warm. I worry about you living in a house with no heat."

"It's all right, I'm never cold. Listen. I've got news. I made a big decision. I'm joining the Jehovah's Witnesses."

Long pause while I thought about that. "That *is* a big decision. Are you sure?"

"You know I've been on a path of enlightenment. I've investigated every possible religion, even visited a synagogue. None of them cried out to me."

"And the Witnesses did?"

"They're kind and loving people. Did you know that when they have birthday parties, no one ever puts their names on the presents? Get it? Everyone is equal. No matter how much or how little they can afford to spend. Isn't that neat? And you know what? I'm going to move to their New York office, where I'll get to work on their *Watchtower* newspaper. See? I'd be a writer, like you."

"Honey, promise me something. If it doesn't work out, you'll come back home?"

"Everything will be fine, don't worry. Gotta go, and thanks for being so understanding. I love you, Mom."

"I love you too, my little girl." But I had tears in my eyes.

1979
Almost any night
My house

IN OUR BASEMENT, which we had turned into a game room for Gavin and Mark, the two boys paused in the middle of a Ping-Pong game, trying unsuccessfully to ignore the yelling upstairs.

They exchanged shrugs. It was becoming a habit to hear their parents fighting. Mark's dad was louder, and Gavin's mom could be heard crying. Night after night.

I was living in limbo. Or purgatory? I wasn't sure which.

My young reporter was pacing my living room, rife with agitation. "How could you stand it? You must have been so conflicted."

"I was."

"You did so much for him and it was never appreciated."

"True. That's just the way it was. My mother's generation had it tougher. Mine had it a little better."

"But you took so much grief from him."

"He was conflicted too. He was raised to expect that he was going to succeed, and he was frustrated that it wasn't working for him."

"But there's no excuse for his behavior. Why didn't you just get in your car and go to Lake Arrowhead? Why didn't you just tell that husband of yours that you were not going to pimp him to the president of Universal Pictures?"

"Easy there, Chelsea. You just don't understand what it was like for us. You're the first generation who doesn't expect men to grope you in the office. It was like the Jurassic Era for women in my time."

"But you made so much money! Why did you turn everything all over to him?"

"Because women weren't supposed to understand finances. That's the way it was."

"I just don't get it. There was women's lib! What about that?"

I sighed. "Yes, what about it? For so many decades, women marched and fought and managed to get laws changed. They did everything they could. But yet, things still hadn't changed enough. In feature films, in 1974, Alice Doesn't Live Here Anymore was a singular movie in which a woman breaks free. . . . And in 1978, An Unmarried Woman, broke another barrier in that it was about a woman not defining herself by a husband. And TV was still way behind that. Women of today don't understand how powerless we were in business and in marriage partners."

Chelsea just shook her head in disbelief.

I mused, "I managed to hire women writers on whatever show I did. Unbeknownst to me, there actually was a groundswell of women's activity happening, poised to erupt well into the eighties. Women were entering the workplace with a vengeance, and nothing would ever be the same again."

We both stopped to sip our tea. I studied my pretty interviewer. "Let me ask you a question."

Chelsea looked up and uncreased her forehead.

"Thinking of getting married?"

She shrugged. "Haven't given it serious thought yet. I might. Or might not."

"What about having babies?"

"Not even on the horizon. I might not. Ever."

"Well, in my generation, people thought there was something wrong with you if you weren't married before twenty-five. And as to having children, it was not an option, it was assumed and expected. Otherwise people talked behind your back."

Chelsea shuddered. I smiled. The seventies were over.

On to the eighties.

Part Three
THE EIGHTIES

An Aside: Steven Bochco

1980 (Eight years after* The Rookies*)

Along came Steven Bochco. How I praised him! He was brilliant, a talented writer who said he was going to do cop shows differently, like they'd never been done before. Sound familiar? Lucky guy, a different network—NBC—and different sensibilities.

Because of Steven being the creator of this exciting new cop show, the networks finally understood if they wanted that show to be consistently good, the writer/creator was needed to run the entire show himself. He had to be at the office every day to make sure the shows continued up to his standards. That was the origin of the term *showrunner*. This put writers in a position of power for the first time ever. So, they invented a different kind of producer, with a new job description. A supervising producer. And it forever changed the freelance market. Now most shows are headed by the creator and written by a staff he hired.

Bochco's exciting *Hill Street Blues* changed cop shows forevermore. He invented the large, tight-group family/cast still imitated by many genre shows today. This show was brilliant. The dialogue was sharp and at times hilariously funny, the direction innovative and displaying what I'd been trying for on *The Rookies*—reality, truth. Not that I would have even come close to what Steven accomplished, but I had been sharp enough to realize the need to upgrade TV and help it grow up.

No more cardboard writing. No more clichés. His characters were real and unforgettable. Stories you laughed and cried with. The viewers got hooked.

The show had a documentary feel to it. Mike Post's theme music was memorable. I could go on raving. Steven's show was an awesome triumph. I knew I was seeing things on TV never done before.

In its first season, *Hill Street Blues* won eight deserved Emmys. The show went for 146 episodes. Besides garnering astronomical numbers of awards and nominations, it landed on various lists as one of the best shows ever made for television.

Meanwhile, at home, my marriage was slowly sinking into oblivion.

THE HOME FRONT

A Dramatic Trip to Our Past with the First Official Female Showrunner, Me

TV LOG LINE: October 11, 1980
The Home Front, NBC
World War II provides the background for two families to dramatically interact.
Executive producer: Charles Fries. Producer: Buck Houghton.
Supervising producer: Rita Lakin. Creator/writer: Rita Lakin.
Cast: Jean Simmons, Craig Stevens.

Wow! So finally there was a name for what I had been doing on *Executive Suite*. Meaning I became (and was called) a supervising producer/showrunner. I think I was the first woman writer to ever supervise and produce her own show.

While my friend Doris was busily crafting a new career for herself, deliriously happy and grateful, I was pursuing an idea I loved. I created a show called *The Home Front*. I had always wanted to write more about the WWII days, as I had with *A Summer Without Boys*. I was excited about the cast, especially the wonderful, internationally famous Jean Simmons. This was the pilot being produced to sell the show. Besides writing, I got to work on the creative side as well: casting, watching the dailies, editing—all those things I'd learned on *Mod Squad*.

I'd just arrived on the first day at my producing job, when my phone rang. It was a near hysterical call from the AD on the set. It was also the very first day of shooting and already there was a problem. "Come down right now!"

Which I did. The set was that of a dance at the ritzy country club. The date was December 7, 1941, and in this scene the party would break up when news of the war was announced.

We had the music and we had our young stars, the "wealthy college kids," plus about thirty extras—young people dancing. Everybody, dressed in their 1940s Sunday night finery, was ready.

The problem? They were supposed to be dancing the popular dance of the era, the Lindy Hop, and we had not hired a choreographer.

I could tell that panic was about to set in. Cast and crew had the deer-in-the-headlights look. There might be blame, and heads could roll. Everyone looked to me. I tend to stay calm in daunting situations and fall apart later, which came in handy.

I thought about it for a few moments, and before I made any SOS phone calls to anyone higher up, I asked if anyone knew how to dance East Coast swing. I was going back thirty years. Not one young actor knew the old-fashioned dance.

"No big deal," said I. "I know how." I joked, "I was quite a swinger in my day." Hearty laughs cleared the air. "I'll teach you."

I asked for a male volunteer to be my partner, someone who had confidence, and I showed him the basic jitterbug steps, and within thirty seconds he caught on. Arthur Murray would have been proud. My cast was given a history lesson. Dancing in the forties meant uncomplicated steps, so I expected they'd be able to learn the dance quickly.

I told my lead actors and my extras, "Just follow me."

The sound track was turned on. And they did. At first they were clumsy, unsure and wondering what the hell they were doing. But Harry James's orchestra playing "One O'Clock Jump" was infectious, and soon they were all tapping feet to it. Easily picking up the steps. By the time we were finished, the guys had mastered flinging their partners under arms and over shoulders. Even the crew was tapping along.

Soon everyone was having a wonderful time, and Harry Harris, the director, was able to shoot the scene.

I was the only one who hadn't been worried. Remember, my mother, Gladdy, a frustrated ballroom dancer wannabe, had taught her daughters how to dance when we were mere babes.

Things were going along wonderfully until the day we went out on location.

When I'd created and sold *The Home Front*, my husband had found that acceptable, because of the money I'd be earning.

The day our crew and I arrived at the rented house in Pasadena where we were about to shoot, the mother of the house came out and informed us her child had woken up with measles, so she canceled us then and there.

We were in a pickle. We had not prepared a cover set—another place to go in case of an emergency. Everyone was at a loss as to what to do. Ten trucks and fifty people lined the streets, waiting for instructions, as production costs clicked higher and higher.

I made an executive decision. I took the entire cast and crew back to shoot in our Beverly Hills home, which would work perfectly for us. Whew, was everyone relieved. And thankful to me. The difficult problem was solved. The money the company saved was estimable.

Not an hour had gone by when hubby Bob arrived. Somehow he'd gotten word we were there, and he stormed though every room in a fit of rage.

"How dare you shoot here without my permission?" he shouted at me, in a deafening voice, denigrating me in front of the entire cast and crew. Spitting cruel, nasty words that cut through me. Then threatening lawsuits against the production company if they ruined anything in his house! *His* house that *I'd* paid for! *He'd* sue! I had to stand there and listen to his rant. I did what I always did when he had a temper tantrum. I froze. Why was it that whenever he behaved like this, I would go numb, unable to respond?

He picked up a cloisonné candy dish and put it in his pocket, as if to insinuate that some one of them might steal it. He mortified me in front of the people who worked for me and called me "boss." Would he have dared if I hadn't been a woman?

I think something died in me, then. The beginning of the end of any feelings I ever had for him.

CHUCK FRIES and his Metromedia company did all they could to push the show. Everyone attached wanted it to be a go. But, alas, when it was on the air, it got lukewarm reviews and low Nielsen numbers. I was hoping the network would take it to the next stage anyway. I knew I could make it succeed. I would learn from the reviews what to fix. I was an inexperienced producer, and I hadn't yet learned how to fight for my project.

Bottom line, it was all about economics. And poof. All gone. I was really sorry, but there was nothing to be done.

And my marriage was winding down.

MY TRAVELS WITH OMAR

Germany, Italy, and a Spectacular Birthday Dinner

1980
Plane cruising at 32,000 feet

Was I dreaming? Was Omar Sharif bending over me in my first-class seat on the production company's private flight to Berlin? Dressed casually in a black Ralph Lauren signature polo shirt and tight chinos, he smelled divinely of some subtle aftershave lotion. He was whispering in my ear. His lips tickled my lobes and I smiled as he invited me to join him in the rear lavatory of this private chartered 727.

"So naughty," he crooned. What could that mean? Oh, Omar, I sighed, you with those moony bedroom eyes. We discovered you in *Lawrence of Arabia*. You devastated us in your immortal love story, *Doctor Zhivago*. In *Funny Girl*, Barbra Streisand called you "Gorgeous." She couldn't resist you. How could I?

Omar smiled that same enticing grin that made women melt with desire.

"What's that? What's a mile-high club?" I mumbled, ever naïve. But I had a good imagination. I could guess.

"Let me show you; it's a very private club," he answered in that sexy accent.

I squinted up, not quite conscious, my eyes barely slits. They widened. I was pulled into wakefulness. Shucks, I had dreamed all that.

Omar Sharif *was* actually leaning over me. The internationally famous movie star was smiling down at me, holding out a champagne bottle.

"Would you care for a drink?" he asked.

We were on our way to shoot a TV spy thriller, *S.H.E.* Bob was the director, and the cast was with us. Omar was the star. Bob was busy conferring with his cinematographer. He hadn't sat with me the entire trip.

The plane suddenly jolted and jarred me upright. I was already a member of a club—the white-knuckles club. Needing to clutch the armrests, even in my sleep. How else could the plane fly, if not with my help?

Fear and lust hit me at the same time while my stomach lurched at the terrifying loop-de-loops of the plane. If this plane crashed, ten million dollars' worth of talent would go down with it.

The pilot on the loudspeaker was warning of possible sleet and snow down below and telling us to fasten our seat belts.

Omar winked and shrugged. "*C'est la vie.*" With that, he made his unsteady way back to his seat, his hand waving the champagne bottle.

Too bad it was only a dream, though I wouldn't have acted on it. Not that my husband would have even noticed.

That was me, so inexperienced. Had the turbulence saved me? Goodness knows what might have happened if . . . I'll never know.

First destination: Berlin

On that whole trip, Bob hardly noticed me; he was too busy trying to turn a weak script into something he could shoot.

Berlin was experiencing a blizzard, with snow as deep as our thighs. Everything blindingly white, we could hardly make out the buildings. I walked past what once was gestapo headquarters. Chilled, from a different kind of cold.

Most of the time we rode the elevator in the hotel to an underground city where there were restaurants and stores. I'd never seen anything like this before. It was crowded with people shopping and eating. Everything aboveground was snowed in.

At one point, in a break in the weather, the entire city came back to life. But we still had to wait for it to clear up.

I took the tour bus ride through East Berlin. All passengers were searched thoroughly before we could even enter the bus. Reading about it didn't give you the eerie feelings that you got actually being there. How unreal it seemed, unlike the pace and wealth of busy West Berlin only that wall away. As we drove by, I could look into empty store windows. Everything looked dismal and sad. Like a ghost town.

We were not allowed off the bus at any time and saw few people.

Eight years later, on November 9, 1989, the wall came tumbling down.

The other bizarre part of the trip was going to the theater one evening to see the play *Fiddler on the Roof*, the by-now world-famous musical about a Jewish community in a small town in Russia. Strange experience. Even though the Second World War had been over for nearly forty years, this play being done in this country freaked me out. The theater was sold out. Horst Buchholz, a famous international star, played the lead, Tevye. Of course it was all in German, but I had seen the play a number of times and knew what every scene was about.

The audience remained utterly motionless throughout. I could hardly sit still. What were these well-dressed people seated around me thinking? Or feeling? I could barely see their faces in the dark theater. Why were they here? Was this meant to be some kind of penance? Were they thinking of parents or grandparents who committed atrocities?

They weren't laughing at the jokes. I didn't laugh either. Both the play and the audience brought me to tears.

I cried softly into my scarf, thinking of my grandmother, whom I would never meet. My father had tried to get her out of Poland in 1939—she would not leave her homeland. Years later, he could no longer reach her. My family knew the worst had happened.

We left moments before the intermission. I didn't want to see any of their faces in the light. Bob had hardly paid any attention to the show. I knew his mind was, as usual, on the script.

THE BLIZZARD made it impossible to film, so onward. To Italy.

The weather was still cold, but at least there was no snow. As soon as we arrived at our hotel in the charming seaside town of Terracina, Omar discovered it was my birthday. He found the best restaurant in town, met the chef, and then planned a special feast for me.

The restaurant was elegant, with a beautiful view of the sea.

I was seated at the head of the table, and the meal was served to the entire cast and crew. First, there was the mushroom and fennel crostini. Next came a soup, ribollita, a peasant bread soup. I was already getting full. And then three different kinds of pastas. I was filled and I pushed my plate away, loosening my belt, sighing.

But no, that was only the beginning. Next was served *il secondo*, the second course, a *filetto di cernia* (grouper fish), was followed by vegetables, eggplant capo-nata. And finally, *il doce*, the dessert. The tiramisu, and zabaglione with berries.

A different wine with every course. Of course. It was a ten-course meal to die for. I was deeply touched. The entire cast and crew wished me happy birthday.

My husband, who had been seated next to me, had not remembered my birthday. I pointed out that tiny omission to him with an acidic tongue.

"Gimme a break. I have a film to prepare!" was his retort.

"A *TV movie*, dear, only a TV movie!"

Things between us were as cold as the weather.

Our hotel room was down the corridor from Omar. Lying next to my inert husband, I played a fantasy in my head, wishing I were two doors down instead.

BYE-BYE BOB

The End of the Marriage

Think this marriage couldn't get worse? Yes, it could.

In year eight, Prince Not-So-Charming got a job directing another TV movie, this time in Australia. I went for a short time, and then went home.

When he finally arrived back from down under, something had changed dramatically. He returned with a beard, a smirk, and an Australian girlfriend, left behind. Someone who'd seen them together described her as a bony stunt-woman with leathery skin. I didn't know about them right away, until he wanted me to find out.

One night he left his briefcase open on his desk. Not that I would have gone into his private papers, but he was behaving so irrationally that I had to figure out what was going on. For weeks, he had been constantly picking fights with me. Would I ever forget that ghastly night in a theater where we were to see *A Chorus Line*, and he chose to unleash a screaming fit at me for no damn good reason (other than that he wanted out).

So Bob left his briefcase where I would discover it.

Well, lo and behold and gee whiz, drumroll here. The briefcase was filled with oozing, oily love letters. She was a nobody, entranced with this American she thought was a somebody. Robert Michael had found true love. So he wrote. And when would he bring her over so they could be together forever?

When? I discovered she'd arrived on my birthday. Her very expensive ticket from Sydney? Paid for with our joint credit card.

Here's where you're supposed to feel sorry for pathetic me.

Before I was married, I was considered kind, generous, carefree, outgoing, and fun to be with. By the time my marriage ended, I'd become a different person. My kids, in later years, admitted they thought I'd been brainwashed by aliens. I walked in as "Woman, hear me roar." I came out as "Pitiful Pearl, the rag doll with her frayed babushka, black socks, and a scowl on her face."

Bob originally told me that he outgrew his first wife. In other words, she was no longer useful. She'd probably supported him as a film editor. And what was I? Next up on the useful trail? I was well entrenched in the Hollywood scene. Marrying me was the strategic step to the top. So he'd thought. Now *I* was no longer useful. Time for him to move on. I wondered what Ms. Aussie was useful for. One could only guess.

When finally I'd been ready for love, the wrong man had walked into my life.

How could I explain my reactions? I should have given up the ghost then. Instead, like some rabid pit bull, I held on to this debilitating marriage—a marriage that had beaten me down to a shadow of my former self.

It took me many agonizing years later to understand why I stayed and fought so hard to keep that marriage. To my amazement and even shock, when it was over, I grieved almost as long and as hard as I did after Hank died. How was that possible? Surely death was more devastating than divorce.

It was all about loss. The pain of both was equally unbearable. I could not stand losing another person from my life. As simple, and as complicated, as that.

Epiphany

Nora Ephron, worthy of liberated women's worship, wrote and directed many women-centric books and movies—*When Harry Met Sally*, *Sleepless in Seattle*, and *You've Got Mail*, to name just a few. In 1983, in an interview, she spoke about her then-dead marriage. When she realized her hubby had cheated on her and dumped her for another woman, she commented, "I've reached that day that I can write about it. When far enough beyond it, you can get to see the humor in it. And in so doing you get the last laugh." She pointed out that women writers had the talent and advantage of revenge. If men were foolish enough to marry a writer, unless they behaved, eventually they'd see themselves in print or on the screen.

First she wrote the novel, *Heartburn*. She described her ex-husband as a man "capable of having sex with a Venetian blind." And his lover, "a giraffe with big feet." How can anyone top that? The icing on the cake was a movie, based on her book, starring Jack Nicholson and Meryl Streep. Imagine Meryl playing you. Oh, how delicious.

When I finally got past the pain of loss in my own marriage, I thought about Nora's Ephron's advice. I, too, needed to exorcise my own demon, so I imagined my own script.

Uhmm, let's see, who should play the parts in my fantasy movie? I was going to have fun with this. I, of course, would be played by my heroine, Anne Bancroft. How about Tom Cruise in *Interview with the Vampire*? Or Anthony Hopkins, the ultimate fiend, in *Silence of the Lambs*? Nora was right—laughter was a great antidote.

Suddenly my movie wasn't a comedy; it was a tragicomedy. And it had already been done. I had been living *Funny Girl*. No wonder I had fantasies of Omar Sharif, who played the hapless husband of a woman who had too much success. (Bob should be so lucky to look like Omar! I wouldn't mind resembling Barbra Streisand.)

The movie, for those who missed it, was about a couple who fell in love. But it was hopeless, because they had both married wrong. He didn't want to hurt the woman he loved, but he couldn't escape the gender trap he was in. In spite of her love, she couldn't beat the odds against her.

So I had my answer, finally. Bob had to save himself. He married again, to a woman who earned little money, who looked up to him as a god and therefore caused no jealousy or pressure.

But, hey, he "done good." Besides now owning half of an expensive Beverly Hills home, he had come to me in a Mazda and rode off into the sunset in a Mercedes.

IN CONCLUSION, I tip a slouch bush hat to Aussie wife number three. Thanks for taking him off my hands. I was returned to being my old cheerful, happy self.

Although I've never married again, I've had a wonderful life, a loving family, lifelong friends, and a very long, successful career. I could finally turn my anger into sympathy for him. I don't know how his life turned out, but as Rhett Butler walked out, he said those famous words to Scarlett O'Hara with pity and resignation: "Frankly, my dear, I don't give a damn." Neither do I.

FLAMINGO ROAD

Freedom from Marital Stress at Last; a Lot of Pink Birds and Barrels of Fun

TV LOG LINE: May 12, 1981
Flamingo Road, NBC
The hot and steamy South is background for secrets and sex in a small town.
Executive producer: Michael Filerman. Producer: Edward H. Feldman.
Supervising producer: Rita Lakin. Teleplay: Howard Lakin.
Cast: Howard Duff, Mark Harmon, Kevin McCarthy, Morgan Fairchild.

Well, to my happy surprise, here I was, a supervising producer/showrunner again. And what good timing. Part of me was still mourning the death of my marriage, and another part still kicking myself for having been so easily misled. But with the return of the real me, I was in great spirits, excited for a fun project like this.

Once again, this project started as a backdoor pilot movie. It did so well in the ratings that we were picked up for a fall series. Ironic, because I felt *The Home Front* was in my comfort zone, and this new show was hardly that, but it was delightful to work on and delicious in its content.

Flamingo Road was another of those properties like *Death Takes a Holiday* that had a provenance. It had been a best-selling novel written by Robert Wilder in 1942 and made into a melodramatic film in 1949 starring Joan Crawford.

And here we were with the TV series. NBC wanted another nighttime soap opera. But times had changed and my vision was not to redo it as a dated melodrama, but as a tongue-in-cheek satire, making fun of all those Southern clichés. Audiences loved it. For the first time, I had a show that had humor. And I discovered something new—I loved doing comedy.

Unlike with *Executive Suite*, with its dreadful tension, having real control of a show like this was a hoot. I liked working with clever executive producer Mike Filerman, who became a lifelong friend. Our line producer, Eddie S. Feldman, was an award-winning producer in film as well as TV. It was a happy grouping all around.

Now that I was the showrunner, I could pick and choose any writers I wanted, writers who were in sync with the tone of the show. I emulated that kindly producer/mentor David Victor's philosophy and gave new writers a break. And I discovered some new women writers as well.

Which brings me to my son. You may have noticed the name Howard Lakin in the credits. Yes, my older son did follow Mom into showbiz, despite my feeble attempts to discourage him. And he did very well on his own. I hired him to write the clever, droll pilot script.

We chose a fun cast, and everyone hired got into the comedic spirit of the show. Mark Harmon was handsome and became a new Hollywood heartthrob. Howard Duff had a great time playing the wicked sheriff, master of dirty deeds. Morgan Fairchild was the villainous Constance.

My favorite review was by James Brown in the *L.A. Times*, who called it "gloriously awful with a sleazy majesty all its own," and went on to say, "There's corruption, sex, and skeletons in the closet, dark secrets, smoldering feuds and musical beds. . . ." He ended with "If you don't fall hopelessly in love with *Flamingo Road*, you don't know great trash when you see it."

Now that's what I call a terrific review.

At that time, I was happily inundated with fans sending me every kind of souvenir. *Flamingo Road* ashtrays, greeting cards, paintings, and statues, etc. Everyone wanted to get into the act! I might say, with little modesty, that I must have been a good producer, because we had a happy cast and crew.

Alas, we only made it through two years. Once again, we were the victim of competing shows. And, ironically, which show did us in? *Dallas! Dallas.* That great big Texas saga. But that was okay, not only did Bob's brother, Art, write and produce this show for a few years, so did Howard later on write and produce it, as well. I was glad two of my family struck oil.

We were discarded for a medical show called *St. Elsewhere.* I couldn't complain, because the show was wonderful. But couldn't NBC have dumped somebody else's series instead of mine?

NEW YORK, NEW YORK

Wonderful Chance Meetings, with Redemption at Last

1982
Los Angeles International Airport

had two unexpected chance meetings almost at the same time. The first was in the Los Angeles airport waiting for a flight to New York. I glanced over to the waiting area, where a man was reading a newspaper, seemingly covering his face. From what I could see of him from my angle, he looked familiar. Sure enough, it was Richard Chamberlain, trying to appear inconspicuous. I hesitated, but I couldn't resist. I walked over.

When I reached him, he looked up pleasantly, but I could tell he wasn't happy about this imposition on his privacy, something I'm sure he experienced a lot.

I quickly introduced myself as the writer of the *Dr. Kildare* "Candle in the Window" episode, assuming that he wouldn't remember. After all, this was eighteen years later.

He warmed up immediately. "Oh, that one," he said, smiling. "Ruth Roman played the unhappy nurse. And that amazing little Ronny Howard? What a great career he has."

Imagine my surprise! After acting in who knows how many hundreds of scripts, and he remembered mine?

"I liked it," Richard said. "Sorry I never had a chance to meet you."

He almost had. I didn't tell him about that naïve young writer who'd made that hasty, tearful retreat from the set.

In spite of my better judgment, my next words slipped out, anyway. "But dear 'Dr. Gillespie' didn't like my script."

Chamberlain laughed out loud about his friend Massey. "Oh, acerbic Raymond. He didn't like many of them. He wasn't too fond of emotion."

"Thanks," I said, gushing in spite of myself. "But you were superb."

I felt so much better. I said goodbye and left him to his privacy.

Two days later
The Russian Tea Room, New York

THE RUSSIAN TEA ROOM was a restaurant at the height of its popularity. Everyone who was anyone famous came for lunch to see or be seen. I learned quickly that the roomy red leather booths in the front were for celebrities only. The tearoom was used in a number of movies: *When Harry Met Sally*, *The Turning Point*, and, most recently, *Tootsie*.

I had come to New York to visit my dear friend Jackie Smith, who was vice president of ABC daytime programming. As tiny and fragile as she seemed, she was nevertheless the first woman in that high of a position of power at any of the networks.

As a treat, Jackie took me to the Russian Tea Room for lunch. She was greeted royally. A major VIP, Jackie was led to one of the important booths in the front.

According to my guidebook, the tearoom was next door to Carnegie Hall, and it was originally built in 1927 by members of the Russian Imperial Ballet as a place for Russians to gather. The restaurant was filled with memorabilia—paintings, samovars, and such. The menu specialized in Russian dishes.

And here was Mikhail Baryshnikov, the famous Russian ballet dancer, two tables away. Just look at those muscles! That chiseled face. Those piercing blue eyes. Larger than life. Stunning. I couldn't help staring at him.

Suddenly, there was a humming sound emanating from the door. Someone else important had just arrived. And who should be led to the number one booth next to ours but Sydney Pollack.

He had obviously come to New York for the premiere of *Tootsie*, since it had just opened to rave notices. He was the director of the wonderfully funny film, which starred Dustin Hoffman, who played a man pretending to be a woman so he could get an acting job. As Sydney sat down in the booth next to ours, the entire room exploded with applause, waiters included.

Wow! I was so close I could have touched his arm. A parade of other celebrities lined up to take turns greeting him, hugging and air-kissing, making deserved and glowing comments about his new movie.

Jackie grinned and poked me. "You worked with him. Say something, I know you're dying to."

"Yeah, sure," I said, sipping and enjoying my Danish Mary, having just discovered aquavit instead of vodka. "As if he'd remember me."

She nudged me again. "You're always so damned unassuming. Stop it. You'll never get anywhere in this world with that hide-your-light-under-a bushel-basket attitude."

"But I don't want to intrude. The man wants to eat his lunch."

Jackie laughed. "If Syd wanted not to be bothered, he'd eat his lunch at the Automat! He came here to be pestered. What's fame for, if not to be recognized and applauded?"

I smiled. If I'd been eating alone, *I'd* have been at the Automat. The Horn & Hardart self-serve, coin-operated cafeteria was the most reasonable popular chain of restaurants in the city. You put your nickels in the slots, opened the glass doors, and there were wonderful choices of good food. Those Harvard beets, yum. I elbowed Jackie. "All right already, stop nagging."

Finally, people left Sydney Pollack alone to eat the chive potato blini with cherries that he'd just been served. But I kept hesitating and glancing in his direction.

Catching me at it, Sydney leaned over into our booth. "I probably know you. But forgive me, I forgot your name."

I froze. This time Jackie kicked me under the table. "Open your mouth. Talk!"

With quavering voice, I whispered to Sydney, "It was so long ago, but you directed a TV episode of mine." I told him my name and reminded him of the episode I'd written. "In fact," I gushed, yet again—I was no better than a typical fan—"what a coincidence. I just ran into Richard Chamberlain in the airport."

His eyes lit up. "Really? *Dr. Kildare.* My first job."

"Mine too."

He leaned even closer. I was enthralled. "Now I remember you. My favorite scene was in the hotel room. Ruth Roman's poignant performance made me cry."

"Me too," I said. I could have cried, too. Right then. From joy.

Before I could say more, Sydney was pulled away by the person who then sat down to join him. Oh my! It was Dustin Hoffman, in almost a replay of the hilarious scene from *Tootsie*, where Sydney, starring as his agent, is horrified by Dustin, dressed as a woman. I loved Dustin's famous line after being made up as a woman for the first time. "I didn't think I'd be so ugly."

I turned back to Jackie, grinning. "Did I make a fool of myself?"

Jackie poked me again. "See! Now, aren't you glad I made you do that?"

I gave her a quick peck on the cheek and happily went back to my potato pierogi and cold borscht. Take that, Raymond Massey! For me, redemption.

Class acts, both those men from my past. I walked on a cloud all day.

Jackie was amused. "I told you life was exhilarating here. You've got to move back to your hometown and take the head writer position on one of my daytime shows."

Believe me, I was tempted. But I turned my friend down; I didn't want to uproot myself again.

Same night
Manhattan street

I REMAINED in Jackie's office the rest of the workday, seeing how seamlessly she handled one complicated problem after another in her daytime shows. I recognized the popular names, *One Life to Live* and *General Hospital.*

She started to walk me back to my hotel that evening. We reached the corner where we each had to make a turn in the opposite direction.

Jackie warned, "It's getting dark now. Too dangerous for you to walk alone along Sixth Avenue in this part of town. Get a cab."

"Big deal." said I. "I grew up in 'this town.' I'll be all right."

Jackie was adamant. "This was always a bad area. It's even worse now." She indicated the line of strip joints and porno theaters, and tourist-trap stores with their huge GOING OUT OF BUSINESS signs that remained in their windows permanently.

I was insistent. "It's still part of the theater district. Look at all the people around us. It's safe."

Jackie was torn then. "All right. At least let me teach you how to walk."

I stared at her, astonished. "Ha-ha. I believe I learned that when I was one year old and I've been doing it nicely ever since."

Ignoring that, Jackie instructed: "First, you never, never look anybody in the eye. You waddle fast. Act as if you're wearing bulky clothes to make you look big and tough."

Which she acted out, swaying and lurching from side to side.

"You look ridiculous."

"Pay attention. Never walk too close to the curb or you can be grabbed and shoved into a passing van."

I was amused. "A passing van. Sure it won't be a passing Porsche wanting to pick me up and take me to Sardi's?" Sardi's was a famous theater district restaurant.

"And you don't want to walk too close to the buildings, either. You don't want to get grabbed by someone lurking in a doorway." She moved us into the center of the sidewalk.

"Lurking. Look bulky. Stay away from the street. Stay away from doorways. Okay. Got it." Then I burst into laughter. "You must be kidding."

She looked me straight in the eyes. "I. Am. Not. Kidding!"

With a few hugs and a "safe trip back to L.A. tomorrow," Jackie left me on my own.

Jackie's warning reminded me of my news from my mom a while back. They were finally moving out of the Bronx.

My mother had written me that I had been right in warning them long ago. The neighborhood *was* deteriorating, and she was afraid, but my dad had been adamant. "I'm not leaving my home. Ever," was his proclamation. He was a man who didn't like change.

Mom and her sisters had been conniving behind his back, phoning back and forth, raving about the joys of Florida retirement. My aunt Ann wanted to move when her marriage ended, wanting a new start. Aunt Rose also wanted to move, because she couldn't bear the idea of her sisters living so far away from her. And her husband, my Uncle Hy, a clothing store proprietor, had read about new businesses flourishing in Florida, so he was willing to jump on the let's-move-south bandwagon.

My dad continued to be the only family holdout. Until the day someone picked his pocket and stole his full wallet at his beloved Belmont Park racetrack. He came home distraught. "Let's move! And now!" he announced. "What are you waiting for?"

I smiled thinking about the three sisters having bought condos in the very same Fort Lauderdale development. It was one thing for one sister to live in Boston, one in the Bronx, and the youngest in Brooklyn, with the safety cushion of distance. But now they would be living in one another's apron pockets. I laughed aloud, thinking that I hoped they wouldn't kill each other. But it turned out well. They all loved Florida.

≈

MY REVERIE ENDED as I became aware that I was no longer on Sixth Avenue. I'd turned onto a side street. Three more blocks to go. I was still chuckling over Jackie's "lesson" when I heard the footsteps. Behind me. I had been vaguely aware of a guy sitting on the stoop of one of the buildings, a guy wearing a sweatshirt with a hood.

I glanced back. He was no longer sitting there. I moved a little faster. The footsteps picked up with my pace. His shoes seemed to have some kind of metal on them, like tap shoes, and I could hear them click.

I couldn't see him. He wasn't at the curb or near the doorways. So much for that theory. He was directly behind me. Following me.

No, it must be a guy who was just walking in the same direction. At my same speed. I stopped again. The clicking stopped. Another theory shot.

I felt the sweat forming. I was about to be mugged! Or even murdered. On my last day in the city. I was never going to see my kids again. Or my family or my friends. Jackie would cry the most at my funeral, thinking I'd died because I hadn't taken her advice.

Suddenly I couldn't remember anything that Jackie taught me. I told myself to think! Okay, it came back to me . . . bulk up. Then waddle.

Forget that. I started to run.

The footsteps caught up to me at the corner. Seventh Avenue had lights and people in sight, but no one close enough to help. I wanted to scream, but nothing came out of my mouth. It was too late. I felt his hand on my shoulder. I froze, waiting for the blow. Let it be fast. Don't make me suffer.

The hand tapped at my shoulder.

"Miss Bancroft?" he asked.

What the hell?

Since I realized I wasn't dead, I slowly managed to get my quivering legs to move. I turned around and the young hooded man whipped out a small album and a pen and held them out to me.

"Miss Bancroft," he said grinning. "I'm taking classes at the Actors Studio and I'm going to be an actor, too. If I could have your autograph . . ."

Huh?

My desperately dry mouth could only manage a croak. "Of course, dear boy."

My shaking hand reached for the pen. In my jumpiness, I almost signed my own name, but I caught myself in time. Suddenly I drew a blank. Was *Anne* with an *e* or not?

I scribbled Anne Bancroft's name in his book.

"I loved you in *The Graduate*," he said, and then he happily dashed off.

I hoped my favorite actress would forgive me for the forgery.

AT A PARTY, years later, I met Mel Brooks. So I decided to ask him, "By the way, Mel, a lot of people tell me I look like your wife. Do I?"

Funny man Mel made a meal out of it, looking me up and down.

"So?"

"So no," he said. "Not even close," and he walked away from this annoying pest.

A CELEBRATION

Alison

Two years later
The week before March 23, 1983

A wondrous event occurred that week. My son Howard and his wife, Jennifer, were expecting a baby at any moment, so the troops gathered. Jennifer's parents arrived from England. I was there representing the new father-to-be. My parents arrived from Florida. Dave and Gladdy, tanned and thriving, were thrilled to become great-grandparents to the new heir.

Jennifer had the hard job of producing said heir. Howard's job was pacing.

Lots of family catching up. My folks reported on retirement life in Florida. Effie and Percy Taylor caught us up with news of Jennifer's four brothers and their wives and Taylor grandchildren. The distances between us made visits rare and very special. The new baby would be grandchild number nine for them. Wow! A first for me.

We talked and shared meals, even played cards, took walks, but the new baby was taking its time arriving. So we talked some more and laughingly took bets on arrival time. Oh, and we managed to drink up a good bottle of wine every night. Maybe he (or she) was waiting for us to go home?

Not a chance. We would continue to stand by, no matter how long. And finally, Alison Elizabeth Lakin decided to greet us early in the morning of March 26. Welcome, dear baby. And brother James Patrick Taylor Lakin sweetly came to us just over four years later.

DYNASTY

"Terribly Tasteful and Tastefully Terrible"

TV LOG LINE: 1987
Dynasty, ABC
Money and power dominate the lives of a family in Denver.
Executive producer: Aaron Spelling.
Creators/executive producers: Esther Shapiro, Richard Shapiro.
Staff written.
Cast: John Forsythe, Linda Evans, Joan Collins.

I ought to mention *Dynasty*, only because it was a famous show. *Flamingo Road* was canceled and I was looking for work again. Then I thought I had a good idea. I would work with this other woman producer, Esther Shapiro, who was riding high with the very successful *Dynasty*. I was looking forward to a woman-to-woman camaraderie. I was eager to hear *her* war stories about being a woman in the business, and I would tell her mine. So I demoted myself from being a producer and took a job as staff writer on the show.

A closeness with Esther? Never happened. We did not connect at all.

I was sorry almost immediately to have taken the job. Not only was I disappointed with Esther, I wasn't too thrilled about having to share my office with another staff writer. Specifically this writer.

Larry Heath (not his real name, but the name he went by) was a strange duck and I never felt comfortable working with him. I didn't know what it was about him, but the vibes were weird. We had to work together, but it was all too stiff and unyielding, and we were definitely not a good match.

It was only later that I discovered that Larry had actually violently murdered his wife and managed to avoid going to prison, or worse. He even wrote a book about it, relating what he said was his true story. It was called *By Reason of Insanity*. Yikes! Not that I was afraid of him, but he was way too odd for me.

Working in story meetings with Esther and a couple, the Pollacks (Mike and Bob—Mike was a woman), I soon realized that this was the wrong environment for me. These were three nonwriters, and their ideas did not match mine.

Esther wasn't into bonding with other women. I'm guessing she was too busy being rich and famous.

Luckily, I had a very short contract, and I left the show as soon as I could. I just wanted out.

NIGHTINGALES

Love Means Never Having to Say You're Sorry. Signed, Yours Truly, Aaron Spelling.
Good Night, *Nightingales*; Goodbye, Rita

TV LOG LINE: June 27, 1989
Nightingales, NBC
Student nurses find love and conflict in a Los Angeles hospital.
Executive producer: Aaron Spelling. Series creators: Rita Lakin, Howard Lakin, Frank Furino.
Supervising producer: Rita Lakin. Teleplay: Howard Lakin.

Talk about going out with a bang—this series turned out to be my unexpected exit from showbiz. Aaron Spelling had been in and out of my career for twenty-five years, so it seems only right that he played a major part in my finale.

I was eager to tackle the premise, another nighttime drama, and a chance to be sophisticated and write a mystery as well. The story line I pitched to Aaron was simple. It was about six dedicated women, student nurses, who, for one intriguing reason or another, wind up working in the same hospital, roommates in an old Victorian building in L.A. named Nightingale House. Each nurse brought into the timeline a suspenseful and secretive backstory.

My son Howard wrote the pilot script. He was a partner this time on the "Created by" credits along with Frank Furino—a longtime writer friend.

The way Aaron pitched *Nightingales* to NBC was not how I would have done it, nor would I have agreed to it. But I didn't know any of this until three years later, when a nonfiction book came out in 1991, called *Three Blind Mice*. It was about the three major networks—ABC, NBC, and CBS—at a crucial time of soaring costs and a dwindling audience, as cable TV was driving their ratings down. The investigative reporter/author Ken Auletta followed a show on each of the networks from inception to end, not knowing how things might turn out for each of them.

Unbeknownst to me, Aaron had allowed Ken Auletta to use my show for his book. Auletta followed Aaron around, day by day, and sat in on all meetings on every aspect of the show, but never with me, even though I was the creative producer. I had no idea who he was. Perhaps I passed him in the halls, but I'd never been introduced to him.

It started with Aaron "taking a meeting" with NBC.

As Auletta wrote in his book, "ABC executive Brandon Stoddard thought Spelling's idea was vulgar, and the viewer would dismiss it as exploitive. So Aaron went to Brandon Tartikoff, president of the entertainment division, and pitched it to him, like this:

"'Student nurses in Dallas in the summer heat wave and there's no air conditioning, so they sweat a lot!'"

"It's a 40 share," exclaimed Tartikoff, describing a megahit. "Let's do it."

So Aaron sold my idea before there was a story or a meeting, or a script or a pilot. Yet again, shades of *The Rookies*.

NOT HAVING ANY KNOWLEDGE of the back-alley politicking that had been going on, my two partners, Howard and Frank, and I were innocently working in a hornets' nest.

Once again, I had a variation of the same conversation with Aaron that I'd had in the past, time and time again. Only this time, I knew it was more important.

Alone in his usual mega-huge office, Aaron faced me, seated behind his always impressive massive desk, leaning back, calm and relaxed, smoking his pipe. Me, pacing. Aaron, as usual, being amused by my passion.

"Aaron, we are talking about nurses. They are to be treated with respect. For heaven's sakes, what were you thinking?"

"They're grown-ups. Over twenty-one. What's the big deal?"

"I even have a sister-in-law who's a nurse. These women save lives. How dare we treat them like tramps?"

He drawled slowly, talking to me with phony compassion. "Rita . . . Rita . . . How many times have we been through this? How many shows?"

"Too many."

"Sex sells. And our actresses are so beautiful. Why shouldn't we see them semi- undressed? In bathing suits. About to get into showers. Opening their blouses because it is soooo hot." Aaron grinned. "It worked with *Charlie's Angels* and *Dynasty* and *Fantasy Island* and *Vegas* and *Love Boat*. . . ."

I folded my arms and gave him a dirty look. He was like a little boy who had all the toys and loved to show them off. When he realized I was tuning him out, he stopped.

But of course he had to get the last word in. "As with every one of my shows, the men in the audience will drool, and the women will be envious."

"Aaron, I hear there are some porno studios in the San Fernando Valley. Leave those movies to them."

"Now, now . . . Nobody ever complained before."

"Because they weren't nurses! You want sex and women in their underwear, give that to the guest-star actresses."

I finally sat down at the edge of one of his stuffed chairs. I didn't dare lean back, or I'd never get out.

I gave it one more anguished try. "We have a show with exciting dramatic stories about our nurses' lives. They could be done with style and, yes, class. We have their medical cases, their romances, the secrets they're hiding, people who are coming after them who mean them harm. Plenty of high-concept story material. We don't need to be distasteful."

Aaron's intercom buzzed. He picked up and then turned to me. "My eleven o'clock is about to start."

Like hell it is, I thought. I knew that gambit. When Aaron was in an unwanted situation, after a certain amount of time, his loyal secretary would pretend he had another meeting in order to set him free.

Aaron stood up. "I promise to take your arguments under advisement." And he once again made promises I knew he wouldn't keep. I foolishly thought that by now I had enough clout to change his mind.

Between Aaron and the greedy network, I didn't have a chance.

From Ken Auletta's book, I learned that there had been wide dissension among the NBC troops. Executive Warren Littlefield, also shocked by the blatant misbehavior of the nurses, was quoted as saying, "We'll be shot for this," but then recanted, saying, "Aaron knew what he was doing." Why did he change his tune?

In the midst of all this, the Writers Guild went on strike and I could no longer work on my own show. While I was trapped at home, the network guys used my office and gleefully played house. They took over and butchered the ideas for series stories to come, assuming the show would sell.

Aaron had been telling our female director, Mimi Leder, what he wanted, and she went along with it. I assumed she saw the show as "cutting edge" and didn't think it was exploitative, which, frankly, surprised me. I expected a woman to recognize it as demeaning.

According to Auletta, then, when the dailies started arriving at the network, a lot of the men who had nothing to do with the show but worked in the NBC building poured in to watch. Littlefield was quoted as calling these daily viewings a "porn fest,"—student nurses romping around in g-strings, stripping scenes, and worse.

I had no idea of any of this was going on. But in spite of the salacious directing, and all the interfering and editing, our original plot held, and the movie was miraculously solid and watchable.

Again, according to Auletta, NBC then did a flip-flop. To Aaron's shock, they abruptly decided they hated it and decided not put it on the air for the next season.

Well, since they'd spent a small fortune of money producing the show, they screened it anyway. And buried it. Put it on as a deadly middle-of-the-summer rerun in what I called the cemetery hours, a time when baseball and vacations and good weather kept people outdoors, and no one was indoors watching anything. The show was in the company of other loser programs along with a load of dull repeats. No publicity, nothing to tell viewers what the show was about or why to watch. NBC wrote it off as a total loss. The only mention was in the usual time slot in *TV Guide*.

Lo and behold, our pilot movie *Nightingales* came in first as the highest-rated show of the week. With eighteen million viewers, it topped all the other shows in that time slot. A curious audience, having heard rumors, turned their sets on to observe what all the whispers had been about.

Naturally, NBC immediately flipped back again, and the show was slated to be on the air for the new season.

I was determined that when the strike was over and I was able to return to my office, the series was going to be done my way! And I'd fight until I got it.

THE DAY the Writers Guild strike ended, I was dressed and out the door, about to head back to my office, when I found a letter marked BY MESSENGER left on my doorstep, soaking wet, since it had rained the night before. It was from Aaron, on his fancy Spelling letterhead.

In his letter, he said this "had been hard to write, having known and loved you for so many years, I couldn't bear talking to you over the phone . . ."

Oh, oh, I thought, this is not good.

"What it comes down to," he continued, "and this is going to hurt me as much as it hurts you. . . ."

Oh, really. I doubt that very much.

". . . they [the network] will not pick up the show unless we bring in an entirely new staff . . . They suggested nicely, of course, that we should bring in a younger person. . . ."

So the network decided that I was too old at fifty-nine. I was fired. For the first time in my entire career. The first and last time!

What really upset me was that Aaron used the oft-quoted line from the romantic film *Love Story*, "Love means never having to say you're sorry." What the hell was that supposed to mean? That he didn't have to apologize for lying and going behind my back to sabotage me?

Hey, as they are wont to say in mafia movies, it was only business. Aaron truly liked me. And amazingly, in spite of everything, that charming *momzer* . . . I liked him too.

And so the aftermath. The NBC-Aaron version of the rest of the series episodes, without me on board, caused outrage. The ratings quickly dropped. People all over the country were incensed that a show would treat nurses like whores. Parents met in PTA meetings to complain about how shocking the show was, unfit for family viewing.

Lee Iacocca, a major successful auto industry CEO, denounced it in a highly publicized press conferences, insisting *Nightingales* be taken off the air. Phil Donahue on his popular daytime talk show spent a whole program with a roomful of nurses furiously damning the show. It was a witch hunt.

Too bad Donahue hadn't bothered to find me and have me on the show to listen to my side of the story.

Nightingales was ripped off the air. I won the battle but lost the war.

A strangeness came upon the world of TV right after the strike. Odd changes were occurring. It was if the well dried up. Jobs were suddenly scarce. My phone stopped ringing. I would try to make appointments with producers I knew, and they didn't answer back.

The network wasn't interested in hearing from me either.

I had a clue. A very friendly secretary of a producer I'd worked with phoned me and told me of a conversation she'd overheard. Her boss was pitching me for a new series job, writer of the pilot and then showrunner, a very good deal, which included the fun of working with him. (He was a delightful, funny guy. David Gerber used to tell me he wanted more *nunces* in my scripts. I had no idea what he was talking about until I realized the word he was trying to say was—*nuances*—more subtle changes of meanings and feelings. But I digress.) My secretary spy quoted the network executive in the meeting as saying, "Rita is getting too old." Gerber defended me, saying that was ridiculous. This was countered with something like—"Well, maybe these older writers are paid way more than necessary. I suggest we go for younger producers, college graduates who will be satisfied with much less money."

Lo and behold, suddenly many shows had young, just-out-of college writers with no experience, appearing as if from out of nowhere. Was it any wonder that the network TV shows started their epic slide?

A coincidence? In 1988 I'd cleared $186,000. In 1989, $3,200.

Years later there would be a major ageism lawsuit against an industry that had been dumping writers because of their age. It was then I realized it hadn't only happened to me. The strike had been used as an opportunity to get rid of a huge number of very highly paid writers. Never mind quality—it no longer was necessary. Only profit counted.

So after twenty-six years of almost nonstop working, I decided it was time to retire. I'd had a hell of a good ride. I was looking forward to spending more time with my grown children with more grandchildren to come, with good times ahead, including world travel that I hadn't time to do when I was younger.

As for the women, as you will see below, there were finally plenty to take my place. Goodbye, reel world. I was returning to live only in the real one.

BY 1989, women had finally found their way into power. Woman's lib may have been assumed as having succeeded in the 1960s, but truth is, it wasn't until the eighties that it was all right for a woman to do better than a man. Seemingly, women were suddenly visible everywhere. In contrast to the college-boy-written shows, there was a fresh subtext to all these renegade new shows. They starred modern women. *Roseanne* starred Roseanne Barr, taking the step up from bombastic stand-up comic to her own blue-collar sitcom.

Candice Bergen played Murphy Brown, a fortyish journalist, highly feminist, highly intelligent, taking on hot issues of the day. Her producer was a woman as well. The series slogan was "Nice and sweet was out."

Suddenly, women were dominating programming. Here is a partial list: *China Beach* (women at war). *HeartBeat* (women in medicine). My show *Nightingales*, as long as we lasted (women in nursing). *Designing Women* (women in business). *The Golden Girls* (women in retirement). *Day by Day*, *227*, *Kate & Allie*, *Falcon Crest*, and more. And I bet women were paid less.

EPILOGUE

I wrote 260 scripts in one job alone. Plus maybe a hundred or more scripts with ups and downs, hits and misses, success and failure, good reviews and bad. I came to the carnival and had a roller-coaster ride of a career at a time when it was almost unheard of for a woman writer to work in TV.

From an unwilling young woman who was forced to go to work, I evolved into someone who knew who she was. I did the best I could as a parent. I created a place for myself. I grew into my job and learned to love it. I'd learned not to be afraid. I was proud of many things: that I stood my ground when I thought situations were wrong, that I helped many women come into a business that had ignored them, that I mentored many young people along their way. I helped start a committee called Open Door during my tenure on the Writers Guild board of directors in the early 1960s for writers to volunteer to teach minorities how to write for films so that they could get jobs. I was surprised to learn I was considered a pioneer by the lesbian-gay community by writing sympathetically about a transgender person in a two-part *Medical Center* episode.

I only wish I'd been more aware. I would have hired more women writers, and even women directors.

But most important to me is that I tried for twenty-five years to convince men to write women honestly and give up the clichés that kept women second-class citizens.

I RECENTLY LEARNED that only 4 percent of the members of the Writers Guild of America in the 1960s and 1970s were women. There were about forty of us women (nearly half teamed with husbands) out of a thousand male writers.

And sadly, nearly half a century later, it's only up to about 22 percent, which is better, but it could be much better still. Maybe we haven't come a long way, baby, yet.

So END MY ADVENTURES. I had done better than my mother's generation. My peers will certainly be able to relate to what I went through. But I hope my story will reach out to the women of today so they can imagine how it used to be just two generations ago and how they should never forget how important it is to continue to push for equality. As Gloria Steinem has said, this is no time to relax—the revolution continues on. No matter how long it takes, hopefully we will never again have to be the only woman in the room.

My interview *was winding down; Chelsea asked a question that stumped me for a moment. "Ms. Lakin," she queried, "it seems as if you were known for being very nice to people and very generous. You never lost your cool in a business where people would just as soon put a knife in your back."*

I immediately quipped, "That's because I'm basically a nice person."

The interviewer waited and I gave the question more thought. "You know, I think it all goes back to the beginning. When I went for my first job as a secretary, I was a widow. I needed to work, I didn't want to, but I had no choice. So I came into the business with very heavy baggage. I had lost the most important person in my life. In my heart, I'd gone through hell, so I guess the things that bothered most people didn't bother me. How upset would I get if someone didn't like my script? I didn't take it personally. I just shrugged and did the rewrite. Does that make sense to you?"

"I think so," she said.

I smiled. "A long time ago, I once met one of the first of the women writers in feature films. She was elderly at that time. I don't remember her name anymore, but she, in a sense, was handing down the torch to me. She gave me this advice: She said, 'Kill them with kindness, and remember always to wear white gloves.'"

Chelsea laughed. "White gloves?"

"Meaning don't ever lose your femininity. The white gloves went out of style, but the kindness part stayed with me forever. There were no rules on how to function in a male's world. I couldn't be one of those women who wore suits and emulated men. That wasn't me. So I tried to behave like a caring human being. You know—do unto others . . .

"If someone wanted to fight with me, I responded with smiles and kind words. That always disarmed them."

"But you always came across as hard to get. You never fought to get jobs. It's almost as if you just waited for them to come to you. Other writers would have killed to get those jobs."

"You want to know my secret? It's not that I was playing hard to get; I was so ambivalent that I just couldn't make up my mind. And that made me seem like I wasn't intimidated by them. They wrongly thought I didn't care whether I'd get the job or not. They believed I was shrewd enough to beat them at their Hollywood game. That made them want me even more."

"You've helped a lot people, especially women, get ahead in the biz. Why would you do that?"

"Why wouldn't I? I was very lucky. Not many people get a career that lasts more than twenty-five years. I wanted to give back to others."

"Can a woman have it all—work, family, marriage, success?"

I paused. "That's a difficult question. It wasn't easy. . . . I don't know. . . . Women today are still pondering that question."

Chelsea turned off her recording device.

"Are we done?" I asked.

Yes, thank you."

"Good luck to you. I hope you get what you want in life. And remember to kill them with kindness."

To my surprise, Chelsea walked over to me and hugged me.

"That's from all of us girls," she said.

Fade out.

Index